Building Skills

1

Course Book

Terry Phillips and Anna Phillips

Garnet EDUCATION

Contents

Introduction

Building Skills Books 1 and 2 will take you from pre-intermediate to advanced level in the four skills, listening, speaking, reading and writing. The course will also provide you with a range of relevant vocabulary and grammar practice.

The course focuses on language competencies as defined by the Common European Framework (CEF). This tells you the skills you need to communicate with others and the situations where these competencies are used.

The course is designed to build skills that help you survive in an academic institution where lectures, tutorials, assignments and research are wholly or partly in English.

The course is organized into unit themes, e.g., Science and Nature, Art and Literature. Each unit is designed to help you build knowledge as well as language.

Within each unit, there are six sections, with two lessons in each section – a total of 12 lessons per unit:

Lessons 1 & 2:   Vocabulary

Lessons 3 & 4:   Listening

Lessons 5 & 6:   Speaking

Lessons 7 & 8:   Reading

Lessons 9 & 10:   Writing

Lessons 11 & 12:   Grammar

The course also has a Workbook for further practice. It covers all the four skills, plus vocabulary and grammar, and also has an audio CD for extra listening practice.

Book Map

Theme/Lexical set	Topics	Texts	Sounds and spelling	Grammar
1 Education, Student Life	• Personal information • Introductions	• Speech • College advice leaflet • Application form	• /p/, /b/ • Short vs. long: /ɪ/ vs /iː/ • *le* at the end of words, e.g., *table* • Spelling the sound /iː/: e, ee, ea, y	• Present simple – facts • Present continuous – present action • Gerund as object
2 Daily Life, Organizing Your Time	• Schedules • Times • Habits and routines	• Speech • Article giving advice • Weekly schedule	• Short vs. long: /æ/ vs /aː/ • Sounds of *a* and *ea*: /æ/, /aː/, / iː/	• Present simple with frequency adverbs and time periods for habits and routines • Imperative – advice
3 Work and Business, Work Starts Now!	• Jobs • Likes and dislikes	• Lecture • Job advertisement • Application form • Job description	• /g/, /dʒ/ • Spelling with *g* and *j*	• Parts of speech • Coordinated clauses – *and, but,* • Subordinated clauses – *because*
4 Science and Nature, The Sun, The Air, The Rain	• Requests for help • Offers and rejections of help	• Radio programme • Popular science text • Table of information	• /θ/, /ð/ • Short vs long: /e/ vs /ɜː/ • Spelling the /ɜː/ sound • Doubling letters in suffixes	• Discourse markers – exemplification • Present simple – facts
5 The Physical World, Where Is Your Country?	• Countries • Location • Places	• Lecture • Encyclopedia articles • Maps • Tables	• /s/, /z/ • Short vs long: /ɒ/ vs /ɔː/ • Spelling the /ɔː/ sound	• Present simple – facts • Prepositions of place • Impersonal pronouns – *there*
6 Culture and Civilization, Festivals	• Events • Birthdays • Festivals	• Student talk • Chronological narrative • Tourist guide information	• /t/, /d/ • Long: /uː/ • Spelling vowel sounds	• Present simple – facts • Past simple – facts • Discourse markers – chronological
7 They Made Our World, A Brief History of Travel	• Dates and periods • Research • Inventions	• Lecture • Chronological narrative • Magazine articles	• /ʃ/, /tʃ/ • Diphthongs with /ɪ/	• Past simple – facts • Pronouns and possessive adjectives
8 Art and Literature, Telling a Story	• Traditional stories	• Radio programme • Chronological narrative • Stories from Shakespeare	• Diphthongs /aɪ/, /eɪ/, /ɔɪ/	• Past simple – facts • Pronoun reference
9 Sports and Leisure, Games We Play	• Games • Sports	• Lecture • Descriptive narrative • Encyclopedia articles	• Diphthongs /əʊ/, /aʊ/ • Spelling /ə/	• Referring back: – *then/there* • Present simple – how to do something
10 Nutrition and Health, A Balanced Diet	• Food and drink • Eating patterns	• Lecture • Informal letters • Information about healthy eating	• Revision	• Revision

Skills Map

Theme/Lexical set	Listening skills	Speaking skills	Reading skills	Writing skills
1 Education, Student Life	• Understanding spoken definitions • Following instructions • Identifying names	• Asking about new words • Checking sounds in a dictionary • Introducing oneself • Giving personal information	• Predicting content – from introduction/first paragraph • Predicting content – from headings • Word-attack skills – asking for the meaning of new words • Following instructions	• Following written instructions
2 Daily Life, Organizing Your Time	• Understanding spoken times	• Saying times	• Predicting content – from introduction/first paragraph • Predicting content – from illustrations	• Describing habits and routines
3 Work and Business, Work Starts Now!	• Identifying important words • Predicting content	• Checking sounds in a dictionary • Expressing likes and dislikes	• Locating information – from headings • Dealing with new words	• Ordering information
4 Science and Nature, The Sun, The Air, The Rain	• Predicting the next word	• Checking pronunciation • Requesting, accepting and rejecting help	• Understanding the point of topic sentences	• Referring to figures and tables
5 The Physical World, Where Is Your Country?	• Understanding spoken spellings	• Spelling words aloud	• Transferring information from text to chart • Skimming topic sentences for main points	• Describing location • Describing places
6 Culture and Civilization, Festivals	• Understanding signpost language (1)	• Showing understanding – echo + comment/ question • Showing lack of understanding – echo	• Using chronological markers	• Describing events
7 They Made Our World, A Brief History of Travel	• Understanding signpost language (2) • Identifying dates	• Talking about research • Showing lack of understanding – questions	• Using a dictionary • Recognizing dates and periods	• Using pronouns and possessive adjectives
8 Art and Literature, Telling a Story	• Following a narrative	• Narrating a story	• Understanding pronoun reference	• Lexical cohesion – replacing noun with noun
9 Sports and Leisure, Games We Play	• Recognizing important words	• Keeping the conversation going	• Active reading – predicting tense forms	• Distinguishing people and things
10 Nutrition and Health, A Balanced Diet	• Revision	• Revision	• Revision	• Revision

Lesson 1: Vocabulary

In this unit, you are going to:

- listen to speeches for new students at college
- talk about yourself, your interests and the subjects you like and don't like
- read a college leaflet and advice for new students
- complete an application form

A **Discuss these questions in pairs.**

1 What was your favourite subject at high school? Why did you like it?
2 Which subjects didn't you like? Why not?
3 Which is your best skill in English – listening, speaking, reading or writing? Which is your worst?

B **◉ 1.1 Listen to the following sentences. Then complete each one using some of the *Key vocabulary*.**

1 The _____ year in my country starts in October. All the students go back to high school then.
2 When does the second _____ start? Is it in February?
3 Which room is the _____ in? The one about learning English?
4 Mr Jones is in charge of the library. He is _____ for all the books and CD-ROMs.
5 Who is the _____ of Year 1? Is it Mrs Wright? Or is she in charge of Year 2?

> **Key vocabulary**
> academic   college   head
> in charge (of)   lecture
> meeting   principal
> responsible (for)   semester
> speech   studies   subject
> year

C **What is the connection between each pair of words? Match each pair to a connection.**

1 history *and* mathematics
2 principal *and* teacher
3 college *and* university
4 lecture *and* speech
5 term *and* semester

a They are both places to study after you finish school.
b They are almost the same – one is British English and the other is American English.
c They are both jobs in a school or college.
d They are both subjects.
e They both mean one person talking to a group of people.

D **Find the odd one out. Then match it with a reason below.**

1	school	university	college	dictionary
2	history	science	test	mathematics
3	learn	teacher	spell	explain
4	explain	speak	listen	tell

a It's not a subject.
b You don't study there.
c It's not a verb.
d It's not about talking.

Lesson 2: Vocabulary

A Look at *Key vocabulary 1* for a minute. Then cover the words and complete the missing letters.

1 advi_____   4 advis_____   7 rela_____
2 assign_____   5 intellig_____   8 respe_____
3 consid_____   6 poli_____   9 instruct_____

B Read the paragraph. Think about the meaning of the red words. Then match each word to its dictionary definition below.

The instructor gave me a bad mark for my assignment. She was very polite, but she said, 'Your work was good but it was two weeks late.' I went to the student advisor. She considered the situation for a moment. Then she gave me some good advice. She said, 'Stop worrying. Relax. There is nothing wrong with your intelligence. You can get good marks. But you must respect the college rules. Don't be late with your assignments.'

Student Advice

How to manage your bank account

• Opening an account
• Setting up a standing order
• Understanding your statement
• Managing your money

1 advice   **a** an idea about a good thing to do in a particular situation
2 assignment   **b** not rude
3 consider   **c** a person who gives advice
4 advisor   **d** a piece of homework for college
5 intelligence   **e** stop working, have a break from activity
6 polite   **f** a teacher at a college or university
7 relax   **g** the ability to understand many things
8 respect   **h** think about
9 instructor   **i** think about another person's feelings when you do
                     something; care about something

C Discuss these questions in pairs.
1 Who do you go to for *advice*?
2 How do you *relax*?
3 Which person in your life do you *respect* most?

D Complete each sentence with a word from *Key vocabulary 2*.
1 A person who teaches at a British university is called a tutor, but at an American university a teacher is called an _____.
2 Fill in the application _____ and send it, with a letter, to the college.
3 He has passed the certificate course and now he is doing a _____.
4 I like the classwork, but I find the _____ difficult.
5 I'm studying English Language and English _____.
6 When you do an assignment, first do a _____ and then write it out again.
7 When you go to university, you choose a _____ to study in – for example, Arts, Engineering or Religious Education.

Lesson 3: Listening

A **Discuss the questions in pairs.**

1 When did your academic year begin?
2 What is the name of the head of your college?
3 Who do you tell if you can't come to college one day?

B **Look at a page from an information leaflet about Greenhill College. What information is missing? Make questions.**

Example:
What is the surname of the principal?

C ⊙ **1.2 It is the start of the college year at Greenhill College. The principal is welcoming the new students. Listen and add the missing information.**

D **Some words and phrases from the speech may be new to you. Match the words and their meanings.**

1 principal   a information about the times of lectures
2 fees   b a teacher at a college or university
3 schedule   c the person in charge of a college
4 instructor   d money you pay to study
5 advisor   e a person who helps if you have problems

E ⊙ **1.3 The principal explains the meaning of the words in Exercise D. Listen to his speech again and check your answers.**

F **Work in pairs. Make a sentence with each of the words in Exercise D. Then give a definition. Use one of the phrases from the Skills Check to introduce the definition.**

Example:
How much are the fees – I mean the money you pay to study?

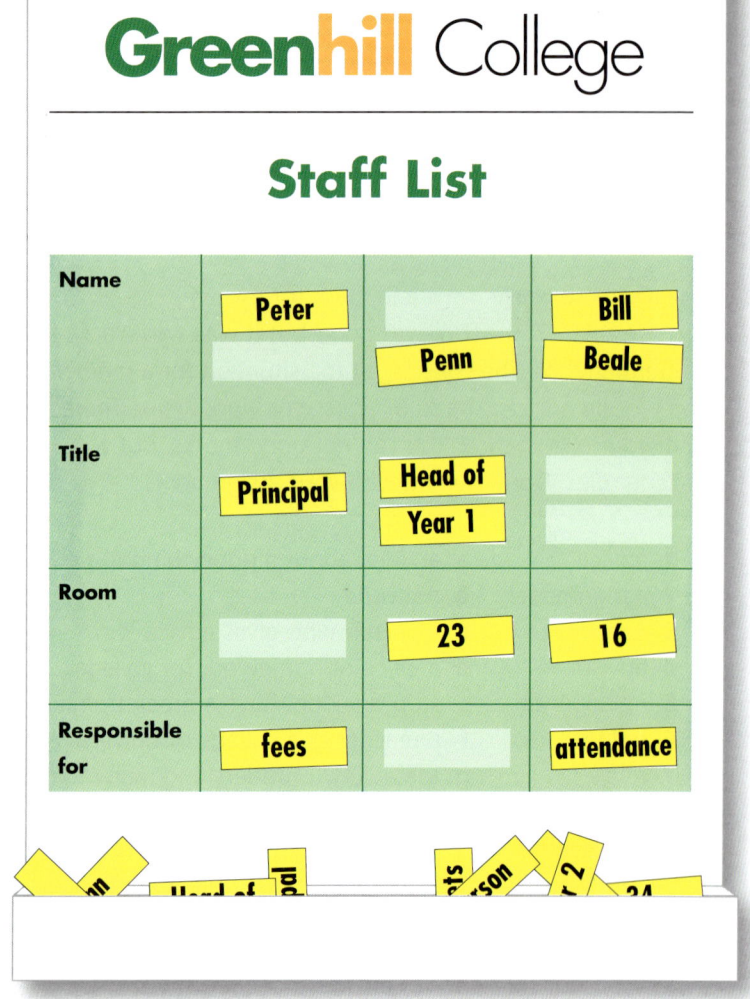

Greenhill College

Staff List

Name	Peter	Penn	Bill Beale
Title	Principal	Head of Year 1	
Room		23	16
Responsible for	fees		attendance

Skills Check

Waiting for definitions

When a person uses an unusual word in a speech or lecture, he or she often explains the meaning in the next few words.

Example:
*I'm the **principal** – that means I am **in charge of the whole place**.*

If you hear a word that is new to you, listen carefully. You may hear a definition. Listen for these phrases:
*That means …   I mean …   In other words …
That is …*

Lesson 4: Listening

A 🔊 **1.4 Listen and tick the words you hear. If you get three ticks in a line, say Bingo!**

Card A

head	I mean	schedule
fees	principal	in charge of
instructor	attendance	advisor

Card B

fees	advisor	principal
head	schedule	I mean
instructor	in charge of	attendance

B **Read Skills Check 1.**

1 These words are from the speech in Lesson 3. Tick the correct column for the missing sound in each word.

Words	p	b	Words	p	b
… ay	✓		… lace		
… ill			… leased		
… enn			… eale		
… ersonal			… olly		
… ean			… rincipal		
… eter			… roblems		
… eo … le			… ehind		

2 🔊 **1.5** Listen and check your answers.

3 🔊 **1.6** Listen to these words connected with education. Is the missing letter *p* or *b*?

a ___ook   d s___ell   g su___ject
b pa___er   e ___ass   h ex___lain
c ___egin   f ___eriod

C **Read Skills Check 2.**

1 Study these examples.

fill	feel
hill	pleased
is	means
this	see
will	me
give	she's
his	he's
if	we

2 🔊 **1.7** Look at these pairs of words. Listen. Which do you hear in each case? Don't worry about the meanings.

a	hill	heal	**f**	kill	keel
b	still	steal	**g**	fill	feel
c	will	wheel	**h**	fit	feet
d	mill	meal	**i**	Bill	Beale
e	pill	peel	**j**	bit	beat

3 How can you spell the short sound? What about the longer sound?

D 🔊 **1.8 Listen to the first part of the principal's speech again. It's much slower this time. Put your left hand up every time you hear /p/. Put your right hand up every time you hear /b/.**

E 🔊 **1.9 Listen to the second part of the speech again. Say /ɪ/ every time you hear the short sound. Say /iː/ every time you hear the long sound.**

Lesson 5: Speaking

A Read the first page of the information leaflet from the college on the right. <u>Underline</u> any words or phrases that are new to you.

B 🎧 **1.10** Paula and Barbara are both starting at Greenhill College today. Listen to their conversation. Tick any of your underlined words from the leaflet.

C 🎧 **1.11** Listen again. Match each word from the leaflet with its meaning.

1 principal	**a**	the people who work at a college
2 staff	**b**	a teacher at a college or university
3 head	**c**	the person in charge
4 schedule	**d**	the person you go to if you have any problems with your studies
5 personal advisor	**e**	the subjects and times
6 instructor	**f**	the head of a college

D Read this part of the conversation. Check your answers to Exercise C.

P: What happens today?
B: Well, first there's a speech from the principal.
P: What's a principal?
B: The head of a college. He's going to welcome us and introduce the staff.
P: What does staff mean?
B: The staff are the people who work at a college.
P: Right. Then what?
B: Then there's a meeting with the head of Year 1.
P: The head?
B: Yes, the person in charge. She's going to give us the schedule.
P: Does schedule mean the subjects and times?
B: That's right. She's also going to tell us the name of our instructor and our personal advisor.
P: Is an instructor a teacher?
B: Yes. It's the word for teacher at a college or university.
P: What about a personal advisor?
B: It's the person you go to if you have any problems with your studies.

E Read the conversation in Exercise D in pairs.

Barbara

Paula

Greenhill College

Information for First-Year Students

The first day:
1. Speech from principal Peter Bean:
   • welcoming
   • introducing staff
2. Meeting with head of Year 1 Mrs Polly Penn:
   • your schedule for Semester 1
   • the name of your instructor
   • the name of your personal advisor
3. Meeting with your personal advisor

Skills Check 1

Saying consonants – /p/ and /b/

These two consonant sounds are very similar. You make both sounds with your lips, but you need more air for /p/. Find and underline all the words in the conversation with the letter *p*. Practise saying the words.

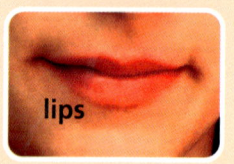
lips

Skills Check 2

Saying vowels – /ɪ/ and /iː/

These two vowel sounds are very similar. The second sound is longer than the first sound. Say these words from the conversation:

is	he's
if	mean
with	people
give	she's
principal	speech

Lesson 6: Speaking

A Find the hidden word that connects all the answers.

1	Maths, English, Religion, Science, etc.
2	You go to your personal _____ if you have any problems with your studies.
3	The head of a college.
4	It tells you the times of all the **1**s.
5	Mrs Penn's the _____ of Year 1.
6	She's _____ of Year 1. (2 words)
7	The staff are the _____ who work at a college.

B Read Skills Check 1. Answer the questions.
1 What is the Skills Check about?
2 Why should you ask people to explain new words?
3 Cover the Skills Check. What is missing in each question?
   - _____ a *principal*?
   - What _____ *staff* mean?
   - _____ *schedule* mean the subjects and times?
   - _____ *head* a job?

C Don't look at the conversation in Lesson 5. Work in pairs. Ask and answer about the meaning of the words in the puzzle in Exercise A. Use the patterns from Skills Check 1.

D Look at the next part of the *Information for First-Year Students*.
1 Read the leaflet and Barbara's notes.
2 🔊 **1.12** Listen to Barbara's speech to the tutor group. Make full sentences from Barbara's notes.
   Example:
   Barbara Peters ⇨ *My name is Barbara Peters.*

E Read Skills Check 2. Find these words with *ea* in your dictionary. Which words have the long vowel sound?

beach   pea   bead   peach
bear   peak   beard   pear

Skills Check 1

Dealing with new words (1)

You hear **new words** every day. Ask people to explain new words. It helps you to increase your vocabulary. Here are some ways to ask:
   What's a *principal*?
   What does *staff* mean?
   Does *schedule* mean the subjects and times?
   Is *head* a job?

You can also repeat the word as a question:
   The *head*?

Greenhill College

Information for First-Year Students
(continued)

First class:
You must introduce yourself to the other people in your group. You must say:
- your name – Barbara Peters
- your nationality – British
- your hometown – Birmingham
- your favourite subject – P.E.
- a subject that you don't like – Biology

Skills Check 2

Checking sounds in a dictionary (1)

In a dictionary, the vowel sound in *fill* is written /ɪ/. The vowel sound in *feel* is written /iː/.

fill   /fɪl/   *feel*   /fiːl/

Lesson 7: Reading

A **Look quickly at the leaflet on pages 136 and 137.**
Choose the best answer to each question.

1 Who wrote the leaflet?   a student OR an instructor?
2 Who is the leaflet for?   new students OR old students?
3 What is in the leaflet?   information OR advice?
4 How many questions   six OR seven?
are there?

B **Look at the introduction on page 136.**

1 Find and underline the words and phrases in a–g below.
2 Read the questions and try to understand the words and phrases.
3 Then match the words and phrases with their opposites.

a away from (home)	**i** stupidly
b sharing (a bedroom)	**ii** a few
c harder	**iii** old
d a lot of	**iv** at (home)
e early	**v** having your own (bedroom)
f sensibly	**vi** easier
g new	**vii** late

C **Look at Skills Check 2.**

1 Read the Skills Check.
2 Cover the Skills Check.
3 Number the actions in the yellow box in order.
4 Uncover the Skills Check. Check your answer.

__ Think: 'What information will be in the text?'
__ Stop.
__ Read the **introduction** or **first paragraph**.

D **Read the introduction again. It is on page 136.**
What information will be in the next part of the leaflet?

E **You met Barbara Peters in Lesson 5.**
Look at Barbara's answers to the questions.
Work in groups. Think of advice for her.

Barbara

Lesson 8: Reading

A Match each verb with a word or phrase.

1	share	**a**	at home
2	work	**b**	bed
3	make	**c**	classes
4	eat	**d**	friends
5	go to	**e**	hard
6	understand	**f**	paragraphs
7	read	**g**	a room
8	live	**h**	sensibly

B What advice did you give Barbara (Lesson 7)? Why?

C Read the introduction to the leaflet again (pages 136 and 137). Look at Barbara's answers to the questions. Which advice paragraphs should she read? (Don't read the paragraphs yet.)

D Read the Skills Check. Answer the questions.
1 Why don't you always have to read everything in a text?
2 How can you find out which parts to read?

E Look at the introduction to the leaflet again.
1 Answer the questions for yourself.
2 Which paragraphs should you read?

F Which paragraphs should your partner read? Ask and answer the questions in pairs.

> Are you living away from home for the first time?

> Yes, I am.

> Do you go to bed early?

> No, I don't. I often go to bed really late.

Skills Check

Preparing to read (2)

Do I have to read it all?
Sometimes you have to read **everything** in a text. But sometimes only **a few parts** are important to you. Look at the **introduction** to a text carefully to find out **which parts** of the text you have to read.

G In the left column below are the paragraph headings for the Advice part of the leaflet. Find a sentence on the right from each paragraph.

1	College life means ... living away from home.	**a**	Always ask before you borrow things from your roommate.
2	College life means ... sharing a room.	**b**	Don't worry if you don't have any friends at first.
3	College life means ... working harder.	**c**	Don't worry if you find college work hard at first.
4	College life means ... making new friends.	**d**	Eat sensibly.
5	College life means ... taking care of yourself.	**e**	If you don't understand something the first time, you can ask your instructor.
6	College life means ... having a second chance.	**f**	You are responsible for managing your time now.

Lesson 9: Writing

A **Ricardo Moreno is a new student at Greenhill College. Ricardo wants to join the college Sports Club.**

1 Look at the application form below.
2 Read Ricardo's personal information in the box on the right.
3 Work in pairs. Match each piece of information to the correct section of the form. **Don't write anything yet.**

0347 382491   18   Alberto Moreno   Arts
Brent Hostel, Dean Road, Greenhill
Diploma in English Literature   Father
Mobile: 07957 834560   Moreno
moreno127@hotmail.com   Mr
PO Box 1986, Madrid   Ricardo
single   Spanish

Greenhill College Sports Club Application Form

Please complete the form in BLOCK CAPITALS. Use black ink only.

Title (delete as applicable)	Mr / Mrs / Miss / Ms	Mr / Mrs / Miss / Ms
First name		
Family name		
Age		
Nationality		
Status		
Permanent address		
College address		
Faculty		
Course		
E-mail address		
Local telephone number		
Next of kin – full name (to be contacted in the event of an accident)		
Relationship to applicant		
Contact details		

B **Find the instructions on the form. Then read the Skills Check.**

1 What are the instructions?
2 What does each instruction mean?

C **Read the lower case letters: *a, b, d,* etc.**

1 Match each lower case letter with the correct block capital.
2 Cover the lower case letters. Write the correct lower case letter under each capital.
3 Some lower case letters are missing. Why?

Skills Check

Following instructions

Always read instructions carefully before you start writing. Forms often say:

Use block capitals = A not a
Write in black ink only = A not A
Tick in the box = ✓
Delete as applicable = ~~Mr~~

a	*b*	*d*	*e*	*f*	*g*	*h*	*i*	*j*	*k*	*l*	*m*	*n*	*q*	*r*	*t*	*y*
L	I	M	N	R	D	E	F	Y	K	T	G	Q	B	H	A	J

Lesson 10: Writing

A **Correct the spelling of these words from Lesson 9.**

1 singel _____
4 diplom _____
2 facalty _____
5 litrature _____
3 colleg _____
6 corse _____

B **Look again at the personal information about Ricardo Moreno in Lesson 9. Copy the information into the correct place on the application form. Use the green column. Follow the instructions carefully.**

C **Read Ricardo's first assignment for his English instructor. Work in pairs. What can he write?**

English Assignment
Write one paragraph about yourself.

D **Read Ricardo's first draft. He is good at spelling, but there is one grammar mistake in each sentence. Find and circle each mistake. Don't try to correct it yet.**

First draft
My name Ricardo Moreno. I am from Spanish. I am live in Madrid. I am having eighteen years. I am single man. I am having two brothers and one sister. Now, I studying at Greenhill College. Am in the Faculty of Arts. I am do a diploma in English Literature. I am liking this course very much.

E **Read Skills Check 2. Then correct Ricardo's first draft.**

F **Ricardo has written his second draft. There are no mistakes now. Compare your corrections in Exercise E. Are they all right?**

Second draft
My name is Ricardo Moreno. I am Spanish. I live in Madrid. I am eighteen. I am single. I have two brothers and one sister. At the moment, I am studying at Greenhill College. I am in the Faculty of Arts. I am doing a diploma in English Literature. I like this course very much.

Skills Check 1

Spelling rules (1)

In this course, we will learn many spelling rules. But often there is no rule. You must just learn the spelling.

In Exercise A, only *single* has an easy rule. The sound *ul* at the end of a word after a consonant (*b, c, d,* etc.) usually has the spelling *le*. Finish these common English words. Say each word. What does each word mean?

app____   peop____
bicyc____   simp____
bott____   tab____
cast____   troub____
circ____   unc____
doub____   vegetab____

Skills Check 2

Writing about present facts and present actions

We normally use the **present simple** to talk about facts that are true now.
Examples:
My name / telephone number / address / e-mail address **is** ...
I **am** ... + nationality / age / status
I **am from** + country
I **am at** + school / college / university
I **am in** + faculty
I **have** ... + family (brothers, sisters, children)
I **live in** ... + hometown
I **like** ... + likes
We normally use the **present continuous** to talk about actions that are happening at the moment.
I **am studying at** + college/university
I **am doing** + course
I **am living in** + temporary address (e.g., a college hall)

Lesson 11: Grammar

A Look at all the tables.

1 What colour is each part of speech?
- noun
- adjective
- pronoun
- preposition
- verb

2 What kind of word …
- can be the subject?
- can come after the verb *be*?
- can come after other verbs?

B Complete each table.

C Look at Tables 1 and 2.

1 Where can you put *not* in each table?
2 How can you make a question with the answer *Yes* or *No*?
3 How can you make a question with a question word (*What*, *Where*, etc.)?

D Look at Table 3. Tick the correct rule for making negative sentences.

___ Add *not* after the verb.
___ Add *not* before the verb.
___ Add *do not* before the verb.
___ Add *does not* after the verb.

Table 1: *Pronoun + verb* (be) *+ adj/noun*

Pronoun	Verb	Adjective/noun
I		Jordanian.
You	are	married.
	is	16.
She		a teacher.
	are	students.

Table 2: *Pronoun + verb* (be) *+ prep + noun*

Pronoun	Verb	Prep	Noun
I		from	China.
You	are		Greenhill College.
	is	in	the Arts Faculty.

Table 3: *Pronoun + verb + noun*

Pronoun	Verb	Noun
I		three brothers.
You		Biology.
We		two sisters.
They		Maths.

Table 4: *Pronoun/noun + verb + prep + noun*

Subject	Verb	Prep	Noun
She		for	a bank.
He		to	Greenhill College.
The lesson		at	8.00 a.m.
The course		in	July.

Table 5: *Pronoun + aux* (be) *+ present participle + other information*

S	Verb		Other
I	am		at Greenhill College.
He	is		Chemistry.
She	is		lunch at the moment.
They	are		football at the moment.

Table 6: *Pronoun + verb + gerund + other*

Subject	Verb	Object	Other
College life	means		away from home.
			a room.
			harder.

Lesson 12: Grammar

A Write a rule for making negative sentences in Table 4.

B Look at Tables 3 and 4 again. Tick the correct questions.
___ Do they love History?
___ Do you has three sisters?
___ Does lessons begin at 9.00 a.m.?
___ Does the course end in June?
___ You do study Chemistry?

C Compare Tables 1 and 5.
In Table 5, how do you make...
- negative sentences?
- questions?

D Compare Tables 5 and 6.
1 Which words are similar?
2 What part of speech are the *~ing* words in each table?

E Write about yourself using a language pattern from each table.
1 Make positive sentences.
Example
I am from Mexico. (Table 2)
2 Make some negative sentences.
Example
I don't go to Greenhill College. (Table 4)

F Join sentencs that go together from Exercise F. Add more where appropriate.
Example
I am married and I have three children.

G Exchange information with your partner.

H Write about your partner.

Lesson 1: Vocabulary

In this unit, you are going to:

- listen to a talk about schedules
- talk about your daily life
- read an article about making the most of your time at college
- write about your weekly schedule

A **Discuss these questions in pairs.**

1 What are you doing this evening?
2 What about tomorrow morning?
3 Have you got any plans for next week?
4 What do you usually do on Saturday and Sunday?
5 Do you do different things in the evening in the summer and the winter?

B 🔊 **1.13 Listen to eight sentences using words from *Key vocabulary*. Number the words in the order you hear them.**
Example:

1 *There is a very good **restaurant** in North Road. The food is excellent.*

C **Complete each sentence using the *Key vocabulary*.**

1 Can you wait a _____? I have to finish this work before I can go out.
2 How long does each class _____ at the college?
3 I usually have _____ at 6.30 in the morning.
4 We don't call them classes. We call them _____.
5 What am I doing today? Let me check my _____.
6 What time do you have _____ in the evening?

D **Work in groups. Put each set of words in a logical order. Explain your order to the other groups.**

1 summer	spring	winter	autumn			
2 yesterday	tomorrow	today				
3 lunch	dinner	breakfast				
4 night	afternoon	midnight	evening	noon	morning	
5 day	year	week	minute	hour	month	second

E **Some words have two different meanings. Say these sentences aloud. Then explain the different meanings.**

1 Periods *last* one hour. The *last* period starts at 3.40.
2 Wait a *second*. I've got to make a *second* phone call.
3 The *past* tense of 'come' is 'came'. He came at half *past* three.
4 *Have* we got a test this afternoon? Yes, so we *have* to revise.

Key vocabulary
breakfast
campus
chess
club
diary
dinner
film
last
music
period
plan
restaurant   *1*
second
sports

Lesson 2: Vocabulary

A **What are the missing vowels in the following six words?**

1 __v__n__ng   4 n__ght
2 m__nth   5 w___k
3 m__rn__ng   6 __ft__rn___n

B **Look at the *Key vocabulary* for one minute. Then cover the box and complete the missing letters.**

1 regula___   4 socia___
2 weeken___   5 brea___
3 spen___   6 weekl___

C **Make words that mean:**

1 every hour _____
2 every month _____
3 every year _____
4 every day (spelling!) _____

D **Choose from the *Key vocabulary* to match each definition.**

1 It's better than being late.
2 It's a rest between things you do.
3 Usually the two days following Friday.
4 It means the same as *use* – time, money, energy.
5 It's the time you spend meeting friends and enjoying yourself.
6 It means *normal*, *usual*, something that happens at the same time each day, week or month.

E **Discuss these questions in pairs.**

1 What do you do regularly every week?
2 How much time do you spend on exercise each week?
3 How do you usually spend the weekend?
4 Are you usually on time for things?
5 Which comes first, college work or your social life?

F **Look at the spelling in the *Key vocabulary*. Which words:**

1 have two vowels the same?
   _____

2 look plural?
   _____

3 end in *e*?
   _____

4 have other words hidden inside?
   _____

G **Match each frequency word to a percentage.**

never	100%
often	80%
sometimes	60%
usually	40%
always	0%

H **Which words from the *Key vocabulary* mean:**

1 one time? _____
2 two times? _____
3 days and times? _____
4 every week? _____

Lesson 3: Listening

A Discuss these questions in pairs.
1 How many classes do you have each day?
2 Do you have the same number of classes every day?
3 What time does the first class start?
4 What time does the last class end?
5 Do you have a break for lunch?

B Here is a planner in which students can write their schedules. Complete the planner by writing in the missing information from the yellow box.

Period	Begins			Tuesday	Wednesday	Thursday	Friday	Saturday
1								
2								
3								
Lunch								
4								
5								
6								

C Students at Greenhill College have to fill in their schedules. Mrs Penn, the head of Year 1, gives the information. She uses the words in the blue box below.
1 What does each word mean? Use some of the words from the yellow box below in each definition.
2 ⊙ **1.14** Listen to Mrs Penn's definitions and check your answers.

> schedule   recess
> period   cafeteria

> between   break   campus   classes
> days   part   restaurant   short   times

D ⊙ **1.15** Mrs Penn is going to give you your schedule. Listen and answer these questions.
1 What time does the first period start?   3 How long is the break between each period?
2 How long is each period?   4 How long is the lunch break?

E ⊙ **1.16** Listen again.
1 Check your answers to the questions in D.
2 Fill in the dark green columns of the planner.

Revision

F The words in the table are from the talk.
1 Put a tick in the correct column, according to the sound.
2 ⊙ **1.17** Listen and check your ideas.

	1	2
	fill	feel
	/ɪ/	/iː/
a each		
b give		
c mean		
d read		
e see		
f six		
g this		
h three		
i begins		
j between		

G The words below are from the talk.
1 Is the missing letter *b* or *p*?
2 ⊙ **1.18** Listen and check your ideas.

a a___out
b ___ecause
c ___egins
d ___encil
e ___etween
f ___reak
g s___ace
h cam___us
i ___art
j ___eriod

Lesson 4: Listening

A Think of a word for each definition. Find the hidden word that connects them all.

1	the days and times of classes	
2	it helps to organize your day/week/month/year	
3	all the buildings of the college	
4	the restaurant on the campus	
5	a short break between classes	
6	the day before Sunday	
7	the day after Tuesday	
8	a part of the college day	

B **Can you understand spoken times in English?**

1 🎧 **1.19** Listen to eight times. Letter the clocks A to H.
2 Study Skills Check 1.
3 🎧 **1.20** Listen to the times again and check.
4 Number the clocks in order (earliest = 1).

six o'clock
ten past eight
quarter past seven
twenty past four
half past eleven
twenty to ten
quarter to three
ten to four

C **Look at the phrases in the blue box. They are all from the talk in Lesson 3.**

1 How do you say each underlined vowel <u>a</u>?
2 Read Skills Check 2. Write S (short) or L (long) for each underlined vowel.
3 🎧 **1.21** Listen and check your ideas.

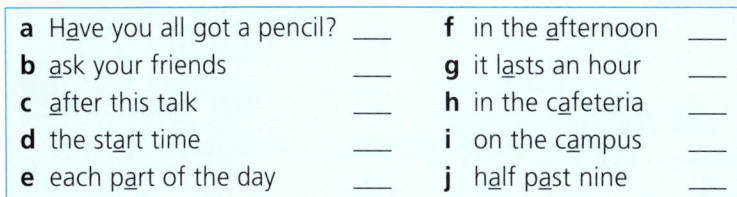

a H<u>a</u>ve you all got a pencil? ____
b <u>a</u>sk your friends ____
c <u>a</u>fter this talk ____
d the st<u>a</u>rt time ____
e each p<u>a</u>rt of the day ____
f in the <u>a</u>fternoon ____
g it l<u>a</u>sts an hour ____
h in the c<u>a</u>feteria ____
i on the c<u>a</u>mpus ____
j h<u>a</u>lf p<u>a</u>st nine ____

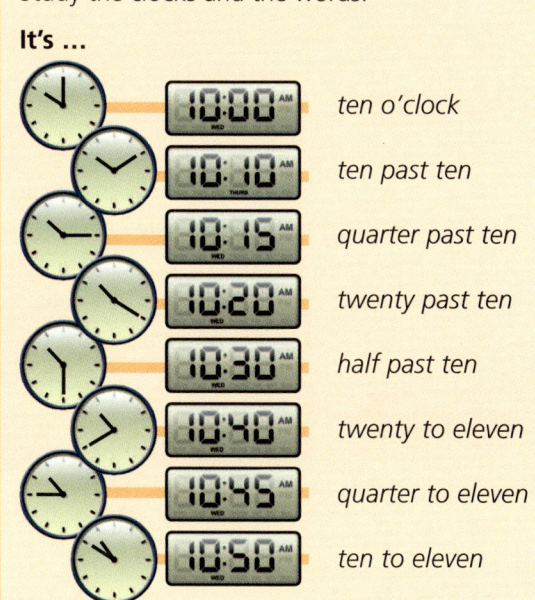

Lesson 5: Speaking

Ⓐ Discuss these questions in pairs.
1 What time do you have breakfast/lunch/dinner?
2 Do you ever miss a meal to play sport or to do college work?
3 Do you go out in the evening or do you do college work?

Ⓑ Martino is a second-year student at Greenhill College.
1 Look at his diary for Monday.
2 🔊 **1.22** Listen to Martino talking about his day. Fill in the missing times.

Ⓒ Complete each of Martino's sentences with a word from the yellow box.
1 It's Monday _____ .
2 I've got a really _____ day.
3 From nine o'clock to eleven ten, I've _____ General Studies.
4 _____ I've got a free period –
5 _____ a period with no class –
6 from eleven twenty to twelve _____ .
7 I have to _____ for a test in the afternoon.
8 Lunch starts _____ twenty past twelve.
9 It _____ an hour.
10 Then I've got PE _____ twenty past one to twenty past two,
11 followed by English from half past two _____ half past three.
12 I've got _____ free period from twenty to four to twenty to five,
13 then I'm _____ handball with Peter from quarter to five to quarter past.

Ⓓ 🔊 1.23 Listen again and check your answers.

Revision

Ⓔ Work in pairs. Say the words in the green box in any order. Your partner must number the words in the order that you say them.

Ⓕ What's the difference between the sound of *p* and the sound of *b*? Say these words – with a *p*, not a *b*!
past   period   play   PE   Peter

Ⓖ Say all the sentences in C aloud. Try to make good sounds for /ɪ/, /iː/ and /p/.

Monday 15th October

9.00 – 11.____: General Studies

11.____ – 12.20: Free period – revise for test

12.20 – ____: Lunch

1.20 – 2.____: P. E.

2.____ – 3.30: English – test!

3.40 – 4.____: Free period

4.45 – ____: Handball with Peter

another   busy   from
got   to   playing
revise   that's   at
tomorrow   twenty
then   lasts

English   free
in   is
means   really
see   studies
thirty   three
twenty   with

Lesson 6: Speaking

A Work in pairs.

1 Number these times in order, starting with the earliest.

___ eleven fifteen   _1_ nine o'clock

___ five past one   ___ quarter to twelve

___ four forty-five   ___ ten ten

___ half past two   ___ twenty to three

2 🔊 **1.24** Listen and check your order.

B Read Skills Check 1. Answer the questions.

1 What is the Skills Check about?

2 Say these times in Pattern 1.

a `10.10`   e `10.40`

b `10.15`   f `10.45`

c `10.20`   g `10.50`

d `10.30`

3 Say the times above again, this time in Pattern 2.

C Work in pairs.

1 Number the clocks on the right in any order. Say the time. Use Pattern 1 and Pattern 2. Your partner must number the clocks in the same order.

2 Write down three more times and say them to your partner. Can he or she write them correctly?

D Read these phrases and sentences from Lesson 5. What is the sound of _a_ in the underlined words?

1 It's <u>Monday</u> tomorrow.

2 <u>That's</u> a period with no <u>class</u>.

3 I <u>have</u> to revise for <u>a</u> test in the <u>afternoon</u>.

4 Lunch <u>starts</u> at twenty <u>past</u> twelve.

5 It <u>lasts</u> <u>an</u> hour.

6 English is from <u>half past</u> two …

7 I've got <u>another</u> free period …

8 then I'm <u>playing</u> <u>handball</u> with Peter from <u>quarter</u> to five to quarter past.

E Read Skills Check 2 and check your answers to Exercise D.

F Can you see any patterns in the spellings? Guess the pronunciation of these unusual words:

ark band bar bat fan mast raft staff

> _Eleven fifteen_ is before _five past one_.

> That's right. But it's after _nine o'clock_.

Skills Check 1

Saying times

With exact hours, we can say:

10.00 = _It's ten._ OR _It's ten o'clock._

We can say other times in two ways:

Pattern 1: _hour + minutes_

10.20 = _It's ten twenty._

9.45 = _It's nine forty-five._

Pattern 2: _minutes + to/past + hour_

9.50 = _It's ten to ten._

10.20 = _It's twenty past ten._

There are special words in Pattern 2 for:

8.15 = _It's quarter past eight._

8.30 = _It's half past eight._

8.45 = _It's quarter to nine._

`11.00`   `3.30`

`12.10`   `9.40`

`1.15`   `4.45`

`2.20`   `5.50`

Skills Check 2

Saying vowels – /æ/ and /ɑː/

The vowel _a_ has two common sounds – a short sound and a longer sound.

The short sound /æ/ is in _have, that, hand._

The longer sound /ɑː/ is in _half, past, after, class, start, last._

But the vowel _a_ has many other sounds.

For example: _day, another, a, an._

Lesson 7: Reading

A **Complete these phrases from Unit 1. Write one word for each phrase.**

  1 share a _____

  2 live away from _____

  3 make new _____

  4 eat junk _____

  5 take care of _____

  6 have a second _____

Skills Check

Reminder

Remember – Read, Stop, Think.

Read the introduction or first paragraph.

Stop.

Think: 'What information will be in the text?'

B **Give advice to a new student at college. Use some of the phrases in Exercise A.**

C **How do you prepare to read?**

  1 Read the Skills Check.

  2 Cover the Skills Check.

  3 Write the three verbs, in order.

  4 Uncover the Skills Check. Check your answer.

D **You are going to read an article from a magazine. Read the title in the excerpt on the right. Answer these questions.**

  1 What will the article be about?

  2 What will the article probably contain – facts, ideas, opinions or advice?

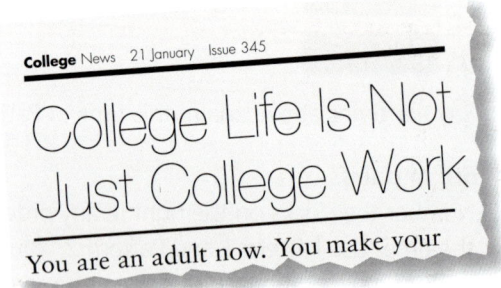

College News 21 January Issue 345

College Life Is Not Just College Work

You are an adult now. You make your

E **There is a diagram with this article. Look at the diagram.**

  1 Describe it.

  2 Can you think of examples of each type of activity?

  - personal care
  - college work
  - family responsibilities
  - social life

F **'Your weekly schedule' points to the centre of the diagram. Why? Work in groups. What do you think the article is going to say?**

Your weekly schedule

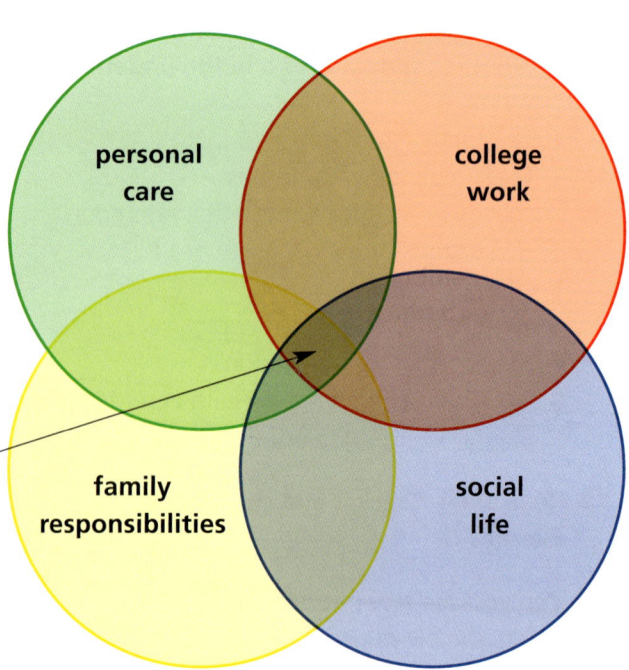

personal care

college work

family responsibilities

social life

Lesson 8: Reading

A Make phrases from the previous lesson with these words.

> care college family life work personal
> responsibilities schedule social weekly

B The phrases below are in the magazine article that you are going to read.
1 Match each phrase to one of the phrases that you made in Exercise A.
   - **a** doing assignments _____
   - **b** enjoying yourself _____
   - **c** helping family members _____
   - **d** looking after yourself _____
2 Read the first part of the article on page 138 and check your ideas.

Skills Check

Preparing to read (3)

Before you read the text of an article, always:
- read the **title** of an article.
- look at any **illustration**.
- read the **introduction** or **first paragraph**.

Think about the information you will find in the text. Your ideas will help you read the text with understanding.

C Read the Skills Check. Look at the article on page 138. Find:
1 the title.
2 the illustration.
3 the introduction or first paragraph.

D Read the whole article. Choose the best summary.
1 Some areas of your life are very important. You must make sure you do those things first.
2 You don't have enough time to do everything, so just do the important things.
3 You must find time for things in all these areas of your life.
4 College work is more important than social life, family responsibilities and personal care.

E Read the article again. Without looking, can you remember a phrase beginning with each verb/verb phrase below?

1 looking after	6 have
2 doing	7 take
3 keeping in	8 get enough
4 helping	9 attend
5 enjoying	10 revise

F Work in pairs. Ask and answer the questions in the check list on page 138. Is your partner neglecting one area of his/her life?

Lesson 9: Writing

A Manuel Garcia is a new student at Greenhill
College. He read a magazine article last week. Look
at the first part of the article.
Discuss the questions.

1 Who is this article for?
2 What is it about?
3 What sort of information will be in this article –
facts, ideas, opinions, advice?
4 What are the 'four areas' in the last line?

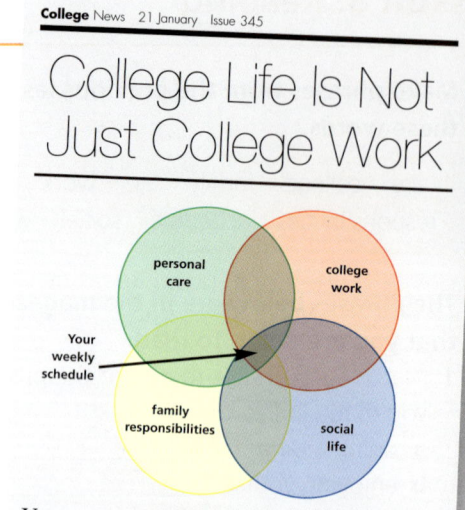

College News   21 January   Issue 345

College Life Is Not Just College Work

You are an adult now. You make your
own weekly schedule. But in that
schedule, you must make time for four
areas of your life.

B Manuel decided to follow the advice in the article.
Look at his schedule for next week (Table 1). Read
the activities in each row. Copy the headings from
the diagram into the correct row.

Example: *The first row = college work*

Table 1: *Manuel's weekly schedule*

Areas	Monday	Tuesday	Wednesday	Thursday	Friday	Saturday	Sunday
college work	attend classes	attend classes	attend classes	attend classes	attend classes	read notes from the week's work	
	take exercise go to bed early	have a sleep	take exercise go to bed early	have a sleep	take exercise		
		go to Film Night		go to Computer Club	see friends at the Sports Club?	meet friends for dinner	go for a walk with friends (afternoon)
			call my father			visit my parents?	

C The words in the box are all from the schedule.

1 What is the connection between them? Think
about the pronunciation of the underlined letters.
2 Test each other in pairs on the spelling of the words.

early   evening   see
family   meet   read
responsibilities   week

D Follow the advice in the article. Plan your weekly
schedule, with activities in all four areas.

Table 2: *My weekly schedule*

Areas	Monday	Tuesday	Wednesday	Thursday	Friday	Saturday	Sunday

Lesson 10: Writing

A **The same letter is missing from all these words from Lesson 9. Which letter is it?**

c__re   soci__l   __ttend   pr__y   e__rly
h__ve   p__rents   f__ther   re__d

B **Manuel has an assignment for his English instructor. Which tense must he use? Think. Then check in Skills Check 2, Unit 1, Lesson 10.**

English Assignment
Write a paragraph about your weekly schedule.

C **Read Manuel's first draft. There is one mistake in each sentence. Find and circle each mistake. Don't try to correct it yet.**

First draft

I attending classes every weekday. At the weekend, I

am read my notes from the week's work. I do never

college work on Sunday. On Sundays, I always to go

for a long walk with my friends. I take exercise three

time a week. I go to bed usually early on Monday and

Wednesday. At Tuesday I go to Film Night at the

college. On Thursday in evening I often go to the

Computer Club. I sometime meet my friends for dinner

on Saturday evening. I call my parents on Wednesday

evening and visit them one time a month.

D **Read Skills Check 2. Then correct Manuel's first draft.**

Skills Check 1

Spelling rules (2)

Each vowel in English can make almost any vowel sound. So if you only *hear* a word, you cannot be sure how to spell it. There are some *patterns*, though. In this lesson, we are looking at patterns for the letter *a*.

1 Words with the short *a* sound (/æ/) are usually spelt with *a*.
   Examples: *have, man, can, bag, sat*
2 Words with the long *aa* sound (/ɑː/) are usually spelt with *a* (+ *r* sometimes).
   Examples: *bath, father, fast, last, car, far, hard*
3 Words with the long *ee* sound are sometimes spelt with *ea*.
   Examples: *read, meat, meal, teach, each*

If you look at a word and think: 'That's a funny spelling,' write the word out ten times and learn it.
(*Learn* – now that's a funny spelling!)

Skills Check 2

Writing about habits and routines

We normally use the **present simple** to talk about habits and routines. We usually say the **frequency** of the habit or routine. In other words, we say **how often** we do something. There are two main patterns:

Pattern 1 – *with frequency adverbs + time period*

	always	visit	my parents	at	the weekend.
	often	go	to the club		Tuesday afternoon.
I	usually	go	to bed early	on	Saturday.
	sometimes	meet	friends		Thursday evening.
	never	do	college work		Sunday.

Pattern 2 – *with time period*

	eat		every	day.
	go to	Film Night	on	Friday.
I	visit	my parents	at	the weekend.
			once	
	meet	my friends	twice	a week.
			three times	

Lesson 11: Grammar

A Look at all the tables.

1 What kind of verb doesn't need a subject?

2 Which of these sentence patterns are possible?
- adjective + verb
- pronoun + adjective + verb
- pronoun + verb + adjective
- pronoun + verb + noun
- pronoun + verb + preposition + other information
- verb + adjective

B Complete each table.

C Work in pairs.

1 Make one new sentence for each language pattern.

2 Repeat step one again.

3 Keep going until you can't make any more sentences.

D Talk about yourself using any sentence pattern …

1 with your partner.

2 with the rest of the class.

E Write some information about yourself using the sentence patterns.

Table 1: *Imperative + noun*

1	Verb	2	Noun	3
	Accept		responsibility.	
	Set		targets.	
			friends.	
			breaks.	
			junk food.	

Table 2: *Pronoun + verb + adjective*

1	Pronoun	2	Verb	3	Adjective	4
	I				late.	
	You				tired.	
	He				ill.	
	She		is			
	They		are			

Table 3: *Pronoun + verb + noun*

1	S	2	V	3	O	4		5
			visit				at the weekend.	
	I		meet				on Fridays.	
					college work		in the afternoon.	
			play		sports			

Table 4: *Pronoun + verb + prep + other*

1	S	2	V	3	Prep	4	Other	5
					in		a restaurant.	
							the library.	
	I		go				work.	
			listen					
			write				my parents.	

Table 5: *Question words + aux + pron + verb + noun*

Question words	Aux	Pron	Verb	Noun
How			visit	your parents?
When	do	you	do	
				at the weekend?

Lesson 12: Grammar

A **Look at Table 1 in Lesson 11.**
 1 How do you make this sentence pattern negative?
 2 Where do you put the negative word(s) – position 1, 2 or 3?
 3 Where do you put the frequency adverbs *always/never* – position 1, 2 or 3?
 4 Write two new sentences in the negative.

 _____

 _____

B **Look at Tables 2, 3 and 4 in Lesson 11.**
 1 Where do you put the frequency adverbs *always/usually/often/never*?
 2 What about *sometimes*?

C **There is one mistake in each of these frequency phrases. Find it and correct it.**
 1 every days
 2 most day
 3 one time a week
 4 twice week
 5 three time a week
 6 every then and now

D **Look again at Tables 2, 3 and 4. Where can you put the frequency phrases in Exercise C?**

E **Look at Table 5 for one minute. Then close this book and draw the table in your notebook.**

F **Work in groups.**
 1 Make a list of adjectives.
 2 Use your list to describe yourself and other students.
 3 Share your descriptions with the rest of the class.

G **Work in groups.**
 1 Make a list of activities and time phrases similar to those in Table 3.
 2 Use your list to describe what you do.
 3 Share what you do with the rest of the class.

Lesson 1: Vocabulary

In this unit, you are going to:

- listen to a talk about work
- talk about jobs you would and wouldn't like to do
- read advertisements for work experience jobs
- complete an application form for a summer job

Key vocabulary
assistant   checkout
clerk   colleague
counsellor   guide
operator   papers
product   rely on   salary
service   telesales
urgent

A **Discuss these questions in pairs.**
1 Have you ever had a job? What was it? Did you like it? Why (not)?
2 What sort of job would you like when you leave college?
3 What sort of job would you hate? Why?

B **Match the pictures and the names of the jobs.**
Write each number next to the correct picture.
1 telesales clerk   5 checkout operator
2 leaflet distributor   6 fruit picker
3 nursery school assistant 7 language teacher
4 tour guide   8 camp counsellor

C **Complete each sentence using the *Key vocabulary*.**
1 People don't like him at work. They can't _____ him. They never know if he will be late, or not come to work at all.
2 It is very important to have good _____ to work with in a job.
3 That work isn't _____. You can do it tomorrow.
4 Where are the _____ for my next meeting? Are they in the file?
5 If you are paid every month, we call that money your _____.
6 Some companies make _____ – real things like computers, televisions or cars.
7 Some companies give _____ – like banks, cleaning companies or car hire companies.

D **Make jobs using words in each column.**
1 telesales   **a** assistant
2 leaflet   **b** clerk
3 nursery school   **c** counsellor
4 tour   **d** distributor
5 checkout   **e** guide
6 fruit   **f** operator
7 language   **g** picker
8 camp   **h** teacher

Lesson 2: Vocabulary

Ⓐ **Study the first extract from a dictionary. Then complete each sentence with one of the words.**

1 A good _____ looks after all the people in the company.
2 If you learn many skills at college, you will be _____ when you leave.
3 That company has 200 _____ in its main office.
4 We would like to _____ you to work as a teacher.
5 What is the length of _____ in this job? I mean, how long do you want me for?

Ⓑ **Study the other extracts from a dictionary. Then guess the meaning of these words and phrases.**

1 requirements
2 benefits
3 career-entry job

Ⓒ **Employers require qualifications and experience.**

1 Do you have any qualifications?
2 Do you have any work experience?
Explain your answers.

Ⓓ **Read the advertisement at the bottom of the page. Find a word from the *Key vocabulary* for each space. You may have to change the form of the word.**

employ (v) to pay someone to do a job
employable (adj) easy to employ, an ~ person has a lot of useful skills for an employer
employee (n) a person who is paid to do a job
employer (n) a person or company who pays someone to do a job
employment (n) **1** employing or being employed **2** a person's job

benefit (v) to get something good from, e.g., a job

career (n) several jobs in one field, e.g., teacher to senior teacher to director of education

enter (v) go into, e.g., a building
entry (n) a way to go in to, e.g., a building; a career

require (v) need

Key vocabulary
applicant assist benefit career employ
employable employee employer
employment experience overtime
qualification requirement salary

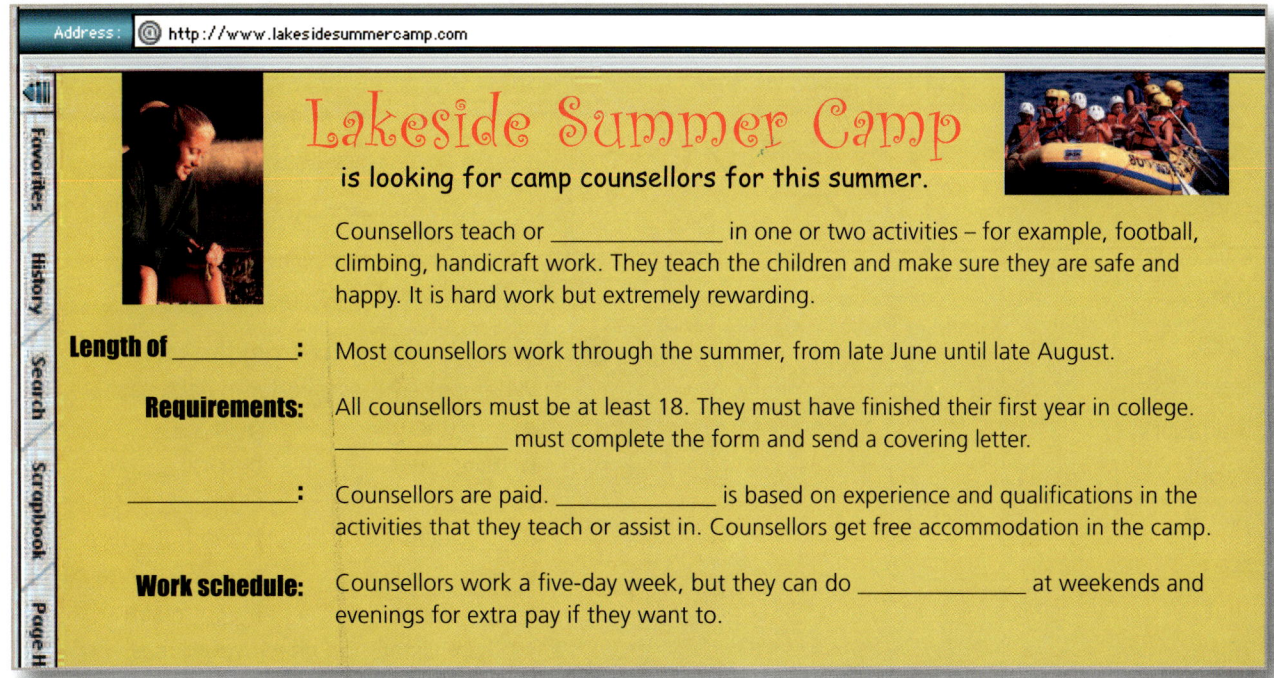

Address: @ http://www.lakesidesummercamp.com

Lakeside Summer Camp

is looking for camp counsellors for this summer.

Counsellors teach or _____ in one or two activities – for example, football, climbing, handicraft work. They teach the children and make sure they are safe and happy. It is hard work but extremely rewarding.

Length of _____: Most counsellors work through the summer, from late June until late August.

Requirements: All counsellors must be at least 18. They must have finished their first year in college. _____ must complete the form and send a covering letter.

_____: Counsellors are paid. _____ is based on experience and qualifications in the activities that they teach or assist in. Counsellors get free accommodation in the camp.

Work schedule: Counsellors work a five-day week, but they can do _____ at weekends and evenings for extra pay if they want to.

Lesson 3: Listening

A **Discuss these questions in pairs.**
1 What are the most important things to do when you have a job?
2 What are the main differences between having a job and going to college?
3 What are the main similarities between the two?

B 🔊 **1.25 Gerald Gardiner is a management consultant. He is at Greenhill College today. He is talking to the first-year students about work. Listen to the first part of his talk.**
1 How many points does he make?
2 Can you remember any of the points?

C 🔊 **1.26 Listen again. How does he define these words? Match each word to a definition.**

1	punctual	**a**	desk, shelves, cupboards
2	manager	**b**	good or bad
3	colleagues	**c**	always on time
4	customers	**d**	ordered by date
5	tasks	**e**	pieces of work
6	quality	**f**	the people who buy things from your company
7	workplace	**g**	the people you work with
8	chronologically	**h**	the person who gives you orders

D **Complete these notes from the talk with a verb in each space.**

E 🔊 **1.27 Listen again and check your answers.**

Revision

F **The words below are from the talk.**
1 Put a tick in the correct column, according to the underlined sound.
2 🔊 **1.28 Listen and check your ideas.**

	A	B	C	D
	fill	feel	have	half
	/ɪ/	/iː/	/æ/	/ɑː/
<u>a</u>re				✓
b<u>a</u>d			✓	
coll<u>ea</u>gues				
<u>g</u>ives				
k<u>ee</u>p				
l<u>ea</u>ve				
m<u>a</u>nager				
p<u>eo</u>ple				
p<u>ie</u>ces				
st<u>a</u>rt				
th<u>a</u>t				
th<u>i</u>nk				

You must:
1 _____ to work every day
2 _____ punctual
3 _____ manager/colleagues
4 _____ customers
5 _____ all tasks
6 _____ all tasks on time
7 _____ responsible for quality of work
8 _____ workplace tidy
9 _____ work files sensibly

G **The words below are from the talk.**
1 What is the missing letter in each case?

a	____unctual	**g**	jo____
b	res____ect	**h**	com____any
c	____uy	**i**	res____onsible
d	____ieces	**j**	work____lace
e	sensi____ly	**k**	com____lete
f	____eople	**l**	____erson

2 🔊 **1.29 Listen and check your ideas.**

Lesson 4: Listening

A Think of a word to complete each sentence. Find the hidden phrase that connects them all.

1	You must be ..., in other words, on time.
2	You must ... things – put them in order.
3	Work with your ..., the people who study with you.
4	Your work must be good ....
5	Keep your ... in order.
6	Your instructor is your ... at college.
7	You must ... people, especially your instructors.
8	You must keep your ... tidy.
9	Think of college as a ....
10	You are ... for your own work – if it's good, or bad.
11	Do all your ... well and on time.

B Read Skills Check 1.

1 Find and underline the important words in these sentences from the talk in Lesson 3.

  a You must go to work every day.

  b You must be punctual.

  c You must respect your manager and your colleagues.

  d You must also respect the customers.

  e You must do all the tasks or pieces of work that your manager gives you.

  f You must complete all your tasks on time.

  g You are responsible for the quality of your work.

  h You must keep your workplace tidy.

  i You must organize your work files sensibly.

2 🎧 **1.30** Listen and check your ideas.

C Read Skills Check 2.

1 Write these words from the talk in the correct place in the table below, according to the sound of *g*:

  go give college get change colleague organize

2 🎧 **1.31** Listen and check your answers.

3 Now put these words into the correct place:

  age page begin charge ago again large big

4 🎧 **1.32** Listen and check your answers.

5 What about these words?

  danger angry wage magazine rig

6 🎧 **1.33** Listen and check your answers.

A	*good /g/*	go
B	*manager /dʒ/*	college

Lesson 5: Speaking

(A) Number these jobs in order (1 = the one you would like the most).

__ telesales clerk   __ nursery school assistant   __ checkout operator   __ language teacher

__ leaflet distributor   __ tour guide   __ fruit picker   __ camp counsellor

(B) Julia Greco is a first-year student at Greenhill College. She wants to get a job during the summer holidays. She has filled in a form on a summer jobs website.

1 Read the website form. What kind of job would she like?

2 What does the computer suggest?

(C) ✹ 1.34 Julia's friend, Carla Fernandez, is talking to her. Listen.

1 Fill in the form for Carla.

2 Complete the suggestion.

I would like a job …

in my own country ☐	abroad ☐
alone ☐	with other people ☐
inside ☐	outside ☐

A good job for you is … |

(D) Complete each sentence with a word from the yellow box.

Carla: Are you going to _____ a job in the college holidays?

Julia: I'd _____ to. What about you?

Carla: Yes, I _____ so.

Julia: What would you like to _____?

Carla: I _____ not sure.

Julia: Would you like to _____ in your own country or abroad?

Carla: Oh, I'd like _____ work abroad.

Julia: _____ you like working alone or with other people?

Carla: With other people, definitely. I don't like _____ alone.

Julia: Do _____ like working inside or outside?

Carla: Um, _____ me think. Inside. No, I'll change that. Outside.

Find-a-job
The summer job finder
online at
www.summerjob.com

Do you want a summer job?
What sort of job would you like?
Answer the questions, press Find
and Find-a-job will do the rest!

I would like a summer job …
(choose one answer in each row)

in my own country ☒	abroad ☐
alone ☐	with other people ☒
inside ☒	outside ☐

Find

A good job for you is …

nursery school assistant
shop assistant

do get you let like
'm think to work
working Do

(E) ✹ 1.35 Listen to this part of the conversation again and check your answers.

Revision

(F) These words are from the conversation. Say each group of words. Which word is the odd one out? What do the others have in common?

1 think	inside	like	click	assistant
2 see	people	Greece	let	means
3 bad	that	have	at	what
4 ask	laugh	France	abroad	are

(G) Say these words from the conversation – with a *p*, not a *b*.

stupid   people   shop   camp   computer

(H) Practise the conversation in D in pairs.

Lesson 6: Speaking

A Work in pairs. Look at the incomplete jobs crosswords on page 149. Describe each job on your crossword to your partner.
  Examples:

> **A:** One across and thirteen across – a person who teaches languages.

> **B:** Two down, eleven down and three down – a person who helps in a school for young children.

B Read Skills Check 1.
  1 Choose the best way to complete each sentence.
    a I like *meet / meeting / to meeting* people.
    b I don't like *selling / to selling / sell* things.
    c Do you like to *working / work / working* alone?
    d Would you like *to be / being / be* a teacher?
    e I wouldn't like *work / to work / working* in a factory.
  2 Say the correct sentences.

C Complete these sentences with true information about you.
  1 I _____ working alone.
  2 I _____ meeting people.
  3 I _____ selling things.
  4 I _____ working outside.
  5 I _____ be a doctor.
  6 I _____ work for the government.
  7 I _____ work in a bank.

D Look at these phrases and sentences from Lesson 5. What is the sound of the underlined letters?
  1 I'm using this web pa<u>g</u>e
  2 a <u>g</u>ood summer job
  3 I think that's a stupid su<u>gg</u>estion!
  4 Are you <u>g</u>oing to <u>g</u>et a job in the colle<u>g</u>e holidays?
  5 What woul<u>d y</u>ou like to do?
  6 I'll chan<u>g</u>e that.
  7 So I <u>j</u>ust click *Find*
  8 I a<u>g</u>ree. I think that is a <u>g</u>ood su<u>gg</u>estion.

E Read Skills Check 2.
  1 Check your answers to Exercise D.
  2 Say the sentences aloud.

Skills Check 1

Talking about likes and dislikes

To talk about likes and dislikes in the **present**, we say:

I	like	working	alone.
	don't like	meeting	people.
		selling	things.

To ask about likes and dislikes in the **present**, we say: ***Do you like ...?***

To talk about likes and dislikes in the **future**, we say:

I	would like	to	be	a	(job).
	wouldn't like		work	as a	
				for	(type of company).
				in	(place).

To ask about likes and dislikes in the future, we say: ***Would you like ...?***

Skills Check 2

Saying consonants – /g/ and /dʒ/

The consonant g has two common sounds:
1 The sound /g/ in *good, get.*
2 The sound /dʒ/ in *college, suggest.*
The consonant j always makes the /dʒ/ sound.
Note: When the consonant d ends one word and the sound /j/ starts the next word, we often make the /dʒ/ sound.
Example: *Would you = wou jou*

Skills Check 3

Checking sounds in a dictionary (2)

If you meet a new word with g, you can check the pronunciation in a dictionary.
The sound in *go* is written /g/.
The sound in *college* is written /dʒ/.
How do you pronounce the g in these words?
age page begin charge ago again large big
Look up these words. Check the pronunciation.
danger angry wage magazine rig

Note: Some words with /dʒ/ are spelt with *j*:
job subject juice just June

Lesson 7: Reading

A Think of a job you would like to do when you leave college. Answer these questions.
1 What *qualifications* do you need?
2 What *experience* do you need?
3 Are there any other *requirements,* e.g., age?
4 What are the *benefits* of the job?

B What should you look at before you read a text in detail? Complete the words.
1 the illust _____
2 the ti _____
3 the intro _____ or first _____

C All the items on the right are from the same text. Is this text:
1 a newspaper report?
2 a leaflet?
3 an advertisement?

D Look at all the items again.
1 Label items A–C with words from Exercise B.
2 What are the items labelled D?
3 Read the Skills Check and check your answer to D2, above.

E Which question will each section answer? Match the questions to section headings a–f.
1 How long can I work for? _____
2 How much money do I earn? _____
3 What are the hours of work? _____
4 What jobs are available? _____
5 How old must I be? _____
6 What qualifications do I need? _C_

F Read the text on page 139. Find the answers to the questions in Exercise E.

G Read the text again.
1 Underline any new words.
2 Ask the teacher about the new words.

H Discuss these questions in groups.
1 Could you work for Get Set this summer? Explain your answer.
2 Would you like to do a work experience course in the summer? If so, in which field?

A

Get Set
WORK EXPERIENCE COMPANY

B
We are looking for students for work experience jobs this summer.

C

D a **The Jobs**

b **Length of Employment**

c **Requirements**

d **Benefits**

e **Work**

f **Schedule**

Skills Check

Preparing to read (4)

Many texts have **section headings**. A section heading is a title for part of the text.
Always read the section headings before you read the text. Think …
What question(s) will this section answer?

Lesson 8: Reading

Ⓐ Study the sentences in the yellow box.

1 Do you understand the words in red?
2 Read Skills Check 1.
3 Read the sentences again. Follow the advice in the Skills Check. Do you understand the sentences?

> **a** You **normally** work a five-day week.
> **b** You can **occasionally** do overtime at the weekend.
> **c** You get **additional** money for this work.
> **d** **Conversely**, you cannot do overtime in a career-entry job.

Ⓑ Study the groups of words in the green box.

1 What is the connection between each group?
2 Read Skills Check 2. Write a heading for each group of words.
3 Add more words to each group.

start	hotel	different
end	restaurant	interesting
do	job	early
get	engineering	late
must be	experience	full-time

Ⓒ Study the sentences in the blue box.

1 Underline the nouns, circle the verbs and box the adjectives.
2 Read Skills Check 3 and check.

> **a** You must be in full-time education.
>
> **b** You receive extra money for this work.
>
> **c** You can do overtime at weekends.
>
> **d** They last through the summer.

Skills Check 1

Dealing with new words (3)

When you find a new word in a text, think:
*Can I understand this sentence **without** the new word?*
Example:
The jobs usually start in June.
Perhaps you don't understand *usually*.
Cross out the word.
The jobs ~~usually~~ start in June.
Can you understand the sentence?

Skills Check 2

Dealing with new words (4)

There are three main kinds of word. They are:
noun (n) – *boy, college. idea*
verb (v) – *go, be, walked, has done*
adjective (adj) – *good, intelligent, nicer*

A new word will probably be a **noun**, a **verb** or an **adjective**, but there are also:
pronouns (pron): *I, you, he, it, them*
prepositions (prep): *in, on, for, with*
articles (art): *a, the, some, any*
adverbs (adv): *quickly, also, usually*

Skills Check 3

Dealing with new words (5)

When you find a new word in a text, think:
Is this word a noun, a verb or an adjective?
The pattern of the sentence will help you.
Study these phrases and patterns from the text in Lesson 7.

Sentences	Patterns
You **receive** ...	pron + **v**
... **jobs last**	**n + v**
... **students can do overtime**	**n + v + n**
... in a **hotel**	prep + art + **n**
... in **full-time education**	pron + **adj + n**
... **jobs are full-time**	**n + 'be' + adj**

When you know the word is, e.g., a noun, you can sometimes **guess** the meaning **from context**.

Lesson 9: Writing

A Jackie Grant is single. She is a student at Greenhill College. She is interested in the camp counsellor jobs at Lakeside Summer Camp (see Lesson 2), but she can't work there for the whole summer. She doesn't want to do overtime at the weekend.

1 Write information from the box in the correct place in the application form below. Use the green column.

2 Follow the instructions on the form to complete the other sections.

> 0347 493675   18   23rd June   18th July   ~~handball~~, piano ~~guitar, cycling~~
> ~~Grade 5 piano; Grade 2 guitar; cycling proficiency certificate~~ JACKIE GRANT ENGINEERING
> GRANGE HOSTEL, GARDEN ROAD, GREENHILL   GREENHILL COLLEGE
> ~~I am captain of the college handball team~~; I play the piano and the guitar.   MARTIN GRANT
> I would like to be a teacher.   jackieg@yahoomail.com   ONE   Yes, I do.

Lakeside Summer Camp
Application Form
Please complete Sections 1 and 2 in BLOCK CAPITALS. Use black ink only.

1. Personal details	Title (delete as applicable)	Mr / Mrs / Miss / Ms	Mr / Mrs / Miss / Ms
	Name		
	Present address		
	Age		
	Telephone		
	E-mail		
	Parent / Guardian (delete as applicable)		
2. Present situation	University / college?		
	What is your major / main subject?		
	How many years have you completed?		
3. Summer job	Which activities are you able to teach?	piano, guitar, cycling	
	Which activities are you able to assist in?	handball	
	I am available for work (tick or delete and complete as applicable)		
	for the whole period		
	from		
	to		
	I would like to do overtime (tick as applicable)		
	in the evenings		
	at the weekend		
4. Background information	What job would you like when you leave college?		
	Relevant experience	I am captain of the college handball team	
	Relevant qualifications	Grade 5 piano, Grade 2 guitar, cycling proficiency certificate	
	Have you got a car?		

B Each group of words has the same sound. But what are the missing letters?

1 t __ __ ch	__ vening	w __ __ kend	del __ te
2 c __ mp	c __ ptain	pi __ no	h __ ve
3 tit __ __	ab __ __	availab __ __	applicab __ __
4 g __ __ den	guit __ __	gu __ __ dian	f __ ther
5 capt __ __ n	d __ lete	gu __ tar	coll __ ge

C Apply for a job at Lakeside Summer Camp. Write true information in the final column.

Lesson 10: Writing

A One letter is missing from each of these words from Lesson 9.

1 Is the missing letter *g* or *j*?

a a__e		**h**	brid__e
b colle__e		**i**	en__ineering
c __arden		**j**	__rade
d __reen		**k**	__uardian
e __uitar		**l**	__ob
f __uly		**m**	__une
g ma__or		**n**	sub__ect

2 Read Skills Check 1. Check your ideas.

B Jackie Grant (see Lesson 9) has to write a covering letter for her application to the Summer Camp. She wants to give lots of information about herself.

1 Read Skills Check 2.
2 Choose the best way to complete each sentence. You can make up information or take it from Jackie's application form (Lesson 9).

a I am eighteen years old *and* _____
_____

b I have completed one year *and* _____
_____

c I would like to do overtime in the evenings *but* _____
_____

d I am not available for the whole of the period *but* _____
_____

e I can drive *and* _____
_____

f My home is in London *but* _____
_____

C Jackie wants to give reasons for some pieces of information.

1 Read Skills Check 3.
2 Think of a suitable way to continue each sentence.

a I am studying engineering because
_____

b I would like to be a teacher because
_____

c I cannot work for the whole of the summer because _____

d I am living in a hostel at Greenhill College because _____

Lesson 11: Grammar

Ⓐ Look at Table 1a.

1 Use these nouns to make statements about a work experience company.

> helpline   website   holiday jobs
> part-time jobs

2 Make *yes/no* questions. (Use *any, many.*)

3 Make the sentences negative. (Use *any, many.*)

4 Add these adjectives to your sentences. Say them to yourself: *useful, short, interesting, friendly*

Table 1a: There + *verb* (be) + *noun phrase*

There	Verb	Noun phrase
There	is	a _____
There	is	a _____
There	are	some _____
There	are	a lot of _____

Ⓑ Look at your work in A and at Table 1b.

1 Write your A4 sentences into **first mention** boxes.

2 How do **first mention** sentences begin?

3 How do **further information** sentences begin?

4 Complete the **further information** sentences.

Table 1b: *First mention + further information*

There is/are + first mention	Pronoun + *is/are* + further information
_____ friendly helpline you can call.	_____ open all day.
_____ a useful website.	_____ easy to use.
_____ short part-time jobs.	_____ for three or four weeks.
_____ interesting holiday jobs.	_____ for six weeks.

Lesson 12: Grammar

A **Look at Table 2.**

1 Add *a* and *the* where necessary. If no article is necessary, write nothing.

2 Match a–c and i–iii to form the correct rules.

   a Use *a/an/some* + noun when you …

   b Use *the* + noun when you …

   c Use zero article when you …

      i … refer to all things/people in a group.

      ii … refer to particular things/people we know about.

      iii … first mention particular things/people.

Table 2: *Indefinite, definite and zero articles*

	Article + noun
Today, we're going to play	_____ game of football.
Well, I don't want to play in	_____ game.
That's because I'm no good at	_____ games.

B **Look at Table 3.**

1 Complete the table with these modal verbs:

> must   can   cannot (can't)

2 State rules in your country.

   • To (drive/get married), …

   • If you are not (age), …

Table 3: *Modal verbs* must, can, cannot (can't)

	Modal verb + verb	
To get a holiday job, you	_____ be	at least 18.
If you work for us, you	_____ get	free accommodation.
If you are not in education, you	_____ work	for us.
To apply for a job, you	_____ complete	a form.

C **Look at Table 4.**

1 Circle these prepositions in the time expressions:

> at   during   for   from … to/until
> in   on   through   until

2 Write about your life. Include time expressions.

Table 4: *Prepositions in time expressions*

	Time expressions
Zara got the job of counsellor at a summer camp.	in April.
Camp started	on June 1.
Now it is early July, so she has been there	for about a month.
She plans to work all the way	through the summer.

UNIT 4 Science and Nature

Lesson 1: Vocabulary

In this unit, you are going to:

- listen to a talk about science as a career and the scientific method
- explain some natural events
- read two articles about the effects of the sun
- Write about information in a table

A Discuss these questions in pairs.

1 What's your favourite colour?
2 What's your favourite type of weather?
3 What's your favourite type of landscape – hills, mountains, the sea …?

B Work in groups.

1 Put the instructions and explanation in a logical order. Use the diagram to help you.
2 Do the experiment.

Instructions and explanation
Colour the sections red, orange, yellow, green and blue.
Make a spinner with five sections.
Spin the spinner. What colour do you see?
When we mix all the colours, we get white.
You should see white, because white light contains all the colours.

Key vocabulary
diagram experiment
explain explanation
graph laboratory
natural science
scientific scientist
sunrise sunset
table test

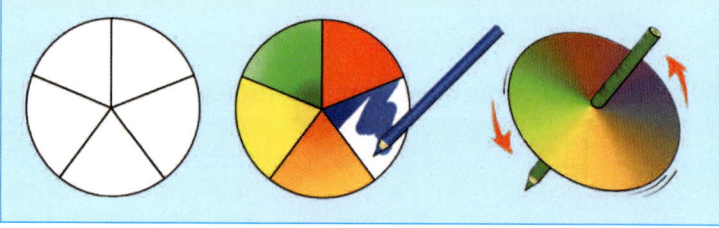

C Discuss this point.

Does the experiment in Exercise B help you to answer these questions about natural events?

1 Why is the sky blue?
2 Why is the sky red, orange and yellow at sunrise and sunset?
3 Why are clouds white?

D 🔊 1.36 **Listen to a paragraph. Then write one of the** *Key vocabulary* **words in each space.**

_____ is the study of how things work in the world.

A _____ usually works in a _____.

He or she _____ things to find out the facts. He or she often puts the facts in a _____, with columns of information, or in a _____, with blocks or lines that represent the information.

Table 1: *Temperatures (in °C)*

	Jan	Feb	Mar	Apr	May	Jun	Jul	Aug	Sep	Oct	Nov	Dec
Abu Dhabi	19	20	23	27	31	33	35	34	32	29	25	20
London	4	4	6	9	12	15	17	17	14	10	7	5

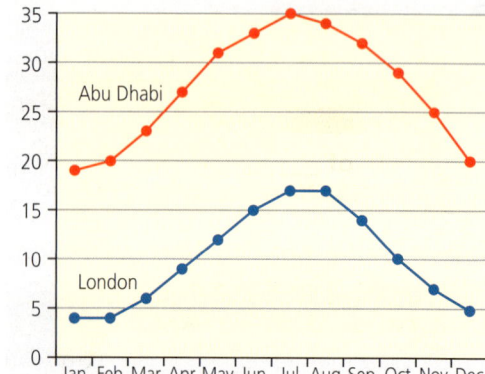

Figure 1: *Temperature (in °C)*

Lesson 2: Vocabulary

A **Discuss these questions.**
What is the weather like in your area in summer / in autumn / in winter / in spring?

B **Look at Figure 1. Read this paragraph.**
This **graph** shows the **average** monthly temperature in two cities, Dubai and New York. In New York, there is a **small increase** in temperature from January to February. There is a **steady increase** in temperature from February to April, then a **large increase** to May. The hottest month is July. There is a **steady decrease** in temperature from August to December.

Key vocabulary 1
average   decrease
graph   increase
large   small   steady
unit of measurement

C **Look at Figure 1 again. Read this paragraph, then complete the paragraph using words from *Key vocabulary 1*.**
The _____ shows that the _____ monthly temperature in Dubai is much higher than in New York. There is a _____ increase in temperature from January to February. There is a _____ increase in temperature from February to July. The hottest months are July and August. There is a steady _____ in temperature from September to December.

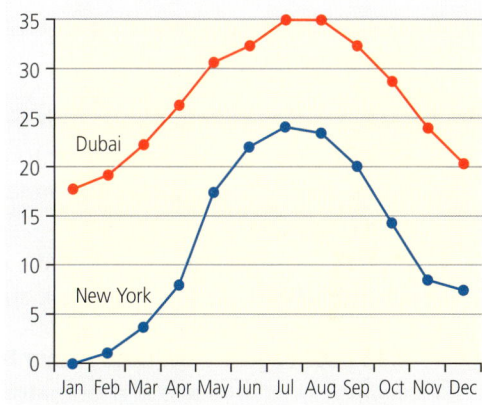

Figure 1: *Temperature (in °C)*

D **Look at the diagram and read the text below. Label the diagram with words from *Key vocabulary 2*.**

Key vocabulary 2
column   latitude
longitude
Meridian   pole
row   source
the Earth
the Equator

Where are Dubai and New York? We can use lines of latitude and longitude to give the position of a place on the Earth. Lines of latitude run around the Earth. The best-known line of latitude is the Equator, which runs around the centre of the Earth. Lines of longitude run from the North Pole to the South Pole. The most important line of longitude is the Greenwich Meridian, which runs through London. International time, or GMT, is taken from this line. So where are Dubai and New York? Dubai is on latitude 25° North and longitude 55° East, and New York is on latitude 40° North and longitude 73° West.

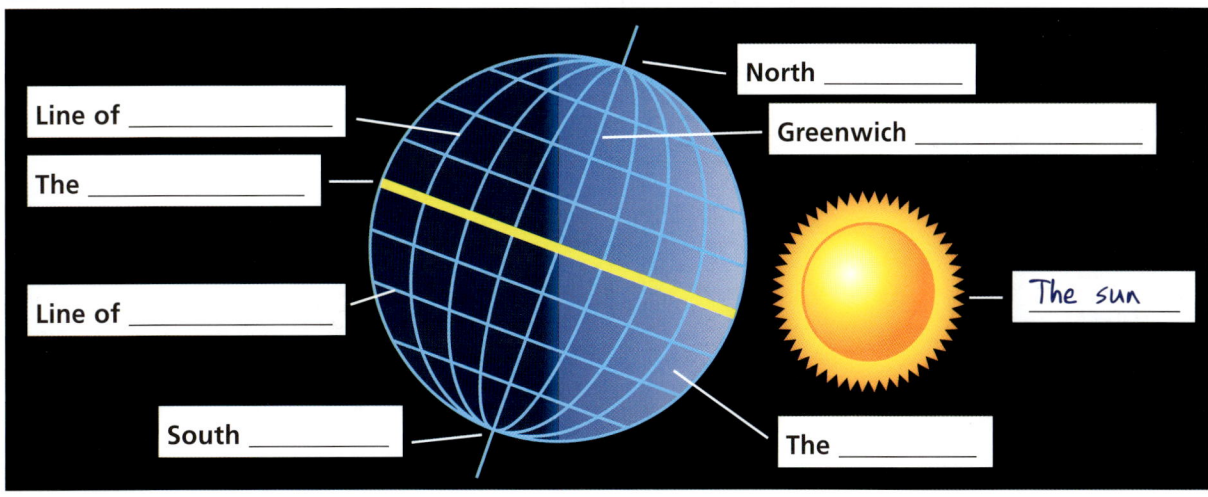

Lesson 3: Listening

A **Discuss the questions in pairs.**
1 What do you think of when you hear the word *science*?
2 Are you interested in science?
3 Would you like to be a scientist?

B **Look at the information on the right. It is about a radio programme. Then work in pairs to discuss these questions.**
1 Where can you see information like this?
2 What time does the programme start?
3 What is the programme about?
4 Who is the programme for?

C **Arthur is going to talk about four points.**
1 🔘 **1.37** Listen to the introduction to the programme. Tick (✓) each point in the programme information on the left when Arthur mentions it.
2 🔘 **1.38** Listen to the first part of the programme. Put your hand up when Arthur starts to talk about a new point.

D 🔘 **1.39 Listen again. How does Arthur Burns define these words?**
1	proving	**a**	a test in a laboratory
2	method	**b**	looking up information, e.g., in a library
3	hypothesis	**c**	an idea of the truth
4	experiment	**d**	information before it is organized
5	research	**e**	a way of doing something
6	data	**f**	what you learn from an experiment
7	conclusions	**g**	showing that something is always true

E 🔘 **1.40 Look at the student notes on the right. Listen to the first part of the programme again. Complete the notes by writing one word in each space.**

Revision

F **The words below are from the talk.**
1 Tick the correct column, according to the underlined sound.
2 🔘 **1.41** Listen and check your ideas.

	A	B	C	D
	fill	feel	have	half
	/ɪ/	/iː/	/æ/	/ɑː/
d<u>i</u>splay	✓			
<u>e</u>ven		✓		
<u>e</u>nough				
gr<u>a</u>ph				
Gr<u>ee</u>k				
h<u>a</u>ppen				
<u>i</u>f				
l<u>a</u>b				
p<u>a</u>st				
pl<u>a</u>nt				

9.15 So you want to be …
a scientist?
In this week's programme, Arthur Burns looks at science as a career.
• What is science?
• What do scientists do?
• What is *scientific method*?
• Is science the right career for you?

9.45 The World in View

Science = Greek/Latin to
_____

Science = knowing things +
_____ things

Scientific method:
_____ a hypothesis.
_____ the hypothesis.
_____ an experiment
or _____ some research.
_____ data.
_____ the results in a table
or a graph.
_____ conclusions.
_____ or disprove the
hypothesis.

G **The words below are from the programme.**
1 What are the missing letters?
2 🔘 **1.42** Listen and check your ideas.
a	____rove	**f**	dis____rove
b	dis____lay	**g**	hy____othesis
c	____oth	**h**	ex____eriment
d	ta____le	**i**	la____
e	____ast	**j**	ha____ ____en

Lesson 4: Listening

A **Think of a word to complete each sentence. Find the hidden word that connects them all.**

1 … is looking up information, e.g., in a library.											
2 You can draw … from a good 3.											
3 You do these in a laboratory.											
4 A … is a way of doing something.											
5 I think it's true, but I don't …											
6 A … is an idea of the truth about something.											
7 Scientists use … method.											
8 We often put these in a table or on a graph.											
9 This is information before it is organized.											

B **Read Skills Check 1. Answer the questions.**
   1 What is it about?
   2 Why should you try to predict the next word?

C **You are going to hear some parts of the radio programme in Lesson 3 again.**
   1 Look at the words in the yellow box. Think of sentences from the radio programme with these words.
   2 🔊 **1.43** Listen to some of Arthur's sentences. Choose the next word from the yellow box each time Arthur pauses. Write the number beside the word.

   | data   graph   know   method   true   world |

D **Read Skills Check 2.**
   1 Put these words from the talk into the correct column, according to the sound of *th*.
   that   the   they   both   then   there   hypothesis   with thing   truth
   2 🔊 **1.44** Listen and check your answers.

A	B
think	this
/θ/	/ð/

E **Answer the questions.**
   1 Which is the odd one out?
   test   when   then   pen   she   bed   many   any   head   again
   2 🔊 **1.45** Listen and check your answers.
   3 Work in pairs. What do all these words have in common?
   bird   first   heard   learn   person   research   surname turn   work   world
   4 Read Skills Check 3. Did you get the right answer to Question 3?

Skills Check 1

What comes next?
We can often predict the next word in a talk. **Examples:** *Science is about knowing things, but even more it is about proving … **things.***
*I know that plants need sunlight to live. At least, I think that's … **true.***
*They can do research, which means looking up … **information.***
If you can predict the next word, you can listen with more understanding.

Skills Check 2

Hearing consonants – /θ/ and /ð/
The consonants *th* have two sounds:
1 The soft sound in *think, thing*: /θ/.
2 The harder sound in *this, the*: /ð/.

Skills Check 3

Hearing vowels – /e/ and /ɜː/
The vowel sound in *then* is usually written with *e*. But there are some common words with *a* or *ea*:
Examples: *many, any, head*
The vowel sound in *her* is written in many different ways: res**ear**ch, w**or**d, b**ir**d, t**ur**n.
In American English, we can hear the *r* sound in these words.

Lesson 5: Speaking

A Martha Smith is reading a newspaper in the college cafe. She has seen an interesting item. Read the item on the right. Then answer the questions in pairs.

1 What is this?
2 How many questions do you have to answer?
3 What else do you have to do?
4 What happens if you win?

B 🔊 **1.46** Martha's friend, Ruth, comes into the cafe. Listen to the conversation. Which question can Ruth answer?

C Look at these sentences from the first part of the conversation.

1 Think of something for Ruth to say in each case.

Ruth: Hi, Martha. _____?

Martha: I'm fine, thanks. Have a seat.

Ruth: _____. What are you doing?

Martha: I'm thinking about this competition.

Ruth: Oh, a competition. I _____ competitions.

Martha: Could you help me, then?

Ruth: _____. I'll give you a hand.

Martha: Thanks. Do you know anything about science and nature?

Ruth: You mean birds and weather and things?

Martha: Yes, things like that.

Ruth: Oh no. _____. I'm afraid _____.

Martha: That's a pity. Neither do I.

Ruth: Well, _____, anyway. What are they asking?

2 🔊 **1.47** Listen again to the first part of the conversation and check your ideas.

Revision

D These words are from the conversation. Say each group of words. Which is the odd one out? What do the others have in common?

1 reading	neither	easier	great
2 because	like	pity	give
3 what	asking	answer	last
4 have	that	hand	anyway

E How do some people say the underlined parts of these phrases?

Could you ...?   Did you ...?
Would you ...?   Do you ...?
Should you ...?

F Practise the conversation in Exercise C in pairs.

A   Why is the sky blue?
B   Why is the sky red at sunrise and sunset?
C   Why are the clouds white or grey?
D   Why does it rain?

Are you a natural scientist?
Nature.com is looking for young scientists.

The rules are simple.
1 Choose one of the questions above.
2 Write an explanation that anyone (not just a scientist) can understand.
3 Draw a diagram to go with your explanation.
4 Send your entry to *Nature.com*. If you win, you will meet a famous scientist.

Lesson 6: Speaking

A **Choose the best reply for each question:**
Yes, please **or** *Yes, certainly*.
1 Could you give me a hand?
2 Can I help you?
3 Could you help me?
4 Would you like some help?
5 Do you need some help?
6 Can I carry that for you?

B **Read Skills Check 1.**
1 Complete these sentences with a suitable word in each space.
   A: Could you _____ me a hand?
   B: Yes, of _____.

   C: Could you help _____?
   D: No, sorry. I'm _____ I can't.

   E: Can I _____ you?
   F: Yes, _____.

   G: I'll give you a _____.
   H: No, _____ you. I can _____.
2 Practise saying the mini-conversations in pairs.

C **Look at these phrases and sentences from the conversation in Lesson 5.**
1 What is the sound of *th* in each case?
   a I'm fine, thanks.
   b I'm thinking about this competition.
   c That's a pity.
   d Neither do I.
   e What are they asking?
   f Why is the sky blue?
   g You mean birds and weather?
   h I don't know that one either.
2 Read Skills Check 2 and check your answers.
3 Practise saying the phrases and sentences aloud.

D **Read these sentences aloud.**
Then Ben's ten men went to bed.
Were her first words 'bird' and 'learn'?
1 Underline the words with the same vowel sound in each sentence.
2 Read Skills Check 3. Check your answers.

Skills Check 1

All about helping!

Ask	Could	you	help	me	?
			give		a hand?
Reply	Yes,	of course.			
		certainly.			
	No,	sorry.		I'm afraid	I can't.
Offer	Can I	help	you	?	
	I'll	give		a hand.	
Reply	Yes,	please.			
	No,	thank you.	I	can	manage.

Skills Check 2

Saying consonants – /θ/ and /ð/

The consonants *th* have two sounds:
1 The soft sound /θ/ in *think, thanks*.
2 The harder sound /ð/ in *that, either, neither, this, they, the, weather*.
If you meet a new word with *th*, you can check the pronunciation in a dictionary.

Skills Check 3

Saying vowels – /e/, /ʃː/, /ə/

We pronounce most words with *e* with the short sound /e/.
Examples: *then, bed, men.*
The letters *er* often come in the middle of a word. We often pronounce the letters with /ʃː/.
Examples: *person, certainly, verb*
The letters *er* often come at the end of a word. We pronounce the letters with /ə/.
Examples: *river, computer, flower, weather*
The sound /ʃː/ is also in many words without the letters *er*.
Examples: *first, learn, burn, word*

Lesson 7: Reading

A **What do tables of information have? Complete the words.**

1 col_____   4 a so_____
2 r_____   5 a u_____ (e.g., degrees)
3 head_____

B **Look at the table on the right. True (T) or false (F)?**

1 There are four columns in this table.
2 There are seven rows in this table.
3 In the first row, there are headings.
4 In the first column, there are capital cities.
5 In the second column, there is information about average rainfall.
6 All the information in this table comes from worldweather.com.
7 Muscat has the highest average temperature of these capital cities.
8 Damascus has the lowest average temperature in the world.

C **The table illustrates the information in the text on page 140.**

1 Which of these sentences do you expect to find in the text? Explain your answers.
  a As you travel north or south from the Equator, the average temperature falls.
  b Cities are often much warmer in summer …
  c In Muscat on July 1ˢᵗ, sunrise is at 5.22 …
  d Kampala is almost on the Equator.
  e Muscat is 2,500 kilometres north of the Equator …
  f The sun rises in the east …
  g There are many factors that affect the average temperature.
2 Look quickly through the text on page 140 and check your answers.

D **Read the text. Deal with any new words.**

E **Complete this summary. Use words from the text.**

There are many _____ that affect average temperature, but the _____ factor is _____ from the Equator. Places near the Equator are _____ because the sun is _____ in the sky during the day.

Why Is It So Hot?

Table 2:
Average temperature in selected capital cities

Capital cities	Average temperature (in °C)	Line of latitude °N	Distance from the Equator (in km)
Muscat	28.6	23	2,530
Abu Dhabi	27.1	24	2,640
Doha	26.6	25	2,750
Manama	26.1	26	2,860
Kuwait	25.6	29	3,190
Baghdad	22.7	33	3,630
Damascus	17.0	33	3,630

Source: Average temperature information from worldweather.com

WHY ARE SOME PLACES HOTTER than other places? Is there one single factor that affects the average temperature at a location? The simple answer is no.

Lesson 8: Reading

Ⓐ **Complete these sentences from the text in Lesson 7 with one word in each space.**

1 Why do some cities have a high average temperature and _____ cities have a _____ average temperature?

2 Is there one single _____ that _____ the temperature at a _____?

3 _____, there is one _____ that strongly _____ the average _____.

Ⓑ **Read Skills Check 1.**

1 What do you often find in a text after a statement of fact?

2 What do you often find after the word *include*?

Ⓒ **Look again at the article *Why Is It So Hot?* on page 140. Find three sentences with examples.**

Ⓓ **Read Skills Check 2.**

1 Find and underline the topic sentences in the article *Why Is It So Hot?*

2 Don't look at the article. There is one mistake in each topic sentence in the green box below. Find and correct the mistakes. Then look again at the article and check.

> **a** There are two factors that affect the average temperature.
>
> **b** However, there is one main factor that strongly influences the average rainfall.
>
> **c** As you travel north or south from the Equator, the average temperature rises.
>
> **d** Why is it so cold at the Equator?

Ⓔ **Topic sentences help you predict the content of a paragraph.**

1 Don't look at the article. Read the corrected topic sentences in Exercise D. What information comes after each sentence? Discuss in pairs.

2 Look again at the article and check.

Skills Check 1

Giving examples

Many paragraphs have this structure:

statement of fact	*As you travel north or south from the Equator, the average temperature falls.*
example(s)	*In Muscat, for example, …*

We introduce examples with:
For example / instance, …
Take …, for example / instance

We introduce several examples with *include*:
There are many factors.
*These factors **include** …*

Skills Check 2

Topic sentences

The first paragraph helps you predict the content of the text.
The **first sentence** of each paragraph often helps you predict **the content of the paragraph**.
The first sentence of a paragraph is called the **topic sentence**.

We can often use the topic sentences to make a **summary** of a text.

Lesson 9: Writing

A Gary Igarov, a student at Greenhill, is writing about weather around the world.

1 Read his paragraph about temperature in one city.

2 Find information in the paragraph to complete the table.

Table 2 shows the average temperature each month in Dhaka, Bangladesh. As we can see, January is the coldest month, at 18.5 degrees Celsius, and April, May and June are the hottest months. The average temperature in April is 29.0, but May is slightly hotter (29.5). There is a steady increase in temperature from January to May and a steady decrease in temperature from September to December. The average temperature for Dhaka is 25.6 degrees Celsius.

B Look at Table 3. Find:

1 the title of the table.

2 the unit of measurement.

3 the wettest month(s).

4 the driest month(s).

5 the average rainfall.

C Here are Gary's notes for a paragraph about rainfall in Dhaka.

1 Number them in a logical order. Look back at the paragraph in Exercise A to help you.

2 Find pairs of sentences to join with *and*.

3 Write a draft paragraph describing the information in Table 3.

As we can see, July is the wettest month.

January, November and December are the driest months.

June, August and September are also very wet.

There is a large increase in rainfall in June and July.

There is a steep decrease in rainfall from September to December.

The average rainfall for Dhaka is 160 millimetres.

Table 3 shows the average monthly rainfall in Dhaka.

D Exchange drafts with your partner.

1 Read the draft. Do you think your partner has:

   a put the information in a logical order?

   b chosen good sentences to join with *and*?

   c copied words correctly from the notes?

2 Talk to your partner about any points.

Table 2: *Average monthly temperature in* _____

Month	_____
Jan	18.5
Feb	20.5
Mar	24.5
Apr	29.0
May	_____
Jun	29.0
Jul	_____
Aug	28.5
Sep	28.5
Oct	27.5
Nov	23.5
_____	19.5
Total	_____
Average	_____

Table 3: *Average monthly rainfall in Dhaka*

Month	mm
Jan	18
Feb	31
Mar	58
Apr	103
May	194
Jun	321
Jul	437
Aug	305
Sep	254
Oct	169
Nov	28
Dec	2
Average	**160**

Revision

E The words below *could* be spelt this way, from the sound, but they are not. Correct the spelling.

1 averidge   6 tabel

2 eech   7 Auggust

3 dri   8 ar

4 steap   9 increese

5 stedy   10 deecreese

Lesson 10: Writing

A **You can make an English word by putting the vowel sound in *her* between each pair of letters.**

1 What is the word? How do you spell it?

   a b __ __ d   **g** w __ __ ld
   b h __ __ __ __ d   **h** f __ __ st
   c th __ __ d   **i** w __ __ k
   d w __ __ d   **j** g __ __ l
   e t __ __ n   **k** h __ __ t
   f b __ __ n   **l** sh __ __ t

2 Read Skills Check 1. Check your spelling.

B **Look at each group of words.**

1 What is wrong with the spelling in each group?

   a hoter   wetest   suny
   b coldder winddy   mistty
   c clouddy rainning colourred

2 Read Skills Check 2. Check your ideas.

C **Gary Igarov has written a paragraph about rainfall in Dhaka. The spelling and grammar are good, but he has made some mistakes in talking about the tables.**

1 Find and correct the mistakes.

2 Read Skills Check 3 and check your answers.

Table 3 is showing the average monthly rainfall in Dhaka. We could see from the table that July is the wettest month and January, November and December are the driest months. January is also the coldest month (look Table 2). There is lots of rainfall in June, August and September. April, May and October are also very wet but, as we are seeing in Table 3, there is less rainfall on average in these months. There is a steep decrease in rainfall from September to December. The average temperature (Table 2) falls during these months. There is a steep increase in rainfall from March to July.

Skills Check 1

Spelling the *er* sound

Many words have the vowel sound in *her* (/ɜː/), but the sound can be spelt in different ways.

1 with *er*: her, person, were, certainly
2 with *ear*: learn, heard, earn
3 with *ir*: bird, third, first, girl
4 with *or*: work, word, world
5 with *ur*: burn, turn, hurt

When you hear the sound *er*, always ask:
Excuse me. How do you spell that word?

Skills Check 2

Doubling letters

We sometimes double consonants when we add endings to words.

Examples: *hot – hotter / hottest*

Look for this pattern at the end of the word:

  C   V   C + C +er
  h   o   t + t +er

We don't double the consonant with these patterns at the end of words:

VCC – *cold*   VVC – *cloud*

Note: C = consonant; V = vowel (a, e, i, o, u)

Skills Check 3

Writing about tables

We put information into tables to make it easier to read. But we often write *about* the information in a table to make sure that the reader notices the important points. We tell the reader to look at the correct table while they are reading. Study the different ways of referring to (talking about) tables:

Table 2 shows the average monthly temperature in Dhaka.

The average monthly rainfall in Dhaka **(Table 3)** is 160 mm.

The hottest month in Dhaka is May **(see Table 2).**

As you can see in Table 2, the average monthly temperature in Dhaka is 25.6 degrees Celsius.

We can (also) see from the table/from Table 2 that the coldest month is January.

Lesson 11: Grammar

A **Look at Table 1.**

  1 Complete the table with appropriate prepositions of movement. Choose from the following:

  across along away from towards down up into out of over under round through

  2 Write more pairs of sentences of your own.

Table 1: *Prepositions of movement*

Speakers		Preposition	
Alan	We can't get	_____	the river here.
Peter	But if we walk	_____	the river, we'll find a place.
Nadia	Our plane flew	_____	a storm on the way to Cairo.
Hanan	We didn't come	_____	it until we were nearly there.
Maria	We went	_____	the mountain very slowly.
Rosa	But then we came	_____	again really fast!
Fuad	We need to swim	_____	here. It's dangerous.
Ahmed	Let's move	_____	the beach. It's safe there.

B **Many expressions, nouns, adjectives and verbs use particular prepositions. Which prepositions often go with these?**

  at / for the first time make friends to / with responsible about / for
  the start for / of take care by / of

C **Look at Table 2.**

  1 Which comments take each of these forms:
   • 1st idea ... 2nd idea that adds (+) to the 1st?
   • 1st idea ... 2nd idea that goes against (–) the 1st
  2 Which words introduce (+) ideas?
  3 Which words introduce (–) ideas?
  4 Which words connect 1st and 2nd ideas in one sentence?
  5 Which words start a new sentence for the 2nd idea?

Table 2: *Connectors – additive and contrastive*

1st idea	Connector	2nd idea
Dubai is a big trading centre,	and	it has a large tourist industry.
It has a large port.	In addition,	there is big new airport.
Riyadh is the Saudi capital,	but	Jeddah is the commercial centre.
Jeddah is on the coast,	whereas	Riyadh is in the desert.
Riyadh is the political centre.	However,	Makkah is the religious heart.

Lesson 12: Grammar

Ⓐ Look at Table 3.

1 Underline the clauses that start with the pronouns *who, which* and *that*.

2 Which of these clauses complete the meaning of the sentence?

3 Which ones add extra information?

4 How do we show that it is extra information? (Think about commas.)

Table 3: *Relative clauses*

	Relative clause	
Egypt is a country	which/that has a long history.	
The Pharaohs were the kings	who/that ruled Ancient Egypt.	
Jordan	, which is west of Iraq,	has several regions.
The Jordanian people	, who live mainly in the north,	have an ancient culture.

Ⓑ Look at Table 4a. Complete the table with the correct forms of *cold*.

Table 4a: *Comparative and superlative adjectives*

Adjective			
comparative	In winter, Moscow is	_____ _____	any Arab city.
superlative	Vostok, near the South Pole, is	_____ _____	place on Earth.

Ⓒ Look at Table 4b.

1 Study the spelling rules for comparative and superlative adjectives with:

a one syllable, and **b** two syllables if they end in *y*. Explain the spelling rules in your own words.

2 Give the comparative and superlative forms of these.   close   cloudy   high   nice   steep   sunny   wet

Table 4b: *Comparative and superlative spellings*

Rules	Adjective	Comparative	Superlative
cold + er/est	cold	_____	_____
dark	_____	_____	_____
large + r/st	_____	_____	_____
late	_____	_____	_____
dry – y + ier/iest	_____	_____	_____
happy	_____	_____	_____
hot + t + er/est	_____	_____	_____
big + g (ending with 1 vowel + 1 consonant)	_____	_____	_____

Ⓓ Look at Table 5.

1 Complete the questions with these question words.   How far   How high   What   When   Where   Why

2 Use the tables on pages 10–11 to answer questions 1–5.

3 Answer question 6 from the first text.

Table 5: *Questions*

Question words	Aux	Noun/pronoun	Verb	Other
_____	does	the sun	rise	in Doha?
_____ time	does	it	rise	in Baghdad?
_____	is	the average temperature		28.6°C?
_____ _____	is	Muscat		from the Equator?
_____ _____	is	the average temperature		in Damascus?
_____	does	Muscat	get	hotter than Damascus?

Lesson 1: Vocabulary

In this unit, you are going to:

- listen to a lecture about a country – its location and physical features
- give a short talk about your own country
- read two encyclopedia articles about countries
- Write about your country.

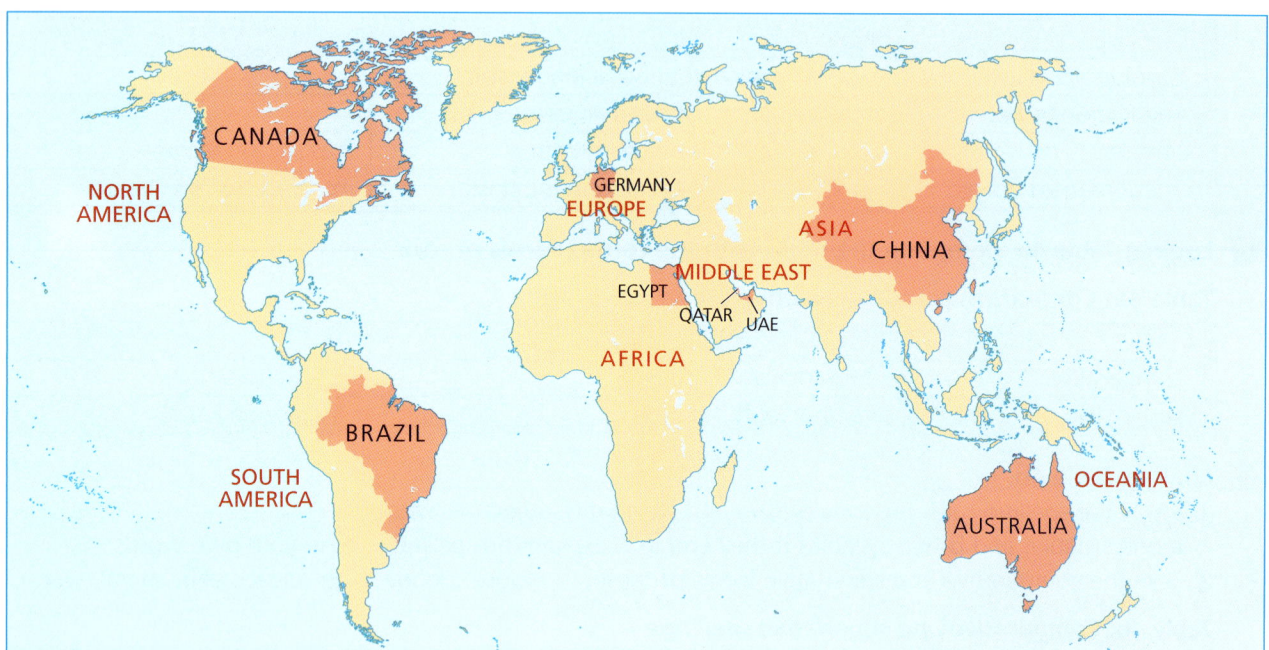

Ⓐ **In your country, are there any …**
1 mountains? **2** rivers? **3** islands? **4** lakes?

Ⓑ **What can you find …**
1 north of your country?   **3** west of your country?
2 south of your country?   **4** east of your country?

Ⓒ **Look at the map of the world. Which countries are:**
1 north of the Equator?   **3** south of the Equator?
2 on the Tropic of Cancer?   **4** on the Tropic of Capricorn?

Ⓓ ☉ **2.1 Listen to descriptions of six countries. Look at the map above. Find each country.**

Ⓔ **Where is your country? Look at the map. Describe the location.**

Ⓕ **Look at the diagram. Country A has a border with Country B, Country C and Country D. Which countries does your country have a border with?**

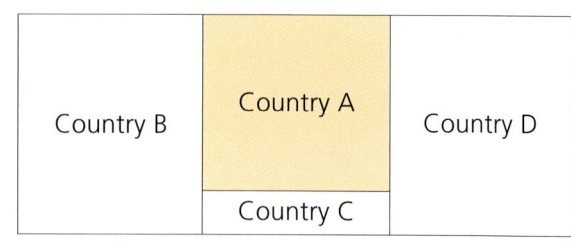

Country B	Country A	Country D
	Country C	

Key vocabulary
Africa America Asia
border   continent
Europe locate location
the Equator Oceania
the Middle East
the Tropic of Cancer
the Tropic of Capricorn

Lesson 2: Vocabulary

A **Read the text. Label the diagram.**

What is **the Middle East**? It is a **region** of the world. It contains many Arab countries, from Egypt in the west to Iraq in the east, and from Yemen in the south to Syria in the north.

The United Arab Emirates is one of the countries in the region. It is located between **latitude** 22° and 26° North and **longitude** 51° and 56° East. What does this mean? Lines of latitude run east to west around the world. The most important line of latitude is **the Equator**. This line is latitude 0°. Lines of longitude run north to south around the world. The most important line of longitude is the Greenwich meridian. The line runs through the city of London. This line is longitude 0°.

B **Look at the Skills Check.**

1 Read the Skills Check.

2 Study the sketches.

3 Make sketches of some of the words from the *Key Vocabulary* and other words from this lesson.

C **How good is your geography? Complete the outline of the map.**

D **Write three sentences to describe the location of one of the countries on the map.**

Skills Check

Dealing with new words (6)

Make sketches of new words to help you remember the meaning.

Lesson 3: Listening

A **Discuss these questions in pairs.**
1 Which country do you come from?
2 Where is your country?
3 What's your hometown/city?
4 Which part of your country is that in?

B **Donna, Anita and Maria are students at Greenhill College. They are talking before a lecture.**
1 🎧 **2.2** Listen. Donna pauses a few times in her questions. Guess the word she is going to say next on each occasion. Listen and check your ideas.
2 Complete the blue table.
3 🎧 **2.3** Listen again. Complete the information about Venezuela and Peru.

Revision

C **The words below are from the conversation.**
1 Tick in the correct column, according to the underlined vowel sound(s).
2 🎧 **2.4** Listen and check your ideas.

Student	Country	Hometown
Anita		
Maria		

The country is in the _____ of South America. It is _____ of Brazil, east of Colombia and west of Guyana. The _____ is Caracas.

The _____ is on the Pacific Ocean. It is _____ of Colombia and Ecuador. The _____ is Lima.

	A	B	C	D	E
	fill	feel	have	half	head
	/ɪ/	/iː/	/æ/	/ɑː/	/e/
c<u>i</u>ty					
d<u>i</u>d					
<u>ea</u>st					
<u>e</u>x<u>a</u>ctly					
s<u>ai</u>d					
sp<u>e</u>ll					
w<u>e</u>st					

D **The words below are from the conversation.**
1 Complete each word with one or two letters.
2 🎧 **2.5** Listen and check your ideas.

a a___out   d ___art
b ca___ital   e sou____
c nor____   f s___ell

E 🎧 **2.6 Listen and complete these words from earlier units.**
1 colle___e   6 me____od
2 dis___lay   7 ___ast
3 ex___eriment   8 ___rove
4 ___ob   9 ___ink
5 mana___er   10 ___unctual

Lesson 4: Listening

A Solve the crossword.

1 5

2 6

3 7

4

B Read Skills Check 1.

1 Say the example words.
2 Say the letter above each word.
3 🔴 **2.7** Listen and put the other letters of the alphabet into the correct column, according to the vowel sound.

A	B	F	Q	I	O	R

C 🔴 **2.8 Listen to the spellings.**

1 Write the letters and find out the names of the countries.
2 Check your answers in pairs.

D Read Skills Check 2.

1 What are the two sounds of *s*?
2 What is the sound of *s* in each of these words from the conversation in Lesson 3?
   *it's   is   small   south   has   east   coast
   what's   sorry   does   spell   say   towns*
3 🔴 **2.9** Listen and check your ideas.

E Work in pairs.

1 Which is the odd one out?
   *on   not   from   what   come   of
   sorry   want   was   wash*
2 What do all these words have in common?
   *for   before   more   small   talk   war
   August   taught   north*
3 Read Skills Check 3. Did you get the right answers to Questions 1 and 2?
4 🔴 **2.10** Listen to the words in Questions 1 and 2.

Skills Check 1

Understanding spoken spellings

Speakers sometimes spell out important words.
Maria: I'm from Tijuana.
Donna: *How do you spell that?*
Maria: T-I-J-U-A-N-A.

You must be able to hear the names of letters correctly. There are seven vowel sounds.

Sounds

A	B	F	Q	I	O	R
w*a*ge	thr*ee*	t*e*n	y*ou*	t*i*me	n*o*	*are*

Skills Check 2

Hearing consonants – /s/ and /z/

The consonant *s* can have two sounds:
1 The sound at the beginning of *s̲ounds: /s/.
2 The sound at the end of *sound̲s̲: /z/.

Skills Check 3

Hearing vowels – /ɒ/ and /ɔː/

1 We often write the vowel sound in *not* /ɒ/ with *o*.
   Examples: *on, from, sorry*
   But there are some common words with *a*.
   Examples: *want, what, was, wash*
2 We often write the vowel sound in *north* /ɔː/ with *or(e)*.
   Examples: *for, before, more*
   But there are some common words with *al, ar, aw* or *au*.
   Examples: *small, talk, war, August, draw*

Lesson 5: Speaking

A You meet someone for the first time. Make a list of the questions you can ask.

B Simon and Zeki are students at Greenhill College. They have just met. Look at the picture. Can you add any more questions to your list in Exercise A?

C Simon and Zeki are talking.

1 🎧 **2.11** Listen to the conversation. Does Simon ask any of your questions from Exercises A or B?

2 🎧 **2.12** Listen again. Complete the information about Zeki in the table.

D Look at the sentences below.

1 Match Simon's questions and Zeki's replies. Number the sentences in order.

2 🎧 **2.13** Listen again and check your order.

___1___ Hi. My name's Simon. Simon Shepherd.

___3___ Can I help you?

_____ Are you going to the Geography lecture?

_____ Yes, me too. When does it start?

_____ Where are you from, Zeki?

_____ Where's that?

_____ And where do you come from in Turkey?

_____ Sorry. What did you say?

_____ How do you spell that?

_____ And how do you say it?

_____ Mersin. Which part of the country is that in?

_____ I come from Mersin.

_____ I said Mersin.

_____ I'm from Turkey.

___2___ Hello. I'm Zeki.

_____ It's in Europe. It's north of Syria and Iraq.

_____ It's in the south.

_____ Mersin.

_____ M-E-R-S-I-N.

___4___ No, it's OK I can manage.

_____ Ten past ten, I think.

_____ Yes, I am. What about you?

Name	Zeki
Country	
Continent/area	
Location of country	
Hometown	
Location of hometown	

Revision

E These words are from the conversation.

1 Say each group of words. Which is the odd one out? What do the others have in common?

   a think   in   hi   it's

   b part   what   Iraq   past

   c me   help   said   spell

   d am   <u>a</u>bout   that   m<u>a</u>nage

   e think   north   south   that

2 🎧 **2.14** Listen and check your answers.

F Practise the conversation in Exercise D in pairs. Cover Zeki's words. Think of a good reply to each of Simon's sentences.

Lesson 6: Speaking

A Say the name of the letter in each row. Find one more letter from the alphabet with the same vowel sound.

A̶ B C D E̶ F̶ G H I J̶ K L M N
O P Q̶ R S T U V W X Y Z

A	ɔ
B	
F	
Q	

B Read Skills Check 1.
1 Check your answers to Exercise A.
2 Practise saying each group of letters.

C Work in pairs. Spell one of the words from each group to your partner. Which word is your partner spelling?

1	HARD	HAD	HEAD
2	SOME	SUM	SWUM
3	GIVE	GAVE	GREY
4	JOB	GAP	CAP
5	PEN	PIN	BEN
6	TRY	DRY	CRY
7	QUICK	QUITE	QUIET
8	FILL	FELL	FALL

Note:
Say "double L."

D Spell to your partner …
1 your first name.
2 your hometown.
3 your country (in English).

E Look at these sentences from the conversation in Lesson 5.
1 What is the sound of s in each case?
  a My name's Simon. Simon Shepherd.
  b No, it's OK.
  c Yes, I am.
  d When does it start?
  e Ten past ten, I think.
  f Where's that?
  g It's in Europe.
  h Sorry. What did you say?
  i I said Mersin.
  j How do you spell that?
  k How do you say it?
  l It's in the south.
2 Read Skills Check 2. Check your answers.
3 Practise saying the phrases and sentences aloud.

F Read Skills Check 3. Then try these tongue twisters.
What I wanted was a wash.
A warm August morning before dawn.
What was your fourth drawing on?

Skills Check 1

Spelling words

Each letter of the alphabet has a name. Sometimes this name is different from the common sound of the letter. For example, *j* has the sound in *job*, but the name = *jay*. There are seven different vowel sounds in the names of letters of the alphabet.

vowel sound in …	letters						
say	A	H	J	K			
me	B	C	D	E	G	P	T	V	Z*
red	F	L	M	N	S	X	Z**
do	Q	U	W				
my	I	Y					
no	O						
car	R						

* American English; **British English

Skills Check 2

Saying consonants – /s/ and /z/

The letter *s* has the sound /s/:
1 at the beginning of a word.
  Examples: *say, sorry*
2 in front of another consonant.
  Examples: *sp*ell, *st*art, pa*st*, *sw*im
  Exception: *sh*e, *sh*ould, *sh*ow
The letter *z* has the sound /z/.
Examples: *z*oo, *z*ero
The letter *s* sometimes has the /z/ sound, too.
Examples: *was, has, does, goes, plays*

Skills Check 3

Saying vowels – /ɒ/ and /ɔː/

The vowel sound /ɒ/ in *not* is usually written with *o*. But there are some common words with *a* instead of *o*.
Examples: *what, want, was, wash*
The vowel sound /ɔː/ in *north* is usually written with *or(e)*. But there are some common words with *al, ar, au* or *aw*.
Examples: *small, talk, warm, August*

Lesson 7: Reading

A Prepare to read the text.

1 Look at the map on the right. Which countries can you see on the map?

2 Find the headings at the bottom of the page. Are any of these words new to you? Look them up in a dictionary.

3 Read the first paragraph of the text and then read the topic sentences. What information will you read about in this text?

B Here are some sentences from the text you are going to read. Which paragraph does each one come from?

1 The highest point of these mountains is Jebel Sawda …

2 It occupies the majority of the Arabian peninsula.

3 To the south, it is bordered by Yemen and Oman.

4 There is another large city, Jeddah, on the Red Sea.

5 There are two large sand deserts.

C Look quickly at the text on page 141. Check your answers to Exercise B.

D Read the text.

1 Deal with any new words.

2 Mark all the places mentioned on the map.

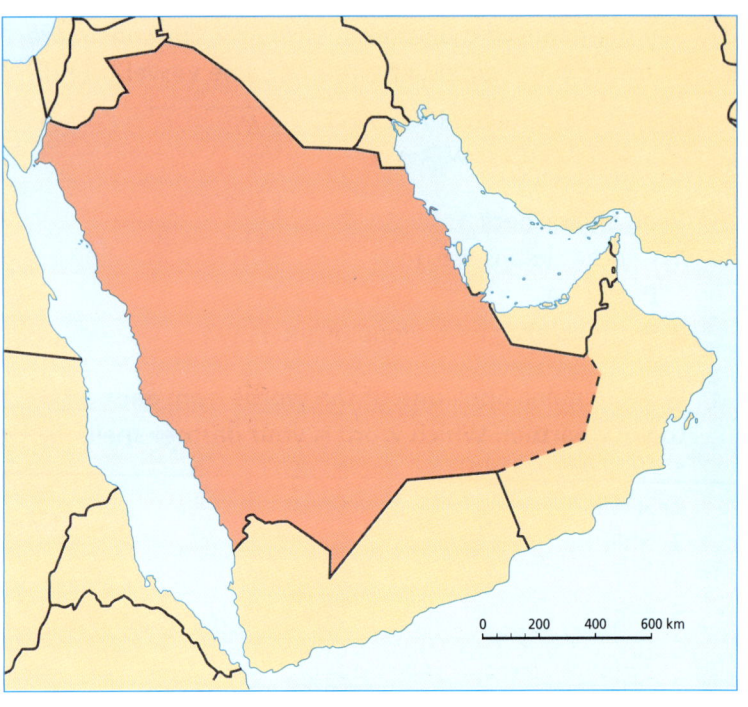

0   200   400   600 km

E Match the verbs and the other words to make phrases from the text.

1 occupies
2 is located
3 covers
4 has
5 is bordered
6 reaches
7 slopes

a a height of 3,133 metres
b a long coastline on the Red Sea
c an area of nearly 2 million square kilometres
d by Jordan, Iraq and Kuwait
e down to the Gulf in the east
f in the centre of the country
g the majority of the Arabian peninsula

Location	Saudi Arabia is a large country situated in the region called the Middle East. It occupies the majority of the Arabian peninsula. It is located between latitudes 16° and 32° North and longitudes 35° and 55° East.
Capital and other main cities	The capital is Riyadh.
Area and borders	The country covers an area of nearly 2 million square kilometres.
Landscape	There are mountains along the coast in the west of the country.

Lesson 8: Reading

(A) **Look at the words in each column.**

1 Make phrases with one word from each column.

2 Does the phrase normally have *the*?

Example: *the Middle East*

a	Middle	**i**	city
b	Arabian	**ii**	coastline
c	holy	**iii**	desert
d	Red	**iv**	East
e	square	**v**	east
f	long	**vi**	kilometres
g	highest	**vii**	marshes
h	Rub al Khali	**viii**	peninsula
i	salt	**ix**	point
j	fresh	**x**	rivers
k	south	**xi**	Sea
l	permanent	**xii**	water

(B) **You are going to complete a table with information from the text in Lesson 7 (page 141).**

1 Read the Skills Check.

2 Which nouns in the text can you use as section headings? Find and underline possible nouns.

3 Which other words can you change to nouns and use as headings?

(C) **Read the information in each section of the table below. Choose a suitable underlined noun for each section.**

Skills Check

Transferring information

We often want to make **notes** of the important information in a factual text. In many cases, we can **record** this information in a **table**. In English, the headings in tables are usually one or two **nouns**. These nouns often appear in the original text.

Example:

Saudi Arabia is a very large <u>country</u> situated in the <u>region</u> called the Middle East.

Sometimes you must change a verb in the text to a noun for the section heading.

Example:

It is <u>located</u> between latitudes …

located ➜ *location*

Country	*Saudi Arabia*
Region	*the Middle East*
Location	*between latitudes …*

Country		Saudi Arabia
Region		the Middle East
		Riyadh
		Jeddah, Makkah
Location	latitude	between 16° and 32° N
		between 35° and 55° E
		nearly 2,000,000 sq km
		Jordan, Iraq, Kuwait
		Yemen, Oman
		Qatar, United Arab Emirates, the Gulf
		the Red Sea
		most of the land is sandy desert
		none, but salt marshes and swamps in the east
		Jebel Sawda (3,133 m)

(D) **Cover the text and the table in Exercise C above. What information can you remember about Saudi Arabia? Test each other in pairs.**

Lesson 9: Writing

A Lucia Mendez is a Spanish student at Greenhill College. She has to write about her country for an assignment. Here are some of the words she has to use.

1 Complete these words with vowels from the box in each space.

   a l __ nd   **d** m __ ddl __

   b w __ st   **e** r __ v __ r

   c tw __   **f** m__nt__n

                                      `a e i o u`

2 Complete these words with one of the pairs of vowels from the box in each space.

   a s ____ th   **d** ____ st

   b degr ____ s   **e** d ____ d

   c betw ____ n   **f** reg ____ n

                                     `ea ee io ou`

B Here are the notes Lucia has collected. Look at the information in the box.

1 Check the spelling of the words in Exercise A.

2 Copy the information into the correct place in the shaded column of the table.

504,782 sq km	The Sanabria in the north
Europe	The River Tagus in the west
France and Andorra	Western Europe
Spain	The Pyrenees in the north and the Sierra Nevada in
Portugal	the south
Gibraltar and Morocco	

Name		Spain	
Continent			
Region			
Land area			
Borders	north		
	south		
	east		
	west		
Natural features	desert		
	rivers		
	lakes		
	mountains		

C Make notes about your own country in the final column.

Lesson 10: Writing

A Read each word. All the bold words have the sound *or*. But what is the correct spelling?

1 Write *or, au, ar, a,* or *ou* in each space.
   a There are **m** _____ **e** mountains in the south.
   b The country has a **b** _____ **der** with Portugal.
   c There is a big mountain range in the **n** _____ **th** of the country.
   d The country is **w** _____ **m** in summer and cold in winter.
   e The hottest month is _____ **gust**.
   f Barcelona is in the north **c** _____ **ner** of the country.
   g There is a **sm** _____ **ll** lake in the south.

2 Read Skills Check 1. Check your spelling.

B Lucia has written the first draft of her assignment. The spelling and punctuation are good, but there are some mistakes in grammar.

1 Read the first paragraph. Find and correct the mistakes.
2 Read Skills Check 2 and check your answers.

Spain is to southwestern Europe. It is located north on the Equator in west. It is border to the north by France and Andorra, and at the south by Gibraltar and Morocco. To the west, it bordered by Portugal.

C Read the second paragraph of Lucia's assignment. She is not sure which way to complete each sentence.

1 Choose and circle the best way for each underlined section.
2 Read Skills Check 3 and check your answers.

There is / It is a river in the west of the country. There is / It is called the Tagus. There is / It is also a lake in the north. There is / It is called the Sanabria. There are / They are mountains in the south. There are / They are called the Sierra Nevada. There are / They are also mountains in the north called the Pyrenees.

Skills Check 1

Spelling the sound *or*

The vowel sound in *north* (/ɔː/) is usually written with *or(e)*.
Examples: *border, more, corner*
But there are some common words with *a(l), ar, au, aw* and *our*.
Examples: *almost, small, warm, August, four*

Skills Check 2

Describing location

We can describe the location of a country in several ways:

1 By continent/ region	*Spain **is in** the continent of Europe. It **is in** southwestern Europe.*
2 By section of the world	*Spain is **located north** of the Equator.*
3 By borders with other countries	*Spain **is bordered by** France and Morocco to the north …*

Skills Check 3

Describing places

We introduce a new piece of information with *There is/are …*
We give more information about something with *It is/They are.*
Examples:
***There is** a river in the west of the country. **It is** called the Tagus.*
***There are** mountains in the south. **They are** called the Sierra Nevada.*

Lesson 11: Grammar

(A) Look at the compass points.

1 Work out the other points and add them.

2 Think of important places and where they are.
Make true statements like these.
- *Makkah is a long way west of here.*
- *Qatar is a short way northeast of here.*

(B) Look at Table 1.

1 How do first mention sentences begin?

2 How do further information sentences begin?

3 Complete Table 1. (Think: singular or plural?)

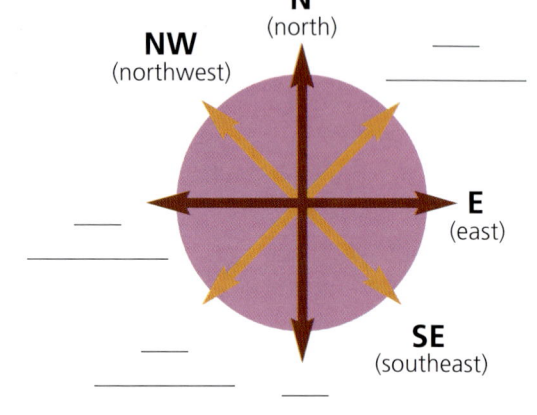

Table 1: *There is, There are, It is, They are*

First mention	Further information
_____ a peninsula between the Red Sea and the Gulf.	_____ called the Arabian Peninsula.
In the peninsula, _____ a very large country called Saudi Arabia.	_____ one of the largest of all the Arab countries.
In addition, _____ several small countries in the Peninsula.	_____ all on the coast of the Gulf.
Finally, _____ two medium-sized countries in this region.	_____ Yemen and Oman and they are both south of Saudi Arabia.

(C) Look at the map of Spain and Table 2.

1 Use these verbs in their correct forms to complete Table 2.

> cover(s)   *lie(s)   occupy(ies)   is/are bordered
> *is/are located   *is/are situated

*These verbs all mean roughly the same. Use each one once.

2 Make similar statements about your country.

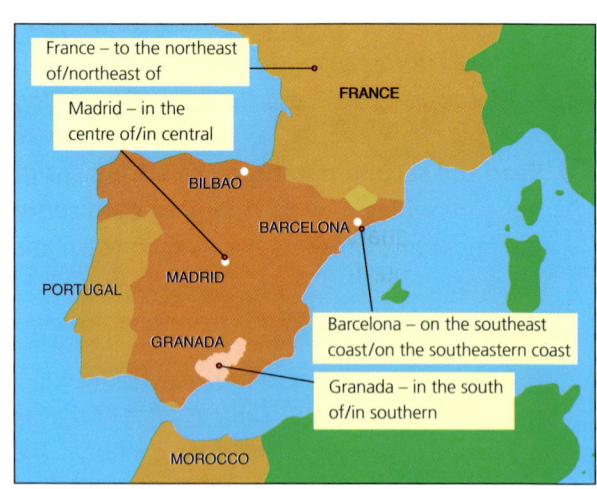

France – to the northeast of/northeast of

Madrid – in the centre of/in central

Barcelona – on the southeast coast/on the southeastern coast

Granada – in the south of/in southern

Table 2: *Verbs to express location*

	Verb	
Spain	_____	in the far west of Europe.
This country	_____	the majority of the Iberian Peninsula.
It	_____	an area of about 500,000 square kilometres.
It	_____	by Portugal and France.
The capital, Madrid,	_____	in the middle of Spain.
Morocco	_____	to the south of Spain.

Lesson 12: Grammar

A **Look at the map of Spain and Table 3.**

1 Complete Table 3 with two phrases for each place.

2 Make similar statements about places in and around your country.

Table 3: *Prepositional phrases to express location*

	Prepositional phrase	
Madrid is	_____	Spain.
France lies	_____	the country.
Granada is situated	_____	Spain.
Barcelona is located	_____	the country.

B **Look at Table 4.**

1 Complete the table. Use these two patterns.
- *be* (... kilometres long)
- *have a* (length of ... kilometres)

Use this information.
- The River Nile – 6,695 kilometres – long/length
- The Pacific Ocean – *4,000 metres – deep/depth
- The Red Sea – *300 kilometres – wide/width
- Mount Everest – 8,848 metres – high/height

*approximate average

C **Look at Table 5.**

1 Write the words in the table.

> a fifth   a quarter   a tenth
> a third   four-fifths
> seven-tenths   three-quarters
> two-thirds

2 Make true statements about things that you know, e.g.:
About a third of my class play football.

Table 4: *Measurements*

The River Nile	is _____
	_____
	has _____
	_____
The Pacific Ocean	is _____
	_____
	has _____
	_____
The Red Sea	is _____
	_____
	has _____
	_____
Mount Everest	is _____
	_____
	has _____
	_____

Table 5: *Fractions*

$\frac{1}{10}$	_____	$\frac{7}{10}$	_____
_____	_____	_____	_____
$\frac{1}{5}$	_____	$\frac{4}{5}$	_____
$\frac{1}{3}$	_____	$\frac{2}{3}$	_____

Lesson 1: Applying listening skills

A Two words are similar. One is different. Circle the odd one out. Write the letter of the reason.

1 schedule	timetable	semester	**a**	It is not a day of the week.
2 cafeteria	recess	restaurant	**b**	It is not a list of days, times and classes.
3 March	Wednesday	Monday	**c**	It is not a place to eat.
4 period	class	planner	**d**	It is not a subject.
5 recess	schedule	break	**e**	It is not a time between classes.
6 General Studies	English	Friday	**f**	It is not part of the college day.

B Discuss these questions in pairs.

1 What do you do after college each day?

2 What clubs do you go to?

3 Why do you go to those clubs?

C 2.15 Mrs Penn runs the extracurricular activities at Greenhill College. Listen and find out:

1 the meaning of *extracurricular*.

2 the extracurricular activities at the college – tick the activities on the notice board.

D 2.16 Listen again and write in the days and times for each activity that you ticked.

E Read the talk on page 162. Check your answers to Exercise D.

F Which of the clubs would you join? Why?

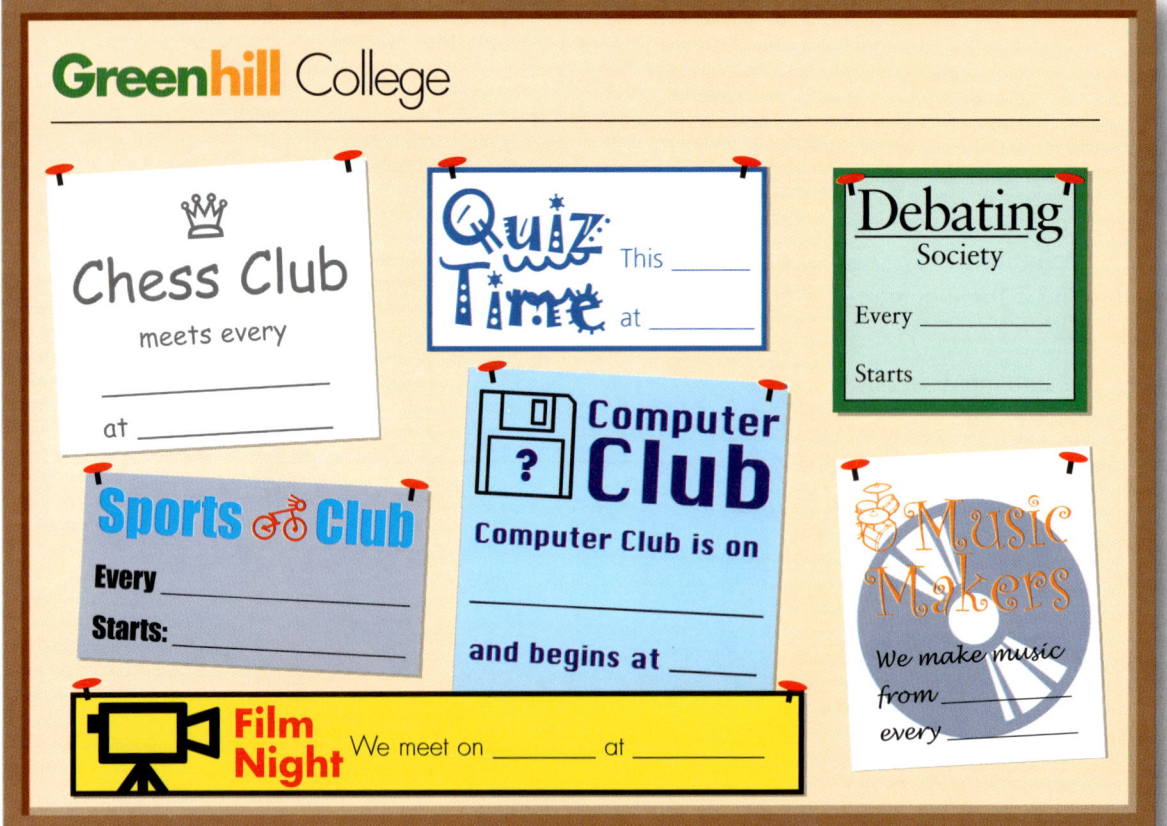

Lesson 2: Applying speaking skills

(A) **Make summer jobs from these words.**

Example: *nursery school assistant*

~~assistant~~ camp checkout clerk counsellor distributor fruit guide language leaflet ~~nursery school~~ operator picker teacher telesales tour

(B) **Work in pairs. Say the words below. Make sure your partner can hear the difference.**

1	go	Joe
2	get	jet
3	ago	age
4	wag	wage
5	rig	ridge
6	colleague	college
7	gust	just
8	goose	juice
9	leg	ledge
10	angle	angel

(C) **Ask your teacher about the meaning of any new words in Exercise B.**

(D) **Work in pairs.**
1 Circle one of the words in each pair in Exercise B.
2 Say the word that you circled. Don't show your partner.
3 Tick the words you hear.
4 Check the circles and ticks. If you got any wrong, say the words again.

(E) **Do the questions from the website form in Unit 3 (page 34) with a partner. Ask the questions, follow the flow chart and tell your partner the suggestion from the computer.**

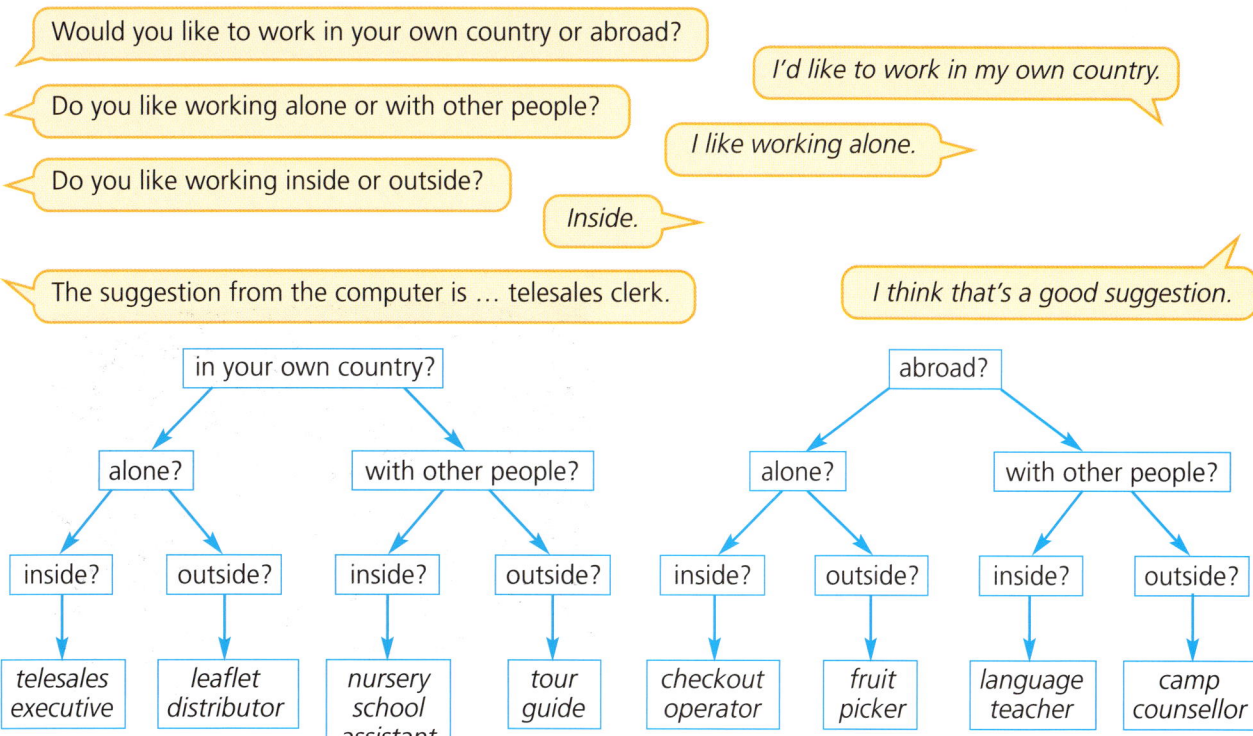

Lesson 3: Applying reading skills

A Find pairs of words. Explain your choices.

> column   high   low   many   north
> one   other   some   south   row

B The items on the right all come from the same article. After each activity below, stop and think: What will the article be about? Discuss with your partner.
1 Read the title. (Stop, think, discuss.)
2 Look at the table. (Stop, think, discuss.)
3 Read the introduction – the first paragraph. (Stop, think, discuss.)
4 Read the topic sentences in paragraphs 2–4. (Stop, think, discuss.)

C Read the article on page 142 straight through.
1 Underline any new words.
2 Do any of your underlined words mean the following?
   a how far
   b a line of longitude
   c not straight
   d a little bit
   e in fact
3 Look up any other underlined words in a dictionary.

D Read the article again and answer the questions.
1 This text answers a question. What is the question?
2 Which two factors affect the time of sunrise?
3 Why is sunrise later in Damascus than in Muscat?
4 Why is sunrise earlier in Tehran than in Abu Dhabi?

E Discuss in groups.
1 What do you often or always do before sunrise?
2 What do you often or always do after sunset?
3 Imagine you live in a country where sunrise is earlier and sunset is later. How does this affect your life?

Why Is It Still Dark?

Table 3:
Sunrise on July 1st in selected capital cities

Capital cities	Sunrise on July 1st	Line of longitude °E	Distance from Greenwich longitude (in km)
Muscat	5.22	59	6,490
Abu Dhabi	5.40	54	5,940
Doha	5.46	52	5,610
Manama	5.48	51	5,720
Kuwait City	5.53	48	5,280
Baghdad	5.55	45	4,950
Damascus	6.31	36	3,960

Source: Sunrise times from worldtime.com

PEOPLE WHO TRAVEL IN WINTER from the Gulf to London are often surprised that the sun does not rise in London until 7.30 or 8.00. Why does the sun rise at different times in different places?

There are two factors that affect the time of sunrise.

The sun rises in the east.

The second factor that affects sunrise time is the distance from the Equator.

Lesson 4: Applying writing skills

A **Solve the crossword.**

Across
1 The line between two countries (6)
5 A line around the middle of the world (7)
6 The opposite of 'south' (5)
9 A large area of water in a country (4)
10 The Middle East is one (6)

Down
2 The Sahara is a big one in North Africa (6)
3 A very high piece of land (8)
4 The UAE is ... in the Gulf (7)
7 There is farming land near the ... Jordan (5)
8 The Dead ... is in Jordan (3)

B **What can you see in the pictures?**

C **Draw a sketch map of your country. Show mountains, rivers, etc.**

D **Look back at the notes you made in Unit 5 (page 62, Exercise C).**
1 Write ten sentences about your country.
2 Join some of the sentences with *and* or *but*.
3 Write a first draft of a paragraph about your country. Leave a space between each line of writing.

E **Exchange drafts with your partner.**
1 Are there any mistakes of fact? Check with the notes that your partner made.
2 Are there any spelling mistakes?
3 Are there any joining mistakes?
4 Correct any mistakes with facts, spelling or joining. Write on the line above the mistake.

F **Look at the corrections on your first draft. Are they right? Write the second draft, correcting the mistakes if necessary. Leave a space between each line of writing.**

G **Show your second draft to your teacher/instructor.**

Lesson 1: Vocabulary

In this unit, you are going to:

- listen to talks about festivals
- give and react to information
- read two magazine articles about traditional events
- write about a festival in your country

A **What happens in your country when someone …**

1 is born?

2 has a birthday?

3 comes of age, e.g., reaches 16, 18 or 21?

4 gets married?

B 🔊 **2.17 Listen to a paragraph. Then complete each space using words from *Key vocabulary 1*.**

In some parts of Pakistan there are _____ events for children. The first _____ is called *Bismillah Khawni*. It takes _____ when the child is four years and four months. The boy or girl wears _____ clothes with flowers on, and family and friends watch him or her say the first chapter of the *Holy Qur'an*. The _____ ends with a special dinner. The second _____ is called *Khtme Qur'an*. This event _____ the child's ability to say the complete *Holy Qur'an*. The child receives gifts and, once again, there is a _____ dinner.

> **Key vocabulary 1**
> celebrate   celebration
> ceremony   event
> festival   special
> take place   traditional

C **Discuss in groups.**

D 🔊 **2.18 Read and listen to the text below. Then complete the text using words from *Key vocabulary 2*. Make any changes necessary**

In some _____, birthdays are very important. In Western _____, for example, people give presents to _____ and friends on their birthday. They often have _____ parties for the _____ person. People say 'Congratulations' or 'Happy birthday' even to people they don't know well. Are birthdays important in your _____?

Some people even believe that date of _____ is connected in some way to _____. These people know how birthdays relate to _____ and they read 'the stars' every day in the newspaper.

Do you know your _____? Do you read 'the stars' every day?

> **Key vocabulary 2**
> birth   culture   luck
> lucky   relative   special
> star sign

Lesson 2: Vocabulary

A Read the text below. Then complete the table with words from *Key vocabulary 1*.

Guy Fawkes Night is a traditional event in England. It takes place every year on November 5th. The event started in 1607. Two years earlier, a man called Guido (or Guy) Fawkes tried to blow up the Houses of Parliament. He failed. Now, every year, people celebrate.

For weeks before the event, people build big piles of wood in the fields. On the day of the event, some children dress up like Guy Fawkes. In the evening, everyone goes to a local field and someone lights the big fire. Then there are fireworks. After that, people have dinner – usually sausages and burgers nowadays!

Where does the _____ take place?	*England*
What is it called?	*Guy Fawkes Night*
When does it _____?	*On November 5th.*
When did the event first begin?	*In 1607.*
What does the event _____?	*People are happy because Guy Fawkes failed.*
How do people _____ for the event?	*They build big piles of wood.*
Do people wear _____ clothes?	*Yes – children dress up as Guy Fawkes.*
What _____ on the day?	*There is a big fire and fireworks.*
What happens after the event?	*People have dinner.*

Key vocabulary 1
celebrate   event
happen   prepare
special   take place
traditional

B Read the dictionary definitions of the words in *Key vocabulary 2*.

1 Write the correct word in each space.

2 Look up in a dictionary any words you don't know and check your answers.

Key vocabulary 2
balloon   festival
harvest   neighbour
parade

a _____ a child's plaything made of rubber; you blow it up into a ball and then you can play games with it

b _____ a lot of people walking through the streets; there is often music and dancing; there are sometimes decorated lorries or carts

c _____ a period of time when people remember something important; there are often parties or special events during the period

d _____ a person who lives next door to you, or in the same area

e _____ the time when farmers cut food crops

C What festivals do you have in your country? Which one is your favourite? What happens during the festival?

Lesson 3: Listening

A Juri Taku is a student at Greenhill College. She is going to talk to her group about a festival in Japan. Make a list of questions you expect to hear the answers to.

B Listen to the talk once.

1 ⚙ **2.19** Juri pauses a few times during her talk. Guess the word that she is going to say next. Listen and check your ideas.

2 Tick the questions from Exercise A that she answers.

C ⚙ **2.20** Listen to the talk again, without the pauses. Make notes in the table below.

Where is it?	
What is it called?	
Who is it for?	
When is it?	
Why is the occasion important?	
What happens on the day?	
Do the people wear special clothes?	
What happens after the ceremony?	

D How does Juri define these words/phrases?

Seijin-no-hi   town hall   kimono

Revision

E Look at these words from the talk.

after   all   although   called   dark   first   girl   hall   or   parties   person   small

1 Write each word in the correct column, according to the (underlined) vowel sound.

2 ⚙ **2.21** Listen and check your answers.

A	B	C
car	talk	word

F ⚙ **2.22** What are the missing letters in each of these sentences? Listen and write the letters.

1 I'm ___oing to talk to you about the Coming of A___e festival.

2 It take___ ___lace on the ___econd Monday of ___anuary.

3 It ___elebrate___ the chan___e from ___eing a child to ___eing an adult.

4 Town hall___ are local ___overnment office___.

5 First, official___ make speeche__.

6 ___en they give small ___resent___.

7 Young women wear traditional dresse___.

8 They usually rent the kimono___.

9 They can cost a___ much a___ a car.

Lesson 4: Listening

A Think of a word to complete each sentence. Find the hidden word that connects them all.

1 We usually spend holidays at home with the …	
2 We give children small …	
3 Sometimes on special occasions, people make …	
4 It means 'well done'.	
5 'You're 17 today! Happy … !'	
6 There are often special … in hotels in the holidays.	
7 At the Coming of Age ceremony, women wear … kimonos.	
8 Do you wear special … on your birthday?	

B Read these sentences from Juri's talk.

  1 Write one word in each space.

    a I'm _____ to talk _____ you today _____ a festival in Japan.

    b _____, government officials make speeches.

    c _____ they give small presents to the new adults.

    d Later, _____ the ceremony, the new adults go to special parties.

    e _____, the young people go home.

  2 Read Skills Check 1. Check your answers.

  3 🔊 **2.23** Listen and check.

C You are going to hear two groups of words from the talk.

  1 🔊 **2.24** Listen to the words in the blue box. Which consonant is missing in each case?

__alk	fes__ival
__ake	par__y
__wen__y	af__er
vo__e	la__er

  2 🔊 **2.25** Listen to the words in the yellow box. Which consonant is missing in each case?

__ark	__ay
a__ult	i__ea
tra__itional	__ie
__inner	un__erstand

  3 Read Skills Check 2 and check your ideas.

D Work in pairs.

  1 What do all these words have in common?
    new   few   true   blue   suit   you   do   who   too

  2 Read Skills Check 3. Check your answers.

Skills Check 1

Follow the signposts (1)

Speakers often help listeners with signpost words – words that tell the listener something about the next part of their talk.

Introducing the topic	I'm going to talk to you today about …
Talking about a sequence of events	First … Then …/Next … Later … After (that/the ceremony) … Finally …

Skills Check 2

Hearing consonants – /t/ and /d/

English speakers always pronounce these consonants differently at the **beginning** of a word. Make sure you can hear the difference.
Examples: *talk, take, twenty   dress, dark*

However, some English speakers pronounce *t* and *d* the same in the **middle** of some words.
Examples: *later* = /leɪtə/ or /leɪdə/

Skills Check 3

Hearing vowels – /uː/

We write the vowel sound in *new* /uː/ in many ways:
Examples:

with *ew: new, few*	with *ou: you*
with *ue: true, blue*	with *o: do, who*
with *ui: suit*	with *oo: too*

Lesson 5: Speaking

A **When do you use each of these expressions?**

Congratulations! Well done! Well tried! Good luck!

Happy birthday! Bad luck!

B **Dario Tedesco is a student at Greenhill College. He is talking to his friend, Tony Drew.**

1 🔊 **2.26** Listen to the conversation. Does Dario use any of the expressions from Exercise A?

2 🔊 **2.27** Listen again. Answer the questions.
   a What is Tony doing?
   b Who is the present from?
   c When is Tony's birthday?
   d What is Dario going to give Tony?
   e When is Dario's birthday?

C **Read Dario's sentences. Think of a good reply by Tony in each case.**

Dario: Hi, Tony. What's the matter?
Tony: _____
Dario: I'll give you a hand.
Tony: _____
Dario: What is it?
Tony: _____
Dario: A present. That's nice. Who's it from?
Tony: _____
Dario: Your father? Lovely. Is it your birthday, then?
Tony: _____ . Well, actually, _____
Dario: Next Thursday? The fourth of August?
Tony: _____
Dario: Great. Happy birthday!
Tony: _____ . Oh, it's _____ .
Dario: A shirt? That's smart. I'll give you a card tomorrow.
Tony: _____
Dario: I want to. Would you like to have a party?
Tony: _____
Dario: Are you sure?
Tony: _____
Dario: OK. By the way …
Tony: _____
Dario: My birthday's on the third of March.
Tony: _____

Revision

D **These words are from the conversation. What does each group have in common?**

1	father	card	March	party
2	your	fourth	August	sure
3	have	happy	hand	thanks
4	Thursday	birthday	third	shirt
5	third	fourth	birthday	thanks
6	Thursday	who's	is	birthday's

E **Work in pairs.**
Student A
Spell ten words from Exercise D to your partner.
Student B
Write the letters down as your partner says them. When you recognize the word, say it.

F **Practise the conversation in Exercise C in pairs. Take it in turns to be Tony.**

Lesson 6: Speaking

A Think of a good reply for each sentence.

I got a present from my father.

It's my birthday today.

My father gave me this shirt.

It's my birthday next month.

B Read Skills Check 1. Practise the mini-conversations in the Skills Check in pairs.

C Cover Skills Check 1. Work in pairs.

Student A
Say the sentences from Exercise A.
Student B
Give a suitable reply, with echo + question/comment.

D Your friend speaks to you, but you don't understand.

1 Make four replies from the words below.

> Could did don't I repeat say Sorry that understand What you you

2 Read Skills Check 2. Check your answers to Exercise D1.
3 Work in pairs.
 Student A
 Say each sentence from Exercise A.
 Student B
 Echo words you are not sure about.

E Read Skills Check 3. Then say these words. Help your partner say each word differently.

1	try	dry
2	tie	die
3	write	ride
4	site	side
5	cart	card

F Work in pairs. What is the correct pronunciation of these words? Some are new.

1 Say each word. Does it have the *oo* sound?
 who you flew do true few blue
2 Check these words in a dictionary.
 but look boot us pull pool use shut

Skills Check 1

I understand!

When a person gives us some new information, we must show that we understand. We can do this by echoing important words. We usually add another sentence – a question or a comment.
Examples:
A: I got a present from **my father.**
B: **Your father?** Is it your birthday, then?
 echo   question
A: It's **my birthday** today.
B: **Your birthday?** Congratulations!
 echo   comment

Skills Check 2

I don't understand!

It is very important in a conversation to show if you don't understand. There are two main ways:
1 Use general sentences:
 A: *It's my birthday next month.*
 B: Sorry? / I don't understand. / What did you say? / Could you repeat that?
2 Echo the words that you are not sure about.
 A: *It's my birthday **next month**.*
 B: Sorry? Did you say **next month**?

Skills Check 3

Saying consonants – /t/ and /d/

These two consonants are very similar. Make sure you can say the two sounds clearly. The sound /t/ uses more air than the sound /d/.

Skills Check 4

Saying vowels – /ʌ/ and /uː/

The vowel sound /uː/ is written in many ways. A word with *ew* is always pronounced with /uː/.
Examples: *new, few, flew, blew*
But the sound can also come in words with the letter *u* and the letter *o*.
Examples: *blue, true, you; too, do, who*
The vowel sound /ʌ/ is often written with the letter *u*.
Examples: *just, but, shut*

Lesson 7: Reading

A Prepare to read the text.

1 Look at the title. Name a traditional event in your country.
2 Look at the subheading. What do you think the *Palio* is? What about *Siena*?
3 Look at the map. Check your answers to question 2 above.
4 Look at the picture. Check your answers to question 2 above again.
5 Read the first paragraph. What extra information do you get?
6 Read the topic sentences. What extra information do you expect in each paragraph?

B Here are some sentences from the text. Which paragraph do you think each one comes from?

___ It only lasts 90 seconds.
___ The Black Death of 1348, however, killed thousands of people.
___ The flags belong to the 17 areas of the city.
___ Then, in the late afternoon, there is a parade in the Piazza del Campo.
___ Thousands of visitors come to the city every year just to see it.

C Look quickly at the text on page 143. Check your answers to Exercise B.

D Read the text. Deal with any new words. Answer these questions.

1 Where is Siena?
2 What is the Palio?
3 When was the first ever race?
4 When does the Palio take place?
5 What sort of clothes do people wear for the event?
6 When does the race start?
7 Where does it take place?
8 How many men take part?
9 How long is the race?
10 When does it finish?

E Make a table of the important information about the Palio for visitors to Italy.

GREAT TRADITIONAL
EVENTS
◁◁ AROUND THE WORLD ▷▷

1: *The Palio in Siena*

Siena is a city of around 56,000 people. It is situated in central Italy, 65 kilometres south of Florence and 271 kilometres northwest of Rome. It is built on a high hilltop.

B
Siena was once an important centre for banking and for art.

C
Siena is famous today for a horse race.

D
For three days before the event, flags fly from houses and shops.

E
On the day of the event, the young men and women of the city dress up in colourful clothes from the Middle Ages.

F
Finally, at exactly 6.30 p.m., the race begins.

Lesson 8: Reading

A **Which words from Lesson 7 mean ...**

1 a square in an Italian town?
2 an old disease?
3 a person who rides a horse in a race?
4 people walking together for a festival, usually wearing interesting clothes?
5 showing something to large groups of people?
6 a period in history?

B **These adjectives and nouns appear as phrases in the text on page 143.**

1 Match each adjective with a noun.
2 Check with the text.

a	high	**i**	afternoon
b	important	**ii**	clothes
c	colourful	**iii**	square
d	late	**iv**	dinners
e	main	**v**	hilltop
f	special	**vi**	centre

C **Some prepositions (*in, at, for, of,* etc.) are missing from these sentences.**

1 Complete each sentence with the missing preposition.
2 Read Skills Check 1. Check your answers.

a (The race) takes place _____ July and August.
b _____ three days before the event, flags fly from houses and shops.
c _____ the day of the event, the young men and women of the city dress up.
d _____ the morning, they walk around the streets.
e _____ the late afternoon, there is a parade in the Piazza del Campo.
f _____ exactly 6.30 p.m., the race begins.

D **Imagine you saw the Palio in Siena.**

1 Read the last two paragraphs again on page 143.
2 Look at Skills Check 2.
3 Tell your partner about the day of the Palio.

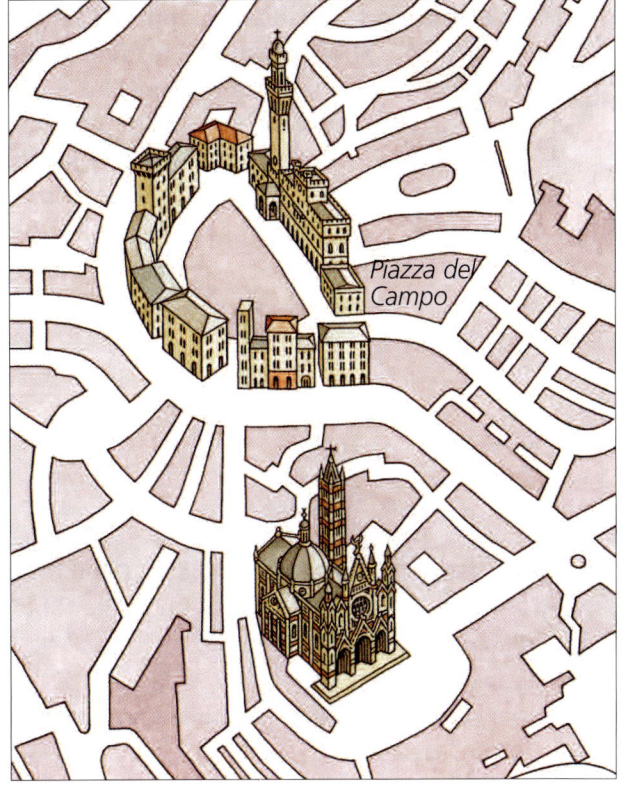

Piazza del Campo

Skills Check 1

Follow the signposts! (2)

Writers often help readers with signpost words in **chronological** texts. A chronological text talks about when actions happen. Writers use **time phrases**.

Examples:
*The race takes place **in** July and August.*
***For** three days before …*
***On** the day of the event …*
***In** the morning/afternoon/evening …*
***At** 6.30 p.m. …*

Skills Check 2

Follow the signposts! (3)

Writers also use **sequencers** in chronological texts:
First …
Then/Next …
Later …
After (that/the race) …
Finally …

Lesson 9: Writing

A **Drew Stevens is a Canadian student at Greenhill College. He has to write about a national festival for an assignment. Here are some verbs and other words he is going to use.**

1 Complete each verb with one or two vowels in each space.

2 Match each verb to one group of words to make phrases.

a w<u>a</u>tch		**i**	sport on television
b s__y		**ii**	the harvest
c s__t d__wn		**iii**	thanks to God
d t__k__ p__rt		**iv**	for the day
e m__k__		**v**	special food
f g__v__		**vi**	special things
g c__ __k		**vii**	in a big parade
h __ __t		**viii**	to a big meal
i pr__p__r__		**ix**	a prayer
j c__l__br__t__		**x**	the meal

B **Here are the notes Drew has made. Copy the table into your exercise book. Then copy the information into the correct place in the table. Sometimes you will have to guess or work it out.**

- Canada and the USA
- Everybody!
- Everyone gives thanks for something.
- Father says a prayer.
- It celebrates the harvest.
- It is the day we give thanks to God for the harvest.
- One day
- Thanksgiving Day
- 2nd Monday in October (Canada) – different day in USA

- We all sit down to a big Thanksgiving dinner in the evening.
- We cook special foods; children make special things.
- We eat the meal – turkey, roast potatoes, pumpkin pie.
- We take part in a big parade in the morning.
- We watch sport on television in the afternoon.
- Yes, for the parades – we wear special clothes and walk through the streets.

Where is the festival?	
What is it called?	
What does the name mean?	
Who is it for?	
When is it?	
How long does it last?	
Why is the occasion important?	
Do the people wear special clothes?	
How do people prepare for the festival?	
What happens on the day(s)? First	
Then/Next	
After that	

C **Make notes about a festival in your own country in your exercise book.**

Lesson 10: Writing

A **Sometimes, one vowel letter can have different sounds.**

1 Which letter is missing from each set of words?

2 What is the sound in each word?

a	h___ppen	l___st	s___ys	w___tch
b	pr___pare	sp___cial	n___w	th___y
c	g___ve	fest___val	l___ke	th___rd
d	m___ney	cl___thes	h___liday	w___men
e	b___y	p___t	___p	___se

B **Sometimes a pair of letters can have different sounds.**

1 Which pair of letters is missing from each set of words?

2 What is the sound in each word?

a	c___ ___ntry	y___ ___	h___ ___se
b	m___ ___n	n___ ___rly	br___ ___kfast
c	ball___ ___n	c___ ___k	g___ ___d
d	th___ ___r	rec___ ___ve	n___ ___ghbour
e	f___ ___lds	fr___ ___nds	countr___ ___s

C **Drew has written the first draft of his assignment.**

1 Complete the sentences with a preposition in each space. Cross out each preposition as you use it.

> at at about for for in on on

a This essay is _____ a festival in Canada and the USA called Thanksgiving Day.

b In my country, it happens _____ the second Monday in October every year.

c It lasts _____ one day.

d _____ weeks before the festival, people prepare.

e Children make special things _____ school.

f People cook special food _____ home.

g _____ the day, there are big parades in many towns and cities.

h Then, _____ the evening, there is a big meal for all the family.

2 Read Skills Check 2 and check your answers.

D **Drew wants to describe the meal in detail.**

1 Write a suitable word or phrase in each space.

a _____, my father says a prayer.

b _____ everyone gives thanks for something – the food, good health, friends and neighbours.

c _____, we eat the first course – turkey and roast potatoes.

d _____, we have the dessert – pumpkin pie.

2 Read Skills Check 3 and check your ideas.

Skills Check 1

Spelling vowel sounds

As we have seen already, one vowel sound can have many spellings. Always learn the spelling of the vowel sound(s) in a new word. Here are some different sounds from a single vowel letter.

a *happen last says watch*

e *prepare special new they*

Here are some different sounds from a pair of vowel letters.

ei *their receive neighbour*

Skills Check 2

Describing an event – using fixed phrases

It is very important to understand the rules for making good sentences. But you should also learn a lot of fixed phrases – sequences of two, three, four or even more words that you can use without thinking about the grammar. In an essay that describes an event, you can use some or all of the following:

It lasts for … + period of time

It happens on … + date

For days/weeks/months before the day/holiday/festival, …

In my country/other countries, …

At school/home/work, …

On the (first/second/final) day, …

In the morning/afternoon/evening, …

Skills Check 3

Describing an event – using signpost words

Writers often use special phrases to introduce information or to show when they are changing to a new point. When we describe an event, we often use these phrases:

This essay is about + topic

Firstly, …

Then/Next/After that …

Finally, …

Lesson 11: Grammar

(A) **Look at Table 1.**

1 How do you complete the first mention question and answer?

2 How do you complete the further information question and answer?

3 Complete the table. Use the verbs in brackets.

Table 1: There + be, *subject pronoun + verb*

	Questions	Answers
First mention	How many people _____ in Negara? (live)	34,000.
Further information	What sort of work _____? (do)	_____ coconuts. (grow)

(B) **Look at Table 2.**

1 Do the sentences end in expressions of movement, place or time?

2 Complete them with these prepositions.

> at   during   for   in   in   on

Table 2: *Time expressions with prepositions*

	Time expressions
The Japanese O-Bon Festival is	_____ August.
This 'Festival of the Dead' starts	_____ or about the 1st.
It goes on	_____ ten days.
People leave food outside for the dead	_____ this period.
There is dancing and drumming	_____ the evening every day.
This all starts when it gets dark	_____ about 7.00.

(C) **Look at Table 3.**

1 Quite a lot of verbs are stative: they express states, not actions, e.g.:

believe   belong to   contain   feel (= have an opinion)   hate   like   love   need   own   realize   remember   seem   sound (= give out a sound)   think (= have an opinion)   understand   weigh (= have weight)

2 Tick (✓) the sentences with the verbs in their stative meanings.

  a **i** I feel you should go. __
    ii I'm feeling great today! __
  b **i** I'm thinking about the problem. __
    ii I think I know the answer. __

3 Put the verbs in brackets in the correct present simple forms to complete the table.

Table 3: *Stative verbs and simple tenses*

	Stative verbs	
Jusuf Walid is at the races, and he	_____	racing bulls. (love)
Sadly, he is poor, and he	_____	any bulls. (own)
The bulls with him today	_____	to his cousin. (belong)
This is his first race, so people	_____	him yet. (know)
They therefore	_____	he will win. (think)
However, Jusuf certainly	_____	he can win. (believe)
His friends and family also	_____	he will do well. (feel)
They are right! At the end, everybody at the bull races	_____	that there is a new champion. (realize)

Lesson 12: Grammar

A Look at Table 4.

1 In which of positions 1–4 can you add these discourse markers?

first(ly)   then   next   after that   finally

2 Where do you put these markers most often?

3 In position 1, what punctuation mark do you usually use after all the markers except *then*?

Note: All the markers except *after that* can also go between the subject and the verb, e.g., *The people first prepare ...*

Table 4: *Chronological discourse markers*

1		2		3		4
	The		people prepare		the fireworks.	
	The		children build		a big fire.	
	The		adults light		the fire after dark.	
	Everybody		cooks food		on the fire.	

B Look at Table 5a, b and c.

1 Complete Table 5a with the correct forms of the auxiliary *do*.

2 Complete Table 5b with these 'wh' question words and the correct forms of *do*.

how long   what   when   where   which

3 Complete Table 5c with *did* and these 'wh' question words and *did*.

when   why

Table 5a: *Present simple – yes/no questions and answers*

Aux		Answer	Aux
_____	the Palio take place every year?	Yes, it	_____
_____	many people go to it?	Yes, they	_____

Table 5b: *Present simple – 'wh' questions and answers*

'Wh' + aux		Answer
_____ _____	it take place?	In Siena.
_____ _____	it happen?	In the summer.
_____ _____	it go on?	All day.
_____ part _____	people enjoy most?	The race.
_____ _____	people do after that?	They eat.

Table 5c: *Past simple – yes/no and 'wh' questions and answers*

Aux/'wh' + aux		Answer	Aux
_____	people dress up in the past	Yes, they	_____
_____ _____	the Palio first start?	Nearly 3,000 years ago.	
_____ _____	it start?	Nobody knows!	

Lesson 1: Vocabulary

In this unit, you are going to:

- listen to two lectures about the history of transport
- talk about research and check new information
- read two texts about the history of space travel
- Write about a famous invention in the field of transport

Key vocabulary
captain   cyclist
helicopter   in the air
invent   invention
inventor   on land
on the sea   ride
rider   track
transport   travel

A Discuss the questions.

1 Can you drive?
2 Have you passed a test?
3 Have you got a car?
4 Have you ever been in a plane? Where did you go?
5 Have you ever been on a boat? Where did you go?

B ⦿ 2.28 Listen to the paragraph. Then complete the text using the *Key vocabulary*. Make any necessary changes.

Nowadays, we can _____ in many different ways. _____, we can _____ on a bicycle or drive in a car. In many countries, we can also go along special _____ in a train. _____, we can sail in a small boat or cruise in a large ship. _____, we can fly in a small plane or in a huge one. How did we get all these forms of _____? Who _____ them? When did each _____ happen?

C Discuss in groups. Which form of transport came first? Which is the most modern?

D Can you fill in any of the information in the table? Do some research before the next lesson.

Table 1: *Inventions in transport*

Invention	Inventor	Date
bicycle		
helicopter		
car		

Lesson 2: Vocabulary

A Complete the transport words in the first column in Table 2.

B Complete the infinitive and past simple forms of the transport verbs in Table 2. Then check using *Key vocabulary 1*.

Table 2: *Methods of transport + verbs*

Transport	Infinitive	Past simple
ca_____	drive	dr___ve
bicyc_____	r___de	r___de
s__ip; b__t	sail	sail_____
pl___n___	fly	fl_____

C Find a word for each definition using *Key vocabulary 1*. Check your answers with a dictionary.
  1 a kind of boat that can go under the water
  2 move a boat through the water using long pieces of wood
  3 a kind of plane with a very powerful engine
  4 make something new
  5 a group of ships with guns
  6 make a car, boat, plane, etc., go at the correct speed and in the correct direction

Key vocabulary 1
control drove flew invent jet navy ride rode row sailed submarine

D Read the article below, which uses words from *Key vocabulary 2*. Then identify the numbered items in the diagram of the Solar System.

Key vocabulary 2
planet Solar System space star the Earth the moon the sun

Travel within the Solar System?

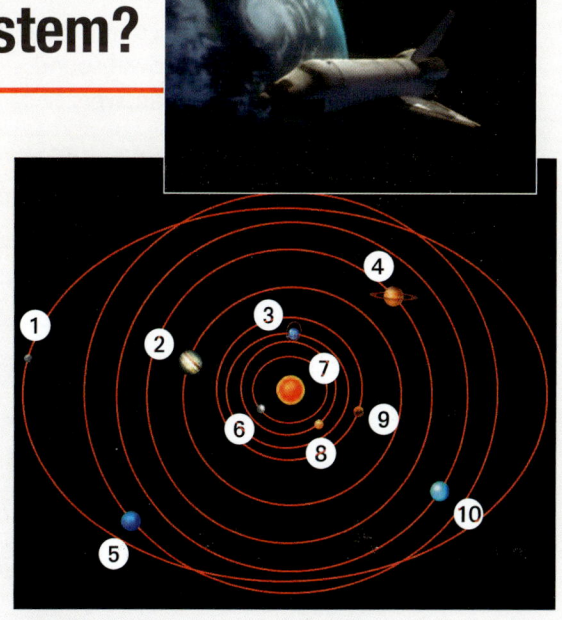

Before considering travel within the Solar System, we need to understand exactly what it is. The sun is a star at the centre of our Solar System. Nine planets orbit the sun. Mercury is the planet closest to the sun. Venus is the second planet. It is the hottest. The Earth is the third planet from the sun. It is the planet that we live on. It has a natural satellite, the moon. The moon orbits the Earth. Mars is the fourth planet. It is sometimes called the red planet.

The next four planets are giant balls of gas. Jupiter, the fifth planet from the sun, is the largest planet in the Solar System. Saturn is the sixth planet from the sun. It has large rings. Uranus is the seventh planet and Neptune is the eighth planet from the sun.

Pluto is usually the furthest from the sun. It is the smallest planet. In fact, it is so small that some scientists say it is not a planet at all.

Lesson 3: Listening

A **Look at these forms of transport.**
1 Number the inventions in order – the earliest = 1.
2 Which of these inventions do you think is the greatest in the history of transport? Discuss in groups.

B **Vicente Fernandez is studying History at Greenhill College. He has a lecture today.**
1 🔊 **2.29** What is the lecturer going to talk about? Look at the notebook. Listen and number the points in order.
2 Which word or phrase does he define as:
  a new way of doing something?
  b area?
  c types?
  d in my opinion?
  🔊 **2.30** Listen again and check your answers.
3 🔊 **2.31** Listen to the second part. When the lecturer stops, guess the next word. Then check your guesses.
4 🔊 **2.32** Copy Table 1. Then listen to the third part and complete the table.
5 🔊 **2.33** Listen to the final part.
  a Which invention does the lecturer think is the most important invention?
  b Why does he have this opinion?

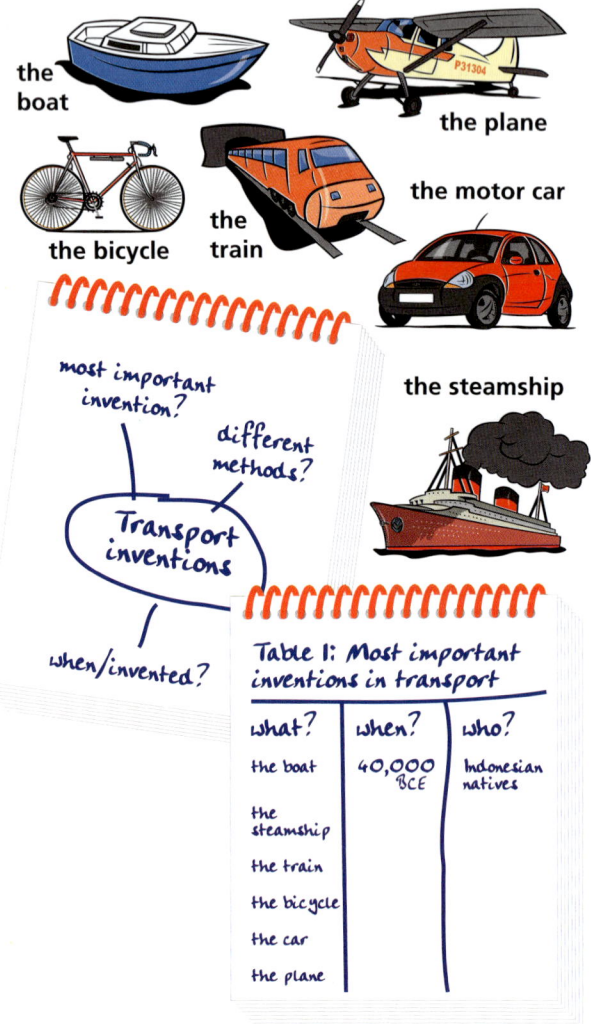

the boat · the plane · the bicycle · the train · the motor car · the steamship

most important invention?

different methods?

Transport inventions

when/invented?

Table I: Most important inventions in transport

what?	when?	who?
the boat	40,000 BCE	Indonesian natives
the steamship		
the train		
the bicycle		
the car		
the plane		

Revision

C **Look at these words from the talk. They all have short vowel sounds.**
1 Write each word in the correct column below, according to the (underlined) vowel sound.
2 🔊 **2.34** Listen and check your answers.

bec<u>au</u>se <u>e</u>ngine eng<u>i</u>ne h<u>i</u>story th<u>a</u>t
tr<u>a</u>ck tr<u>a</u>nsport w<u>a</u>s w<u>e</u>nt wh<u>a</u>t wh<u>e</u>n
wh<u>i</u>ch w<u>i</u>nd

A	B	C	D
ship	land	tell	on

D **Look at these words from the talk. They all have long vowel sounds in British English.**
1 Write each word in the correct column below, according to the (underlined) vowel sound.
2 🔊 **2.35** Listen and check your answers.

<u>a</u>fter c<u>a</u>lled conc<u>er</u>ned c<u>our</u>se <u>ea</u>ch
f<u>a</u>r fl<u>e</u>w l<u>a</u>st m<u>or</u>e m<u>o</u>ve p<u>eo</u>ple
st<u>ea</u>m transp<u>or</u>t <u>u</u>se w<u>a</u>lk w<u>or</u>ld

A	B	C	D	E
sea	car	first	talk	new

Lesson 4: Listening

Ⓐ **Think of a word to complete each sentence. Find the hidden word that connects them all.**

1 and **2** – Karl Benz invented it. (2 words)	**1**											
	2											
3 You can do this on two legs.	**3**											
4 The Wright brothers flew the first one successfully.	**4**											
5 and **6** – J.C. Perier invented it in 1775 to sail on the sea. (2 words)	**5**											
	6											
7 It is more than 40,000 years old.	**7**											
8 All the other answers are different ways of …	**8**											
9 The *Rocket* was the engine that pulled the first …	**9**											

Ⓑ **Read the introduction to the lecture in Lesson 3.**

1 Write one word in each space.

> I'm _____ to _____ to you today about inventions. _____, I'm going to talk _____ different methods of transport. After _____, I'll _____ you when each method was invented. _____, I'm going to _____ which invention was the most important. _____ , first, what are the main methods of transport?

2 ⊙ **2.36** Listen to the introduction again and check your answer.

3 Read Skills Check 1. Notice the signposts in the introduction.

Ⓒ **Vicente started to make notes during the introduction. Has he organized them well? Explain your answer.**

Inventions in transport
Different methods   When?
Most important?

Ⓓ **What are the missing letters – *sh* or *ch*?**

1 Work out the missing letters.

2 ⊙ **2.37** Listen and check your ideas.

a ____eck		**e** mu____		
b ea____		**f** ____ip		
c Engli____		**g** ____ort		
d mat____		**h** whi____		

Ⓔ **You have heard all the words below in the course.**

1 What do the words have in common? Which is the odd one out?

invention	conversation	congratulations
action	definition	information
celebration	description	connection
civilization	question	location
condition	education	

2 Read Skills Check 3. Check your answers.

Lesson 5: Speaking

A **Charles Sheldon is a first-year student at Greenhill College. He is researching inventions on the Internet.**
1 Which invention is the website about?
2 How many pieces of information does it give?

B **Work in pairs. What information is missing from the website? Choose a type of information from the list for each space.**
- a year   • a number   • a name
- a month   • a day   • a country

C 2.38 **Richard Shaw, Charles' friend, has just come into the library. Listen to the conversation between Charles and Richard. Complete the missing information on the website.**

D **Read this part of the conversation.**
1 Complete the sentences with a word in each space.

Charles: _____ you know that there are over a billion bicycles in the world?
Richard: Sorry? _____ many bicycles are there?
Charles: One billion. It says here that Kirkpatrick Macmillan invented it in 1839.
Richard: Pardon? _____ did he invent it?
Charles: In 1839. But it seems that Leonardo da Vinci drew a picture of a bicycle more than 300 years earlier.
Richard: _____ drew a picture of a bicycle?
Charles: Da Vinci. D-A V-I-N-C-I. He was a painter and inventor from Italy. Good heavens!
Richard: _____?
Charles: Apparently, the speed record for a bicycle is 268 kilometres an hour.
Richard: Sorry? _____ many kilometres an hour?
Charles: Two hundred and sixty-eight kilometres an hour.
Richard: _____ you sure?
Charles: Absolutely. According to this, he was riding behind a car.
Richard: Maybe. But you shouldn't believe everything you read on the Web.

2 2.39 Listen and check your ideas.

Revision

E **Say these words from the conversation.**
1 Put the words into five groups, according to the (underlined) vowel sound.

> believe car drew earlier more example
> forty pardon read sure speed thirty
> two who world

2 2.40 Listen and check your answers.

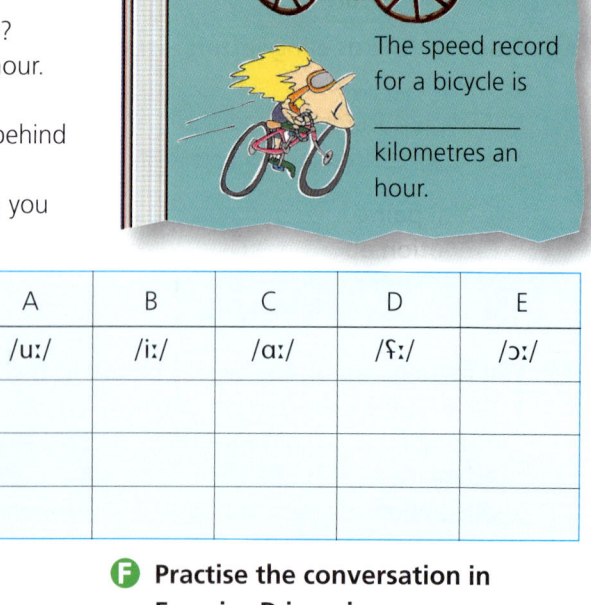

http://www.allaboutbikes.com

Four things you didn't know about ...
The Bicycle

There are over _____ bicycles in the world.

The bicycle was invented by Kirkpatrick Macmillan in _____ .

Leonardo _____, the famous Italian painter, drew a picture of a bicycle in 1493.

The speed record for a bicycle is _____ kilometres an hour.

A	B	C	D	E
/uː/	/iː/	/ɑː/	/ɜː/	/ɔː/

F **Practise the conversation in Exercise D in pairs.**

Lesson 6: Speaking

A **What can you remember about the invention of the bicycle?**

B **Read this part of the conversation from Lesson 5. How does Charles introduce each piece of information from the website?**

1 Complete each word or phrase.

   a _____ you know _____ there are over *a billion* bicycles in the world?

   b It _____ here that Kirkpatrick Macmillan invented it in *1839*.

   c But it _____ that *Leonardo da Vinci* drew a picture ... more than 300 years earlier.

   d App_____, the speed record for a bicycle is *268* kilometres an hour.

   e _____ to this, he was riding behind *a car*.

2 Read Skills Check 1. Check your ideas.

C **Richard doesn't hear, or doesn't believe, the information *in italics* in the sentences in Exercise B.**

1 Think of questions for Richard to ask.

2 Read Skills Check 2. Check your answers.

Example:

There are over *a billion* bicycles in the world.
Sorry? How many bicycles are there?

D **Read these words from the conversation.**

> *Charles   information   invention   sure*
> *picture   research   Richard   shouldn't*

1 Put the words into two groups, according to the underlined sounds.

2 Read Skills Check 3. Check your answers.

3 Practise saying the words aloud.

E **Work in pairs. You each have some extra information about bicycles. Cover your partner's information. Tell your partner your extra information. Use phrases from Skills Check 1 to introduce it. If you don't understand or don't believe some of the information, ask a checking question (Skills Check 2).**

Student A

- More than half of the bicycles in the world are in China.
- Kirkpatrick saw someone on a bicycle without pedals and thought, 'There must be a better way.'

Skills Check 1

Talking about research

We often want to tell another person about research we have done. Learn these ways of introducing information:

Did you know that ...?   *It says (here) ...*
Apparently, ...   *It seems that ...*
According to (this) ...

Skills Check 2

Checking questions

We check statements if we didn't hear them correctly – or don't believe them!

Examples:

> *There are over a billion bicycles in the world.*
> Sorry? <u>How</u> many bicycles are there?

> *Leonardo da Vinci drew a bicycle in 1493.*
> Pardon? <u>Who</u> drew a bicycle in 1493?

With normal information questions, the voice goes down at the end. But with checking questions, it goes up.

Skills Check 3

Hearing blends – /tʃ/ and /ʃ/

These two sounds are similar.

Examples:

> *check, match, which, each*
> *ship, she, short, English*

The sound /tʃ/ also appears in words with *~ture*.

Examples: *picture, lecture*

The sound /ʃ/ also appears:

a in words with *~tion*.

   Examples: *information, invention*

b in some words with *su*.

   Examples: *sure, insurance*

Student B

- Some people say that another man did the da Vinci drawing between 1967 and 1974.
- A Dutchman called Fred Rompelberg set the world record in 1995.

Lesson 7: Reading

Ⓐ Prepare to read the text.

1 Look at the title. Tell your partner three facts that you know about space travel.

2 Look at the subheading. Find pictures of two of the items in the illustrations for this lesson.

3 Read the first paragraph. Answer these questions in pairs.

    a When did the Chinese first make gunpowder?

    b What can you use gunpowder for?

    c The article is about space travel. What connects gunpowder and space travel?

4 Read the topic sentences. Then read each statement below. Is it true or false? If it's false, correct it.

    a Paragraph 1 will probably be about Chinese rockets.

    b Paragraph 2 will probably be about Arab traders.

    c Paragraph 3 will also probably be about Arab traders.

    d Paragraph 4 will probably be about one man.

    e Paragraph 5 will probably be about the future.

Ⓑ Read the text on page 144.

1 Deal with any new words.

2 Check your ideas in Exercise A4.

Ⓒ Which word or phrase in the text means …

1 people you are fighting in a war?

2 periods of 100 years?

3 very old?

4 from the Middle Ages?

5 e.g., petrol, oil?

6 gas with the symbol O?

7 Earth, Mars, Venus, etc.?

Ⓓ Make a table of the information in the text.

Date	Event
800 BCE	Chinese invented gunpowder.
c10th–c13th	

A Brief History of Space Travel
Part 1
Fireworks, cannons and rockets

Fireworks

Cannon of the Middle Ages

Castle

In about 800 BCE, a Chinese person mixed sulphur (S) and potassium nitrate (KNO_3), and carbon (C). He set fire to the mixture. It exploded. The mixture was gunpowder.

1   The Chinese mainly used the new invention in fireworks, but they also made rockets.

2   Between the 10th and 13th centuries, Arab traders in China learnt about gunpowder.

3   The Europeans also put gunpowder in new guns called cannons.

4   Werner von Braun, a German scientist, studied the rockets of the ancient Chinese and the cannons of medieval Europe.

5   On September 8th, 1944, the first rocket hit London.

Lesson 8: Reading

Ⓐ How many facts can you remember from the last lesson?

1 Read Skills Check 1.

2 Think of five more facts from the text in Part 1 of *A Brief History of Space Travel*.

3 Check your ideas with the text on page 144.

Ⓑ What is the infinitive of each of these verbs from Lesson 7?

1 Write the infinitive.

2 Read Skills Check 2.

3 Use a dictionary to check your answers.

Past simple	Infinitive
lit	light
blew	
made	
led	
took	
put	

Ⓒ What do you expect to come after these words in a text about history?

1 Match each preposition to a type of time information.

  a in   **i** a day or date

  b on   **ii** a time period

  c around   **ii** a year or a month

  d between **iii** an approximate date

  e over   **iv** two dates or time periods

2 Read Skills Check 3 and check your answers.

3 Give more examples of each type of time information.

Ⓓ What are the important dates in the history of your country or your city/town? Make some past tense sentences with prepositions + time expressions from Exercise C.

Skills Check 1

Past simple for history

We use the past simple for **facts from history**.

Examples:

*In about 800 BCE, a Chinese person **mixed** three natural substances.*

*He **lit** the mixture.*

*It **blew** up.*

*The mixture **was** gunpowder.*

Skills Check 2

Using a dictionary for verbs

Look up an irregular past tense verb in a dictionary. You will find something like this:

lit /lɪt/ *past* and *past part.* of light

You must look up *light* to find the meaning.

Note: Some irregular verbs have the same form for the infinitive and the past simple. In the dictionary you will find something like this:

put /pʊt/ *vb* **puts, putting, put**

The last word in **bold** is the past simple form.

Skills Check 3

Recognizing dates and periods

Writers often give **the date** or **the period** of a fact from history.

Look for these time expressions.

Year	*In* 1936 …
Month	*In* December …
Day	*On* September 8th …
Period of time	*Over* 1,000 **years later** …
	Between the 10th and 13th **centuries** …

Sometimes the writer does not know the exact date.

Examples:

***Around** 800 BCE …*   OR   ***In about** 800 BCE …*

Lesson 9: Writing

glider

kite

wing   engine

biplane

propeller

A Michael Marsh is studying Science at Greenhill College. He has to write a paragraph about a famous invention. What questions should he answer about the invention and the inventor? Make a list.

B Michael has made a list of information he wants to include in his paragraph.

1 Number the areas in a logical order.
__ development of the invention
__ the historic moment
__ the inventor(s) – later life, death
__ the inventor(s) – birth, early life

2 Look at some extracts from Michael's research sources below. Match each area in 1 to one of the research extracts.

C Read the extracts. Complete the sentences with the missing letter(s) in each space.

a
On December 17th, 1903, Orville Wright flew the plane for 12 sec___nds. It tr___velled more th___n 35 m___tres. The inven___on of the plane chan___ed the w___ld for ever.

b
Wilbur Wright was b___n in 1867 in the USA. He lived for some y___rs in Indiana. Then his family m___ved to Ohio w___n he was v___ry y___ng. His br___ther, Orville, was born f___r years lat___. The tw___ young boys b___lt bicyc___s. Later they sold bicycles in their own sh___p. The brothers st___ted to t___k about building a plane in about 1896.

c
The brothers built bi___er and be___er planes. They sold them to the US gov___nment. They sold them to ___ther countr___s. Wilbur died in 1912. Orville lived to s___ the ___et a___e. He died ___ust ___fter World W___ Two, in 1948.

d
F___st, the Wright brothers built a bicycle with win___s. They fl___ it like a kite. Th___n they built a glider. They l___rnt how to control the glid___. Then they p___t in an engine. Finall___ they built a biplane with two propel___. They c___ed it *The Flyer*.

D Which of your questions in Exercise A can you answer now about this invention?

E Many sentences in these extracts are very short. You can join some of them with *and* or *but*. Choose the best way to join each pair of sentences.

1 He lived for some years in Indiana.   and / but   Then his family moved to Ohio.
2 They built bicycles.   and / but   They sold bicycles in their own shop.
3 They built a bicycle with wings.   and / but   They flew it like a kite.
4 They learnt how to control the glider.   and / but   Then they put in an engine.
5 Wilbur died in 1912.   and / but   Orville lived to see the jet age.
6 They sold them to the US government.   and / but   They sold them to other countries.

Lesson 10: Writing

A How do you spell these words?

1 Choose one spelling in each case.

   a night or nite

   b Wright or write

   c high or hie

   d explane or explain

   e wate or wait

   f plain or plane

   g train or trane

   h chainge or change

   i boi or boy

   j point or poynt

2 Read Skills Check 1 and check.

B Michael wants four sections in his paragraph.

1 Write the correct section letter next to each note.

   a the inventors – birth, early life

   b development of the invention

   c the historic moment

   d the inventors – later life, death

2 Number the notes in order in each section.

C Michael has written some sentences for his assignment.

1 What is wrong with these sections? Can you correct them?

   a Wilbur Wright was born in 1867 in the USA. Wilbur Wright lived for some years in Indiana. Wilbur Wright's family moved to Ohio when Wilbur was very young.

   b First, the Wright brothers built a bicycle with wings. The Wright brothers flew the bicycle like a kite.

   c Finally the Wright brothers built a biplane. The biplane had two propellers. The Wright brothers called the biplane *The Flyer*.

   d The Wright brothers built bigger and better planes. The Wright brothers sold the planes to the US government.

2 Read Skills Check 2. Check your answers.

___ built bicycle with wings / flew it like kite

___ built biplane with 2 propellers and engine

___ built a glider and learnt how to control it

___ built bicycles

___ built bigger and better planes

___ called the biplane 'The Flyer'

___ December 17th, 1903 = Orville flew biplane

___ family lived in Indiana; moved to Ohio

___ biplane flew for 12 seconds

___ Orville lived to see the jet age; d. 1948

___ put engine in glider

___ sold bicycles in their own shop

___ sold planes to US government, etc.

___ started to talk about building plane c. 1896

___ travelled > 35 metres

a Wilbur Wright b. 1867; Orville W. b. 1871

d Wilbur died 1912 (age = 45)

A Look at Table 1.

1 Complete the list of ordinal numbers. Be careful with these spellings.

eighth   fifth   second   third   twelfth   twenty-first   twentieth

Table 1: *Cardinal numbers*

1st	_____	9th	_____	17th	_____
2nd	_____	10th	_____	18th	_____
3rd	_____	11th	_____	19th	_____
4th	_____	12th	_____	20th	_____
5th	_____	13th	_____	21st	_____
6th	_____	14th	_____	22nd	_____
7th	_____	15th	_____	23rd	_____
8th	_____	16th	_____	24th	_____

B Look at Table 2.

1 Look at these comparative and superlative adjectives.

bigger   cheaper   largest

Write them under the correct rules, and then add their other forms.

2 Add the forms of *sunny* to complete the table.

Table 2: *Regular adjectives with comparative and superlative forms*

Rules	Cold + er/est	Late + r/st	Dry – y + ier/iest	Hot + t + er/est (ending with 1 vowel + 1 consonant)
adjective	_____	_____	_____	_____
comparative	_____	_____	_____	_____
superlative	_____	_____	_____	_____

C Look at Table 3.

1 Add these irregular comparative and superlative forms.

better   furthest

2 Learn these forms if you do not already know them.

Table 3: *Irregular adjectives with comparative and superlative forms*

Adjective	Good	Bad	Far
comparative	_____	worse	further/farther
superlative	best	worst	_____/farthest

Lesson 12: Grammar

(A) Look at Table 4.

1 Complete the table with:
   a the correct position of each planet from the Sun;
   b what is special about each, e.g., that (the) Earth is the best for the development of life. (Refer to Course Book page 31 if necessary.)

Table 4: *Statements with cardinals and superlative forms*

Venus is the	_____	planet from the Sun and is	_____
Earth is the	_____	from the Sun and is	the best for the development of life.
Jupiter is the	_____	from the Sun and is	_____
Pluto is the	_____	from the Sun and is	_____

(B) Look at Table 5.

1 Compare the rules with the rules in Table 2.
2 Add the past simple forms of these to the table.

call   carry   change   drop   hurry   invent   land   move   plan   refer   try   use

Table 5: *Past simple – regular forms*

Happen + ed	*Live + d*	*Study – y + ied*	*Travel + l + ed* (ending with 1 vowel + 1 consonant)
_____	_____	_____	_____
_____	_____	_____	_____
_____	_____	_____	_____

(C) Look at Table 6.

1 Many common verbs have irregular past simple forms. Complete the table with past simple forms of the verbs.
2 Some past simple forms are irregular because they are the same as their infinitives. Underline the example in the table. Here are some more.
   cost   cut   hit   hurt   shut
3 Here are some more examples of patterns among irregular verbs.
   • come/came – become/became
   • grow/grew – blow (up)/blew (up)
   • tell/told – sell/sold
   However, it is best just to note and learn irregular past simple forms with their infinitives as you meet them.

Table 6: *Past simple – irregular forms*

Infinitive	Past simple	Infinitive	Past simple
bring	_____	light	_____
build	_____	make	_____
drive	_____	meet	_____
fly	_____	put	_____
go	_____	say	_____
learn	_____	see	_____

Lesson 1: Vocabulary

In this unit, you are going to:

- hear two radio programmes about traditional stories
- hear two stories
- tell a traditional story
- read about two Shakespeare plays
- tell a story from world literature

A Discuss the questions.

1 Do you like reading? What sort of books do you like best?
2 Do you like films? Do you tell your friends the story of a film you have seen?

B 🔊 2.41 **Listen to the paragraph. Then complete it using Key vocabulary 1.**

Everybody likes a good _____. There are _____ in the _____ of every culture. Children learn them at home or at school. Many of these stories have a _____ – in other words, a lesson for life. For example, help people and they will help you. There is usually one main _____ – one person who does most of the actions. We often don't know the name of the _____ of these traditional stories. People often _____ the best stories into many languages, so, in the end, the same story _____ all around the world.

C Identify regular and irregular past tense forms.

1 Find and underline all the regular verbs in Table 1.
2 Practise saying these verbs in the past tense in pairs.
3 Write the correct infinitive next to the irregular past forms in Table 1.

D Play the Past Tense Game.

Work in small groups. The chairperson says an infinitive from Table 1. The first person in the group to say the past tense correctly gets a point.

E Match words from *Key vocabulary 2* to each definition.

1 a person who tells stories
2 a person who listens to a story
3 a person who appears in a story
4 a person who writes a story
5 all the traditional stories in a particular culture
6 a beautiful piece of writing

Key vocabulary 1

appear character literature
moral stories story
translate writer

Table 1: *Some irregular verbs*

Infinitive	Past tense
leave	left
give	gave
	made
	put
	sent
	did
	found
	went
	ran
	brought
	came
	felt
	told
	drew
	built
	got
	took
	said
	met

Key vocabulary 2

character folklore listener
literature storyteller writer

Lesson 2: Vocabulary

A What do you know about William Shakespeare? Do the quiz. Choose one or more answer in each case.

		A	B	C
1	What was his first name?	William	Henry	Andrew
2	When was he born?	1564	1764	1964
3	Where was he born?	London	Manchester	Stratford
4	Which university did he go to?	Oxford	Cambridge	none
5	When did he get married?	at 18	at 28	at 38
6	What was the first name of his wife?	Anne	Anna	Annie
7	How many children did he have?	1	2	3
8	Which of these plays did he write?	*Hamlet*	*Romeo and Juliet*	*Macbeth*
9	How many plays did he write?	5	35	53
10	What type of plays did he write?	funny plays	about kings and queens	sad plays

B Read the text and check your answers to Exercise A.

William Shakespeare was born on April 23rd, 1564. He was born in Stratford, a town in the centre of England. He is probably the most important person in English literature. However, we know very little about his childhood or early life. We do know that he did not go to university. He got married at 18 to Anne Hathaway. Their first child, Susanna, was born one year later, in May 1583. His twins were born in February 1585. He wrote his first play in 1589. It was called *Henry VI*. In 1594, he moved to London. He became an actor, but he continued to work as a playwright. He wrote 35 plays altogether. People know his characters, including Romeo and Juliet, Hamlet, and Macbeth, all around the world. He wrote comedies – funny plays; histories – about the lives of kings and queens; and tragedies – plays with an unhappy ending. He died on his birthday in 1616.

C Look at the *Key vocabulary*. Give a definition for each, then check with a dictionary.

D Read this text. Then complete the text using some words from the *Key vocabulary*. Make any necessary changes to the words.

There are many famous _____ by the _____ William Shakespeare, but perhaps the most famous is *Hamlet*. The main _____ is Hamlet, the prince of Denmark. The _____ is quite simple. Hamlet _____ his uncle, Claudius, because Claudius _____ Hamlet's father. Nobody is happy at the end – it is a _____.

> **Key vocabulary**
> character comedy
> history literature kill
> play playwright plot
> tragedy writer

Lesson 3: Listening

Ⓐ Look at the pictures in Lesson 1. Have you heard of these characters? What stories do you know about them? What is the connection between all three characters?

Ⓑ You are going to hear part of a radio programme. Read the information and answer the questions.
  1 What is this programme about?
  2 Who is the presenter?
  3 What are you going to hear on the programme?

Ⓒ Here are some statements about *The Arabian Nights*.
  1 Decide if each sentence is true or false.
    a *The Arabian Nights* is also called *The Hundred and One Nights*.
    b Stories are from different countries.
    c An Egyptian wrote down all the stories.
    d Aladdin found a lamp.
    e Sindbad had problems with 40 thieves.
    f *The Arabian Nights* is well known in the Western world.
  2 🔊 **2.42** Listen to the first part of the programme and check your answers.

Ⓓ 🔊 **2.43** Listen again. Complete the table.
Table 2: *History of The Arabian Nights*

Date	Event	Writer
	some stories appeared	anonymous
1500	stories written down	an Egyptian
	translated: Arabic →	
1885	translated: Arabic →	

Ⓔ How does Jenny define these words/phrases?
anonymous folklore generation to generation

Ⓕ 🔊 **2.44** Listen to the story. Which sentence about the story is true?
  1 At the end of the story, the poor man knew a thief took his donkey.
  2 The thief changed into a donkey because he hit his mother.
  3 The poor man was a nice man but a little stupid.
  4 At the end of the story, the poor man got his donkey back.

9.30 Literature around the world

This week, Jenny Ingram talks about the history of *The Arabian Nights*. She also introduces one of the stories from the collection, *The Thieves and the Donkey*.

Revision

Ⓖ Here are words from the radio programme.
  1 🔊 **2.45** Listen to the words in Column A.
  2 🔊 **2.46** Listen to the words in the orange box. Write each word in a space in Column B.
  3 🔊 **2.47** Write each word from the yellow box in a space in Column C. Listen and check.

A	B	C
lived		
means		
led		
words		
man		
passed		
not		
called		
young		
rude		
took		

> back bought his looked m<u>a</u>rket m<u>o</u>ther
> pr<u>o</u>blem thief went who world

> bird English f<u>a</u>ther few lamp put
> said son steal stopped st<u>o</u>ry

Lesson 4: Listening

A Discuss. In the story in Lesson 3 ...
1 how many characters are there?
2 who are the characters?
3 which collection does it come from?
4 who wrote the collection?

B Can you remember the story?
1 Tell the story in pairs.
2 Make a note of every past simple verb from the story.
3 Choose five of these past simple verbs. Make a new sentence with each.

C In the story from Lesson 3, there is ...
1 a young man/thief.
2 an old man/thief.
3 a poor man.
   🎧 **2.48** Who did what? Listen to the story in Lesson 3 again. Answer each question with 1, 2 or 3.
   __ **a** Who saw a poor man at the market?
   __ **b** Who went up behind the poor man?
   __ **c** Who untied the rope from the donkey and put it around his own neck?
   __ **d** Who took the donkey away?
   __ **e** Who suddenly stopped?
   __ **f** Who said, 'Who are you'?
   __ **g** Who said, 'I am your donkey'?
   __ **h** Who untied the rope?
   __ **i** Who said, 'Go back to your home'?
   __ **j** Who was surprised to see the donkey for sale again?
   __ **k** Who said, 'I told you not to be rude to your mother again'?

D 🎧 **2.49** Look at these words from the talk. Listen. Tick the correct column, according to the stressed vowel sound.

	1	2
	night	day
away		
became		
behind		
buy		
eighty		
famous		
generation		
made		
tie		
time		
translate		

Skills Check 1

Following a narrative

You must understand *who* did *what*.

1 If there are two or three men or women in a story, narrators use adjectives **in front of** the noun. Listen for:
   age *a young man, a old man*
   appearance *a big man, a small man*
   other description *a rich man, a poor man*, etc.

2 Sometimes narrators give you extra information **after** the noun.
   appearance *a man with a beard*
   possessions *a man with a donkey*

3 Sometimes narrators tell you the occupation of a character.
   occupation *a policeman, a thief*, etc.

4 Sometimes narrators use different words for the same character:
   Example:
   *Once there were two **thieves**, ...*
   a young man *and* **an old man**.

5 Listen also for the pronouns. You must understand who each pronoun refers to.
   Example:
   *Once there were two **thieves**, ...*
   They *were at a market.*

Skills Check 2

Hearing diphthongs with /ɪ/

There are three diphthongs (or double vowels) ending in /ɪ/.
/aɪ/ – *night, why, find*
/eɪ/ – *day, wait, make*
/ɔɪ/ – *boy, toy, oil*

Lesson 5: Speaking

Ⓐ Meliai, a Greek student at Greenhill, is reading a book of stories.
1 What's the name of the book?
2 What's the connection between Chotzas, Hodja, Joha and Goha?
3 Who is the *character* in this case?
4 What does *wise fool* mean?

Ⓑ 2.50 Leila, an Iranian, is talking to her friend, Meliai. Listen to the start of the conversation. Answer the questions.
1 What is Leila's favourite Joha story?
2 What's a tiger?
3 What's going to happen next in the conversation?

Ⓒ 2.51 Listen to the next part of the conversation. Define these words: *hunting, shooting, guns*.

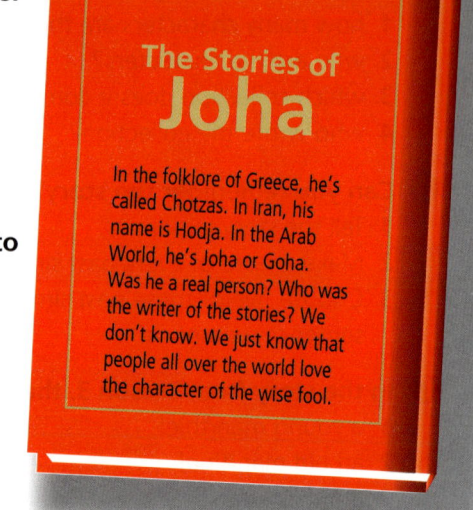

The Stories of
Joha

In the folklore of Greece, he's called Chotzas. In Iran, his name is Hodja. In the Arab World, he's Joha or Goha. Was he a real person? Who was the writer of the stories? We don't know. We just know that people all over the world love the character of the wise fool.

Ⓓ 2.52 Listen to the final part of the conversation. Number the events from the story in order.

	'Can I come with you?' asked Joha.
	'Oh, sorry,' he said. 'I didn't see the word NOT.'
	'What are you hunting?' he asked. 'Tigers,' they replied.
	'What is the matter with you?' said the man. 'Didn't you see the sign?'
	'You can,' said the leader. 'But you must be careful with your gun.'
	A few minutes later, Joha shot him and hurt his arm.
	He got a big piece of paper. He tied it to a rope.
	He put the rope around his neck.
	He wrote on the paper in big letters: I AM NOT A TIGER.
	Joha looked at the man, then came closer and looked at the sign.
	Joha said, 'I'll be careful,' and he went and got his gun.
2	Joha said to the men, 'Are you going hunting?' 'Yes, we are,' they replied.
1	Joha saw some men with guns.
	One of the villagers decided to make fun of Joha.

Revision

Ⓔ These words are from the conversation. Say each group of words. Which is the odd one out? What do the others have in common?

1 big	still	village	like
2 piece	see	replied	leader
3 tell	he	neck	said
4 your	hurt	birds	person
5 man	matter	have	paper
6 charge	asked	arm	am

7 forgot	lots	come	what
8 saw	poor	or	one
9 fun	guns	hunt	put
10 who	got	shoot	few
11 put	looked	would	shoot

Ⓕ Tell the story in D in pairs. Take turns.

Lesson 6: Speaking

A Play noughts and crosses with words from Lesson 5. Make a sentence from the story in each case.

hurt	hunt	gun
tiger	leader	shot
reply	neck	rope

B Who says each of these sentences from the conversation in Lesson 5?

1 Write S for the storyteller (Leila) or L for the listener (Meliai).

_____ **a** Do you know the one about …?

_____ **b** I haven't heard that one.

_____ **c** I'd love to.

_____ **d** It's so funny.

_____ **e** Now, where was I?

_____ **f** Oh, I forgot to say …

_____ **g** OK. Go on.

_____ **h** That's really funny.

_____ **i** Would you like to hear it?

_____ **j** You said …

2 Read Skills Check 1 and Skills Check 2. Check your answers.

C Read these words from the conversation.

> came dec<u>i</u>de my f<u>a</u>vourite great l<u>a</u>ter like make
> p<u>a</u>per repl<u>ie</u>d right say sign they t<u>i</u>gers

1 Put them into two groups according to the (<u>underlined</u>) vowel sound.

2 Read Skills Check 3. Check your answers.

3 Practise saying each group of words aloud.

D Work in pairs.

> **Student A**
> You know the story of _Joha and the Tiger._
> Tell Student B about the story, then tell him/her the story. Answer any questions about the vocabulary.
> Use some phrases from Skills Check 1 and Lesson 5 Exercise D to help you with the story.

> **Student B**
> You don't know the story of _Joha and the Tiger._ You want to hear it, but you don't know any of the words in Exercise A above. Use some phrases from Skills Check 2.

Skills Check 1

Telling a story

Here are some useful phrases.

Checking with the listener	Do you know the one about …? Would you like to hear it?
Talking about the story	It's so funny/clever/ scary …
Asking the listener for help	Now, where was I?
Filling in the gaps	Oh, I forgot to say …

Skills Check 2

Listening to a story

Here are some useful phrases.

Talking about the story	I don't know that one. I haven't heard that one.
Checking understanding	Refer to: Page 15 Skills Check 2 & Page 91 Skills Check 2
Asking the storyteller to continue	Go on.
Helping the storyteller	You said …
Reacting to the story	That's great. That's really funny/ clever/scary.

Skills Check 3

Saying diphthongs – /aɪ/ and /eɪ/

The two sounds are similar.

Examples:

/aɪ/ = _like, my, right, sign, tigers_

/eɪ/ = _say, they, make, came, great_

Note that there are many ways to spell these two sounds.

A Prepare to read the text.

1 Look at the illustrations, the title and the first paragraph.

2 Which of these sentences do you expect to find in the text? Tick (✔) one or more.
   ☐ However, the plan went wrong.
   ☐ Shakespeare wrote many other plays.
   ☐ Romeo Montague fell in love with Juliet Capulet.
   ☐ Juliet's friend had an idea.
   ☐ William Shakespeare died in 1616.

B Read each topic sentence. What will be in the rest of the paragraph?

C Read the text on page 145.

1 Check your answers to Exercise A.
2 Check your ideas from Exercise B.

D Number the illustrations in the correct order.

E Guess the meanings of these words:

1 performances   5 body
2 hated   6 wake/woke
3 sword   7 poison
4 marriage   8 tragedy

F Tell the story of *Romeo and Juliet* in your own words.

Love Story Lasts 400 Years

R*omeo and Juliet* is one of the most famous tragedies in the world. William Shakespeare wrote it between 1590 and 1595. There have been thousands of performances in the 400 years since then. The story is simple and very sad.

A Romeo Montague fell in love with Juliet Capulet.

B Then something terrible happened.

C Juliet's father wanted her to marry a man called Paris.

D Juliet's friend had an idea.

E However, the plan went wrong.

F Something good came out of the tragedy.

Lesson 8: Reading

A **Make sentences about _Romeo and Juliet_ using words from each column.**

Example: _Romeo and Juliet fell in love._

1	2	3
Romeo	didn't know	in love.
	fell	each other.
Juliet	got	a young Capulet.
	had	the city.
The Montagues	hated	married.
	killed	her to marry.
The Capulets	left	about her marriage.
	took	an idea.
Juliet's father	wanted	back to the city.
	went	poison.
Juliet's friend	came	up.
	woke	wrong.
The plan	found	Romeo dead.

B **Read Skills Check 1.**
1 Find and underline regular verbs in Column 2 of Exercise A.
2 Find and circle irregular verbs in Column 2 of Exercise A. What is the infinitive of each irregular verb?

C **Read Skills Check 2.**
1 Find and underline all the pronouns in the text on page 145. What does each pronoun refer to?
2 Find the phrases a–g in the text. For each of these phrases, find another word or phrase with the same meaning in the text.

a	the idea	**i**	Juliet
b	the accident	**ii**	the plan
c	your husband	**iii**	Romeo
d	his wife	**iv**	the death of Romeo and Juliet
e	the tragedy	**v**	Romeo and Juliet
f	the two families	**vi**	killing the young Capulet
g	the two young people	**vii**	the Montagues and the Capulets

3 Cover the right column. Can you remember the other way of referring in each case?

D **What have you learned in this lesson? Cover the Skills Checks and explain them in groups.**

Skills Check 1

Recognizing past tense verbs

Stories have many verbs in the past simple.
1 The past simple of **regular verbs** ends in ~ed.
   Examples: _happened, tried, hated, killed_
   Look for words ending in ~ed in a story. They are probably verbs.

2 You must learn to recognize **irregular** past tense verbs.
   Examples: _fell, went, came_
   Look for words after nouns/pronouns. They are probably verbs.

Skills Check 2

Following a narrative

You must understand _who_ did _what_.
1 Writers use **nouns** the first time a person is mentioned. They often use **pronouns** the second + time.
   Example:
   Romeo Montague _fell in love with_ **Juliet Capulet**. **He** _married_ **her** _in secret._
   Underline pronouns and think: Who does this refer to?
2 Writers use different words for the same person or thing.
   Example: _Romeo heard that_ **his wife** _was dead._
   his wife = Juliet
   Underline 'new' people and things in a story and think: Is this really a new person/thing? Or is it a new word for an 'old' person/thing?

Lesson 9: Writing

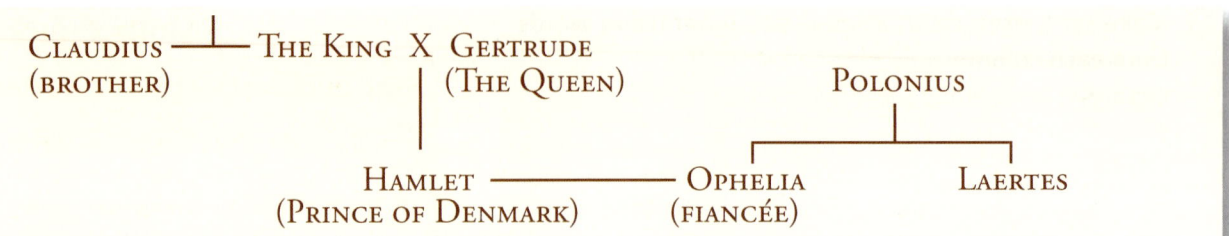

CLAUDIUS ——┬── THE KING X GERTRUDE   POLONIUS
(BROTHER)   (THE QUEEN)

HAMLET ————————— OPHELIA   LAERTES
(PRINCE OF DENMARK)   (FIANCÉE)

Ⓐ Pia is studying World Literature at Greenhill College. This semester, she has to study *Hamlet* by William Shakespeare.

Look at the family tree of the main characters in the play. Complete these sentences about the characters.

1 Hamlet was _____ of Denmark.
2 Hamlet's father was the _____.
3 Hamlet's mother was called _____.
4 Hamlet's _____ was called Claudius.
5 Hamlet's fiancée was called _____.
6 Ophelia's father was _____.
7 Laertes was _____.

Ⓑ Pia has to tell the story of the play. Read her first draft.

1 She has not used many pronouns or possessive adjectives (see Skills Check 2 on page 95). Replace nouns where possible. Write above the noun.
2 Pia's sentences are very short. Join some pairs of sentences with *and* or *but*.
3 You can join some pairs of sentences with *because*. Sometimes you have to change the order of the sentences first.

Ⓒ Cover Pia's draft. Choose the correct spelling of these words.

1 died	dyed
2 becaim	became
3 married	marryed
4 sor	saw
5 said	sayed
6 talk	tak
7 tried	tryed
8 killed	kiled

Ⓓ Can you remember the story? Cover Pia's draft. Look at the family tree to help you.

The king died.

Claudius became king.

Claudius married Gertrude.

Hamlet hated Claudius.

Claudius married Gertrude too quickly.

Hamlet saw the ghost of Hamlet's father.

The ghost said, 'Claudius killed me.'

The ghost said, 'You must kill Claudius.'

Hamlet went to talk to Hamlet's mother.

Hamlet wanted to kill Claudius.

Hamlet killed Ophelia's father by mistake.

Ophelia was very sad about Ophelia's father.

Ophelia died.

Laertes tried to kill Hamlet in a sword fight.

Hamlet killed Laertes.

Hamlet was hurt in the fight.

Hamlet finally killed Claudius.

Hamlet fell down himself.

Hamlet died.

Lesson 10: Writing

A Can you remember the characters in *Hamlet*?
Match the words that refer to the same
person.

1 Ophelia   a Hamlet's mother
2 Laertes   b Hamlet's uncle
3 Claudius   c Ophelia's brother
4 Polonius   d Ophelia's father
5 Gertrude   e Hamlet's fiancée

B Look at these two short sentences.

The king had a brother.
His name was Claudius.

1 Give the same information in one sentence.
2 Read Skills Check 1. Check your answer.

C Combine the information in each pair of
sentences into one sentence. Write the new
sentences in your exercise books.

1 Claudius married Hamlet's mother.
Her name was Gertrude.
2 Hamlet killed Polonius.
Polonius was Ophelia's father.
3 Hamlet killed Ophelia's brother.
Ophelia's brother was Laertes.

Skills Check 1

Combining information

You can often combine information about a
person into one sentence.
Example:

Short sentences	Longer sentence
*The **king** had a **brother**.*	*The king had a*
*His name was **Claudius**.*	*brother, Claudius.*

Notice how we use the comma (,) in this sentence.

Skills Check 2

Replacing one noun with another noun

We can use **different** words for the **same** person
or thing.
Examples:
***Claudius** married **Gertrude**.*
*Hamlet hated **his uncle** because he married*
***his mother** so quickly.*

*Ophelia died and **her brother** wanted to kill*
*Hamlet, but Hamlet killed **Laertes**.*

D Read Skills Check 2. Then read this version of the Hamlet story.
Join the words in red to one of the characters in each case.

Hamlet   Gertrude

Hamlet was the prince of Denmark. His
father, the king, died. The king's brother,
Claudius, became king and married Hamlet's
mother, Gertrude. The young prince hated his
uncle for marrying his mother so quickly. Then
the ghost of his father appeared to the young
man. He said, 'Claudius killed me. You must kill
my wife's new husband.'
Hamlet wanted to kill his stepfather, but he killed
Polonius, Ophelia's father, by mistake. Hamlet's
fiancée died because she was so sad about her
father. Her brother, Laertes, tried to kill his
father's murderer in a sword fight, but Hamlet
killed him. However, he was hurt in the fight,
too. Finally, Hamlet killed his father's killer then
fell down himself and died.

Claudius   Polonius

Ophelia   Laertes

Lesson 11: Grammar

A **Look at Table 1.**

1 Complete the *Yes/No* and 'wh' questions for the answers. Use *was/were* and these question words.

what	when	where	which

2 Write similar questions and answers about someone famous in your history.

Table 1: *Past simple of be – questions and answers*

Questions		Answers
_____ _____	Shakespeare's first name?	William.
_____ _____	he born?	In 1564.
_____ _____	he born?	In Stratford.
_____ _____	his plays popular?	Yes, very.
_____ _____	the most popular 400 years ago?	Perhaps Macbeth.

B **Look at Table 2.**

1 You need past simple verb forms for statements. You need infinitives for questions and negatives. Complete the table of verbs from Unit 3.

2 For regular forms, go back and check the spelling rules in Unit 2, page 19.

3 For irregulars, check spellings in your dictionary.

4 Correct these other forms of verbs from Theme 3.

feel – ~~feeled~~ fall – ~~falled~~ fight – ~~fighted~~ hear – ~~heared~~ know – ~~knowed~~ sleep - ~~sleeped~~

Table 2: *Past simple forms and infinitives*

	Infinitive	Past form	Infinitive	Past form
Regular forms	hate >			< agreed
	stop >			< killed
	try >			< moved
Irregular forms	have >			< came
	say >			< left
	take >			< thought
	write >			< went

C **Read the text below. Then look at Table 3.**

Complete the *Yes/No* and 'wh' questions and answers in the table. Use the underlined verbs and these question words.

how long	how many	when	where

Shakespeare <u>grew up</u> in Stratford, but he <u>moved</u> to London in 1594, <u>lived</u> there for 16 years and <u>wrote</u> most of his plays there. Finally, he <u>went</u> home to Stratford in 1610 and died there in 1616.

Table 3: *Past simple of main verbs – questions and answers*

Questions		Answers	
_____ _____	Shakespeare _____?	He _____	in Stratford.
_____ ___	he _____ to London?	___ _____	there in 1594.
_____ _____ _____	he _____ there?	___ _____	there for 16 years.
____ _____ plays ____	he _____?	___ _____	35.
____	he _____ home?	Yes, ___ _____	back in 1610.

Lesson 12: Grammar

A **Look at Table 4.**
  1 Complete the table with pronouns and possessive adjectives from the texts on pages 8–9.
  2 Complete the following mini-dialogues.
   a A: I'm cold. What about ___?
     B: Yes, ___ am, too. Let's warm _____ by the fire.
   b A: Where's Salwa? ___ was here an hour ago.
     B: ___ father called, so she went to see ___.
   c A: Tom, ___ friends came to see ___ today.
     B: Oh, no! What were ___ names?
   d A: Tell ___, what happened to Ahmet?
     B ___ fell off that wall and hurt _____ badly.

Table 4: Pronouns and possessive adjectives

	Subject pronouns	Object pronouns	Reflexive pronouns	Possessive adjectives
Singular 1st	_____	me	myself	my
2nd	_____	___	yourself	_____
3rd	_____, _____, it	_____, _____, _____	_____, _____, itself	_____
Plural 1st	we	us	ourselves	our
2nd	you	you	yourselves	your
3rd	_____	them	themselves	their

B **Look at Table 5**
  1 Complete the sentences with *s* and *'s*.
  2 Join the pairs of sentences. Change the second sentence in each pair.
   a Claudius killed the king. The king was the father of Hamlet.
     Claudius killed the King, Hamlet's father.
   b He married Gertrude. She was the wife of the king.
   c Hamlet finally killed Claudius. He was the killer of his father.

Table 5: Plural s and apostrophe s

Shakespeare___	play___	are still very popular.
I borrowed	my friend___	set of tape___ of the plays.
Reader___ today	still love	the great man___ storie___.

Lesson 1: Vocabulary

In this unit, you are going to:

- listen to two lectures about sport
- talk about sports
- read about two board games
- write about a traditional game in your country

A Discuss these questions.

1 What do you do in your spare time?
2 What sort of things do you read regularly?
3 What sports do you play?
4 What sports do you watch?

B Underline the *Key vocabulary* in the picture. Then cover the picture and explain the seven words.

C ✎ 3.1 Listen to a paragraph. Then complete with words from the *Key vocabulary* or others you know. Change the form of the word if necessary.

There are many different kinds of _____. We play some sports with a _____ – for example, football, tennis, _____ and _____. We _____ some sports with other _____ in a team. For example, football is a _____ sport. Sometimes we need a piece of _____ to take part in a sport. We need a bicycle, of course, for _____, and we need a stick for _____.

Key vocabulary
court cycling
equipment golf
hit ice hockey
indoors net
player point
out of court
outdoors riding
rugby running
score serve
team winner

D Work in groups of three. You each have three sentences.

1 Look at your three sentences. Learn them. Ask your teacher for help with the pronunciation of new words.
2 Say your sentences to your group.
3 Work out the name of the game.

Student A
- One player serves the ball.
- The winner is the player who gets the most points.
- There is a low net across the middle of the court.

Student B
- This game is normally for two players.
- The players take turns to hit the ball.
- When the ball goes out of court, you score a point.

Student C
- You can play indoors or outdoors.
- You need a small, yellow ball.
- You play in a special place called a court.

Lesson 2: Vocabulary

A **Read the text below. Then label Items A to E in the illustration.**

> These people are playing a game. It is a game for four players. They are using small playing pieces. They have different colours – red, blue, green and yellow. They are playing on a board with lots of squares.
>
> How do you play a game like this? The players take turns. One player moves one of his pieces – one, two or three squares, for example. Then another player has a turn. He moves one of *his* pieces. What happens if he lands on the same square? His opponent has to take his piece back to the start.
>
> The objective of this game is to get all your pieces home first. In this game, home is in the middle of the board.

A _____

B _____

C _____

D _____

E _____

B **Answer these questions about the game in Exercise A.**
1 How many players are there?
2 What do you call a person you are playing against?
3 How do you play the game?
4 How do you win this game?
5 Do you play this game in your country? What is it called?

C **Complete the text about a traditional game using the *Key vocabulary*. Make any necessary changes to the words. You can use the same word more than once.**

There are many traditional children's _____ in England. Some are _____ games. This means the children divide into two groups. However, many are for single _____. Some need special _____, for example, a ball or some stones, but many don't need any _____ at all.

The favourite _____ of many English children is 'What's the time, Mr Wolf?' The _____ of the game are very simple. The children _____ one child to be the wolf. The other _____ make a line and say, 'What's the time, Mr Wolf?' The wolf can say anything, for example, 'Six o'clock.' But when the wolf says, 'Dinner time!' the children run away and the wolf _____ to catch one of them.

> **Key vocabulary**
> choose equipment
> game land objective
> piece player rule
> team try turn

D **Do you know the game in Exercise C? Is there a game with similar rules in your country?**

Lesson 3: Listening

A **Put these sports into groups. Explain your choices.**

cycling   motor racing
football   running
golf   swimming
long jump   tennis

long jump   motor racing   golf

B **Manuel Molinero is studying Sports Education at Greenhill College.**
He has a lecture today about different types of sports.

1 **3.2** Listen to the introduction. Write the missing words in *Categories* and *Definitions*.
2 **3.3** Listen to Part 2. When the lecturer stops, guess the next word. Then listen and check.
3 **3.4** Listen to Part 2 again. Complete the *sub-categories* section with headings under each arrow.
4 **3.5** Listen to Part 2 again and write one example for each sub-category.
5 **3.6** Listen to the summary of the lecture and check your answers.

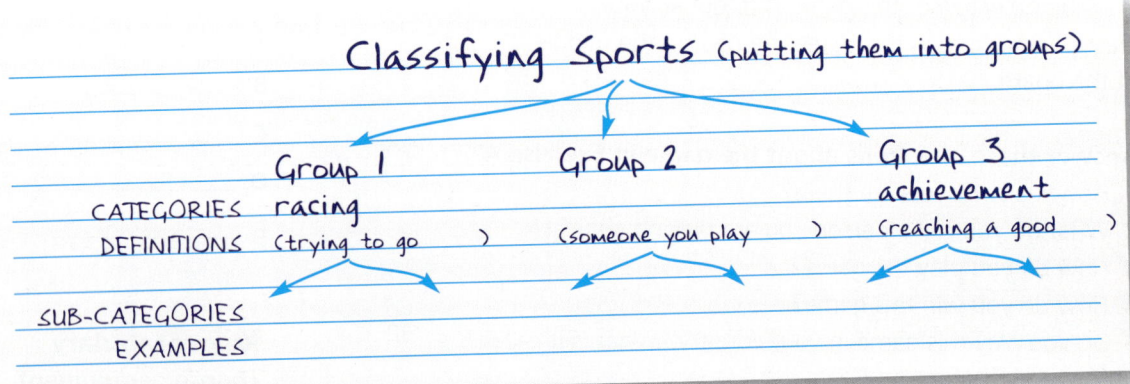

C **Write in examples of other sports of each sub-category.**

Revision

D **All these words from the lecture contain the vowel letter *a*. But what is the sound in each word?**

1 Tick under the word with the same vowel sound.
2 **3.7** Listen and check your answers.

	1 /iː/	2 /æ/	3 /ɑː/	4 /ɒ/	5 /ɔː/	6 /e/	7 /ɜː/	8 /eɪ/
against								
ball								
class								
heard								
quantity								
racing								
reach								
target								
team								
that								

Lesson 4: Listening

A **How can a lecturer tell listeners that a word is important?**
1 Think of at least three ways.
2 Read Skills Check 1. Check your ideas.

> He can say, 'This word is important!'

> She can say the word more slowly.

B 🎧 **3.8 Listen to Part 1 of the lecture from Lesson 3 again. Put your hand up when you hear an important word.**

C 🎧 **3.9 Listen to Part 2 of the lecture again. How does the lecturer show that these words are important? Tick one or more ways.**

Key word	Slowly	Loudly	Explanation	Example	Repetition
racing	✓	✓	✓	✓	✓
machine					
opponent					
person					
target					
quantity					

Skills Check 1

Recognizing important words

It is impossible to hear and understand everything that a lecturer says in a foreign language. You must decide which words are important and then check the meaning later, if necessary. The lecturer usually helps you to recognize important words. He/she does one or more of these things:
1 says the word **more slowly**.
2 says the word **more loudly**.
3 **explains** the meaning of the words.
4 gives an **example** of the word in use.
Don't worry if you do not hear the word clearly the first time. A good lecturer usually …
5 **repeats** important words.

D **Look at these words from the lecture.**
1 Do they have the sound in *no* or the sound in *now*? Tick in one column for each word.
2 🎧 **3.10 Listen and check your ideas.**

	A	B
	no	now
	/əʊ/	/aʊ/
so		
power		
opponent		
how		
know		
go		
also		
OK		

Skills Check 2

Hearing vowels – /əʊ/ and /aʊ/

These two diphthongs are very similar.
Examples:
/əʊ/ *hole, go, so, OK*
/aʊ/ *how, now, power*

Lesson 5: Speaking

Ⓐ Mino is a Sports Education student at Greenhill College. She is talking to her friend, Munira.
🔊 **3.11 Listen to the first part of Mino and Munira's conversation. Answer the questions.**
1 What's Munira's favourite sport?
2 What about Mino?

Ⓑ What do you know about the favourite sports of the girls?
1 Can you answer any of the questions below about football? Discuss and write notes in the second column.
2 What about baseball? Discuss and write notes in the third column.
3 🔊 3.12 Listen to the second part of the conversation. Complete the information about baseball.

	Football	Baseball
a Is it a team game?		
b Is it a ball game?		
c Do you play it indoors?		
d Do you play it in a special place?		
e Do you need any special equipment?		
f Do you score goals?		

Ⓒ Look at the sentences below.
1 Match Munira's questions and Mino's replies.
2 🔊 3.13 Listen to the first part of the conversation again and check your answers.
3 Practise this part of the conversation in pairs.

a	Hi, Mino. How are you?	**i**	Brazil. Two goals to one.
b	What are you watching?	**ii**	Hello, Munira. I'm fine.
c	Who's winning?	**iii**	It's Brazil versus Germany.
d	Is it a good game?	**iv**	P-I-T-C-H.
e	Sorry. What's a pitch?	**v**	The place where they play.
f	How do you spell it?	**vi**	Yes, it's quite exciting. But the pitch is terrible.
g	How do you say it? Pitich?	**vii**	No, pitch.

Revision

Ⓓ All these words from the conversation have the letter *a*. But there are many different sounds.

> all   any   ask   ball   base   bat   called   each   favourite   game   hand   hard
> heard   place   play   really   say   shape   team   that   watch   what

1 Work out the different sounds.
2 🔊 3.14 Listen and check your ideas.

Lesson 6: Speaking

A What can you remember about the game of baseball? Ask and answer in pairs.

B Read this version of part of the conversation from Lesson 5.

1 What is wrong with Mino's reply in each case?
2 Read Skills Check 1 and check your ideas.
3 Complete each of Mino's answers with a polite ending. Then find an extra piece of information from the box.
4 Practise the full conversation in pairs.

Munira: Is it a team game?
   Mino: Yes.
Munira: Is it a ball game?
   Mino: Yes.
Munira: Do you play it indoors?
   Mino: No.
Munira: Do you play it in a special place?
   Mino: Yes.
Munira: Do you need any special equipment?
   Mino: Yes.
Munira: Do you score goals?
   Mino: No.

C Read these words from the conversation.

ab<u>ou</u>t d<u>o</u>n't d<u>ow</u>n g<u>o</u> g<u>oa</u>l h<u>o</u>ld h<u>ow</u>
kn<u>ow</u> m<u>o</u>st n<u>o</u> n<u>ow</u> r<u>ou</u>nd s<u>o</u>

1 Put the words into two groups, according to the (underlined) vowel sounds.
2 Read Skills Check 2. Check your answers.
3 Practise saying the words aloud.

D Work in pairs.

> **Student A**
> Ask about the game of football. Use the questions in Exercise A.

> **Student B**
> Answer the questions politely. Add extra information to each answer.

Change roles.

Skills Check 1

Keeping the conversation going

Never answer *Yes/No* questions with *Yes/No* answers!
Always:
1 be polite = *Yes, it is; No, I don't.*
2 add extra information.
Example:
Is it a team game?
Yes, it is. There are nine players on each team.

- You get one run each time you go round all the bases.
- You need a baseball bat.
- There are nine players on each team.
- You play it with a small hard ball.
- You play outdoors because you hit the ball a long way.
- You play on a big pitch with a diamond shape on one side.

Skills Check 2

Saying diphthongs – /əʊ/ and /aʊ/

These two vowel sounds are very similar. Make sure you can say the two sounds clearly.
Examples:
no, know, don't, go
how, now, round, down
The first sound begins with /ə/.
The second sound begins with /æ/.
Both sounds end with /uː/.

Lesson 7: Reading

A You are going to read a text about a game. Look at the illustrations from the text. Can you name any of the things?

B Look at the section headings underneath the illustrations. Which section do you need to read if you want to find out the following information?

1 How many pieces are there in the game?
2 Which country does the game come from?
3 What are the pieces called?
4 What happens at the end of the game?
5 What do the players do in the game?

C Look at the topic sentences (B – F) from each section. Which section does each topic sentence come from? Write the letter next to each topic sentence. (One section has two paragraphs, so it needs two topic sentences.)

D Do you know this game? Have a guess!

E Look quickly at the text on page 146. Check your answers to Exercise B.

F Read the text carefully. After reading each paragraph, stop and think: *What is this game?*

G We have seen that writers often use different words for the same thing. What words does the writer here use for ...

1 the playing pieces?
2 the other player?
3 the game?

H Label the things in the illustrations. Use words from the text.

A

a) History
b) The playing pieces
c) How to play
d) How to win

B From India, it passed to Persia in the 6th century.

C The game is for two players.

D The names of the pieces show the history of the game.

E The objective of the game is simple.

F People first played this game in India over 2,000 years ago.

Lesson 8: Reading

A **What information can you remember from each section of the text about chess? Work in groups.**

1 History
2 The playing pieces
3 How to play
4 How to win

B **What is *active reading*?**

1 What do you understand by the expression? Discuss in pairs.
2 Read the first part of Skills Check 1. Check your ideas.

C **Predicting tense forms**

1 Read the rest of Skills Check 1.
2 Look back at the section headings in Exercise A. What tense forms were in each section?
3 Find each paragraph in the text on page 146 and check your ideas.

D **Referring back**

1 Look again at the text on page 146. Find and underline all the pronouns in the first two paragraphs of the text. What does each pronoun refer to?
2 Read Skills Check 2.
3 Find the words *then* and *there* in the first two paragraphs of the text. Does the word refer back in each case? Or does it introduce the next action/a new piece of information?

E **Can you play chess? Do you like it? How do some of the pieces move?**

Skills Check 1

Active reading

Active reading means …
• predicting content, *then*
• reading, *then*
• comparing content with predictions.

Predicting tense forms is part of predicting content. You can usually predict the tense forms in a paragraph from …
• the heading
• the topic sentence

Examples:

Heading	Topic sentence	Tense?
Origins	*People first **played** this game in India over 2,000 years ago.*	Past simple
The playing pieces	*The names of the pieces **show** the history of the game.*	Present simple

Skills Check 2

Referring back

We have seen that **pronouns** refer back to previous nouns. We can use **other words** to refer back:

then = referring back to a date or time
there = referring back to a place

Examples:

Then, *they used real soldiers.* = 2,000 years ago
There, *Arab traders learned the game.* = in Persia

But be careful!
The word *then* can also introduce the next action.
The word *there* can also introduce a new piece of information.

Examples:

*One player moves, **then** the other player.*
***There** are now more than 40 million players in Russia alone.*

Lesson 9: Writing

A Dave Wang is studying Education at Greenhill College. He is researching children's games around the world. What information should he find out about the games? Make a list.

B Here are Dave's questions.

> a What the rules are?
> b What equipment are they needing?
> c What is name of game?
> d Where it comes from?
> e Who is play it?

1 Rewrite the questions with the correct grammar.
2 Put the questions in a logical order.

C Look at the illustrations. Read Dave's notes. Do you know any of the games?

D Read Dave's draft of a paragraph about *Umm al lal*. Change some nouns into pronouns or other nouns.

The name of this game is Umm al lal. *The game comes from the UAE. The game is a game for girls. The girls do not need any equipment. First, the girls choose one girl to be the mother and the girls choose another girl to be a wolf. The other girls are the mother's children. Then the wolf tries to catch one of the girls and the mother tries to protect all the girls.*

E Read Dave's draft of a paragraph about *Pie Kalah*.
1 Add *First/Then/After that/Finally*.
2 Join some sentences with *and*.

Pie Kalah is a game from Liberia in West Africa for girls or boys. The children need one small stone. They divide into two teams. One team gets the stone. They move into a circle. They hide the stone from the other team. They pass the stone from one child to another. They say, 'Find the stone' to the other team. They try to find it.

F Write a paragraph about *Kelereng*. Use:
1 pronouns/other nouns
2 *and*
3 *First/Then/After that*

Name	Umm al lal
Country	UAE
Players	girls
Equipment	none
Rules	1. children choose girl = mother
	2. children choose another girl = wolf
	3. other girls = mother's children
	4. wolf tries to catch child; mother tries to protect them

Name	Pie Kalah
Country	Liberia (West Africa)
Players	girls or boys
Equipment	1 small stone
Rules	1. children divide into 2 teams
	2. 1 team gets 1 stone
	3. 1 team moves into circle; hides stone from other team
	4. they pass stone from one child to another
	5. they say "Find stone"; other team tries

Name	Kelereng
Country	Indonesia
Players	boys
Equipment	2 small stones
Rules	1. children draw small circle on ground
	2. each child puts one stone in circle
	3. children take turns to throw other stone into circle; try to hit stone; try to knock it out of circle

Lesson 10: Writing

A We can make one vowel sound with many different vowel letters.

1 What are the missing letters in these words?
2 What is the vowel sound in each case?
3 Read Skills Check 1. Check your answers.

a ___round
b equipm___nt
c ___noth___
d gramm___r
e ill___strat___n
f childr___n
g moth___
h ord___
i oth___
j par___graph
k play___
l pr___tect

B Read Dave's second draft of a paragraph about *Umm al lal*.

1 Choose between the words in brackets in each case.
2 Read Skills Check 2. Check your answers.

There is a game in the UAE called Umm al lal. *It is a game for girls. They do not need any equipment. First, the girls choose (one girl / the girl) to be the mother and (the other / another) girl to be a wolf. The (other / another) girls are the mother's children. Then the wolf tries to catch (other / the other) children and the mother tries to protect (each / all) of them.*

C Read Dave's second draft of a paragraph about *Pie Kalah*.

1 Write one or two words in each space.
2 Read Skills Check 2 again. Check your answers.

Pie Kalah is a game from Liberia in West Africa for girls or boys. _____ children need one small stone. They divide into two teams. _____ team gets the stone. They move into a circle and they hide the stone from _____ team. They pass the stone from _____ child to _____ child. They say, 'Find the stone' to _____ team and they try to find it.

D Read your paragraph about *Kelereng*. Check that you have distinguished between people and things.

Skills Check 1

Spelling the sound /ə/

This sound is called **schwa**. It is the most common sound in English. You can hear it in almost every word with more than one syllable.

But how do you spell it? The simple answer is … there are no rules. You must learn the spelling of each word with schwa.

Examples:

a = **a**nother; **a**round; par**a**graph
e = equipm**e**nt; childr**e**n
o = pr**o**tect
u = ill**u**stration

Notes:

1 The letter *i* does not usually make the schwa sound, except in the ending ~*tion*.
   Example: *illustra**tion***

2 There is one very common pattern: at the end of a word, the sound schwa is usually spelt *er*.
   Examples:
   *moth**er**; oth**er**; anoth**er**; play**er**; ord**er***
   Exceptions: *gramm**ar**, doct**or***

Skills Check 2

Distinguishing between people and things

You often need to explain *who did/does what*.

1 You need special words when there are two people or things.
2 You need an extra word when there are more than two people or things.

Number	Examples		
Two	one child	the other child	
	one stone	the other stone	
More than two	one child	the other children	
	one child	another child	the other children

3 You sometimes need to talk about all the people or things in the whole group.
   Examples:
   each child; each one,
   all of the children; all of them

Lesson 11: Grammar

A **Look at Table 1.**

This is about a Japanese game, *go-mokonarabe*. Use these verbs to complete the sentences. Put them in the correct forms of the present simple.

be   contain   come   have   take   try   use

Table 1: *Present simple: 3ʳᵈ-person singular and plural*

Go-mokonarabe		
This is a game that	_____	from Japan.
The players	_____	a pot of stones each.
One pot	_____	full of white stones.
The other pot	_____	black stones.
The players	_____	it in turns to put a stone down.
Each player	_____	to finish a line of five stones first.
Both players also	_____	stones to stop each others' lines.

B **Look at these sentence parts.**

- the game (come from) where
- players there (be) how many
- what (contain) the pots
- you at this game (win) how

1 Put the parts in order and the verbs in the correct forms, and make questions about *go-mokonarabe*.

2 Answer the questions from what you now know.

3 Make up similar questions and answers about a game from your country.

C **Look at Table 2.**

1 Read the sentences. What game are they about?

2 Use these modal verbs to complete the sentences. (In one, you can use either *cannot* or *must not*.)

can   cannot (can't)   must   must not (mustn't)

Table 2: *Modal verbs – can, must (positive and negative)*

You	_____ run	with the ball,
or you	_____ pass	it to another team member.
Your team	_____ try	to attack the other team's goal,
and at the same time, you	_____ let	the other team near your goal.
The rules say that you	_____ hit	the ball with your head and feet,
but that you	_____ touch	it with your hands.

Lesson 12: Grammar

A **Look at Table 3.**

  1 Read the sentences. Could they be about the same game as in Table 2? Could they be about others?

  2 Complete the table with these words.

> one   another   each other   some   the other   the others

  3 What is the difference between *another* and *the other*?

Table 3: One, another, the other, *etc.*

_____	team plays from the left, and	_____	team plays from the right.
_____	player starts and usually passes the ball to	_____	team member.
_____	players stay back, while the job of	_____	is to attack.
	As they move forward, they pass the ball to	_____ .	

B **Look at the picture of the game *Umm al lal* on page 68 of the Course Book. Then look at Table 4.**

  1 Choose from these forms to complete the sentences.

> all of   another of   both of   one of   the rest of   two of

  2 Look around your class. Make similar statements.

  There are two people in front of me. Both of them are writing.

Table 4: One of, another of, all of, *etc.*

_____	the girls is the wolf.
_____	the girls is the mother.
_____	them are the mother's children.
_____	them are wearing yellow dresses.
_____	them are having fun.

C **Look at Table 5.**

  1 Answer the questions. Use the words in brackets. Also use *then*, *there* and other pronouns.

  2 Write about your life, using *there* and *then*.

  Years ago, we lived on a farm. I liked life there.

  Later, we moved to the city. I was only six then.

Table 5: There, then *and other pronouns*

Did the girls play chess on Wednesday? No, they didn't play chess then. They did that on Thursday.	(Thursday)
Did Noura watch the film on Sunday? _____	(Saturday)
Did Fuad go running in the park? _____	(on the beach)
Did the boys have their football practice in the gym? _____	(at the stadium)

Lesson 1: Vocabulary

In this unit, you are going to:

- listen to two lectures about food groups and healthy eating
- learn some vocabulary that you will need to talk about making meals
- do a quiz and read two articles about healthy eating
- write about your eating habits

A Do a quiz. Name as many foods as you can. You have one minute for each one.

1 drinks   **3** vegetables
2 fruit   **4** meat

B 🔊 **3.15** Listen to a paragraph. Then complete the text using the *Key vocabulary* and other appropriate words.

Why do we eat? What a silly question! We eat because we are _____. Well, that answer is true, in a way. But why do we feel hungry? We feel hungry because the _____ needs more energy. The whole body needs _____ to move. Every part of the body needs energy to work correctly. We get energy from _____. However, we have to be careful. If we don't use all the energy from food, the _____ keeps it. How does it keep it? It keeps it as _____. It is easy to use *new* energy from _____. It is much harder to use the _____ in fat. So, what's the answer? We must eat the right *amount* of _____, and we must take _____ to use the extra energy. The food we normally eat is called our _____. Of course, we must eat the right *kind* of food as well. If we eat the right amount of the right kind of food, we will have a healthy _____. But what's the right *kind* of food? That's another question.

> **Key vocabulary**
> body cut diet energy
> exercise fat gram
> hungry pepper piece
> put on tomato

C The paragraph talks about the problems of too much food. Can you have too little food? What happens (if anything)?

D How do you make a cheese and tomato sandwich?

1 Read *You need*. Find the items in the picture and label them.
2 Do you think you would like this sandwich? Why (not)?
3 How much is 100 grams? Name something in this room with the same weight.
4 Read *The method*. Number the pictures in order.
5 Cover *The method*. Look at the pictures. Work in pairs. Tell each other how to make the sandwich.

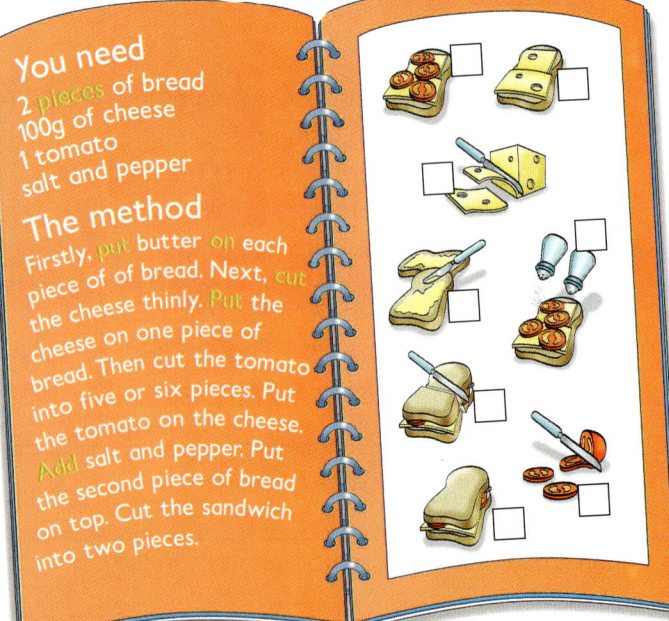

You need
2 pieces of bread
100g of cheese
1 tomato
salt and pepper

The method
Firstly, put butter on each piece of of bread. Next, cut the cheese thinly. Put the cheese on one piece of bread. Then cut the tomato into five or six pieces. Put the tomato on the cheese. Add salt and pepper. Put the second piece of bread on top. Cut the sandwich into two pieces.

E Discuss in groups

1 What's your favourite sandwich?
2 How do you make it?

Lesson 2: Vocabulary

A **Look at the pictures**
1 Label them with some of the *Key vocabulary* words.
2 Check with your dictionary.

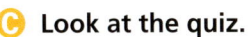

B **Look at these words.**
1 Put them in a logical order.
2 Check with your dictionary.

> lunch   breakfast   dinner

C **Look at the quiz.**
1 Ask and answer in pairs. Tick (✔) your partner's choice in each case.
2 Tell your partner his/her score.
3 Read *Understanding your score*. Do you agree?

eggs

Key vocabulary
biscuit bowl burger cake cereal chip chocolate cook crisp dinner fried lunch pasta potatoes salad soup steak sweet

Section A

1 How much butter do you have on bread?
a Lots
b A little
c None

2 How often do you eat biscuits or cakes in a week?
a 5 or more times
b 2–4 times
c Sometimes or never

3 How often do you eat sweets or chocolate in a week?
a 5 or more times
b 2–4 times
c Sometimes or never

4 How often do you eat chips or crisps in a week?
a 5 or more times
b 2–4 times
c Sometimes or never

5 How often do you eat burgers in a week?
a 5 or more times
b 2–4 times
c Sometimes or never

How to score

A = 5 points; B = 3 points; C = 1 point

Understanding your score You need a low score for Section A. A score below 10 is very good. If you get a score of 20 or more, you need to reduce the amount of sugar and fat in your diet. You need a high score for Section B. A score of 20 or over is very good. If you get a score of 10 or less, you need to increase the amount of bread, cereals, potatoes, fruit and vegetables in your diet. Overall, your score in A must be lower than your score in B.

Section B

1 How many slices of bread (or equivalent) do you eat most days?
a 5 or more
b 2–4
c 1 or fewer

2 How often do you eat rice or pasta in a week?
a 5 or more times
b 2–4 times
c Sometimes or never

3 How many potatoes (the size of an egg) do you usually have at a meal?
a 5 or more
b 2–4
c 1 or fewer

4 How many times a week do you eat cereal for breakfast?
a 5 or more times
b 2–4 times
c Sometimes or never

5 How many portions of fruit and vegetables do you eat every day?
a 5 or more
b 2–4
c 1 or fewer

chips

crisps

burger

potato

fruit

vegetables

Lesson 3: Listening

A **Look at the names of foods in the box.**

apples beef butter bread carrots cheese chicken eggs lamb milk oranges pasta peas rice

1 Put the foods into groups. Explain your choices.
2 Add some more foods to each group.

B 🔊 **3.16 Noura Hamed is studying Food Sciences at Greenhill College. She has a lecture today about food. Listen to the first part. When the lecturer stops, guess the next word. Did you guess correctly?**

C **Read this summary of the first part.**

1 Complete the notes.
2 🔊 **3.17** Listen to the first part again and check.

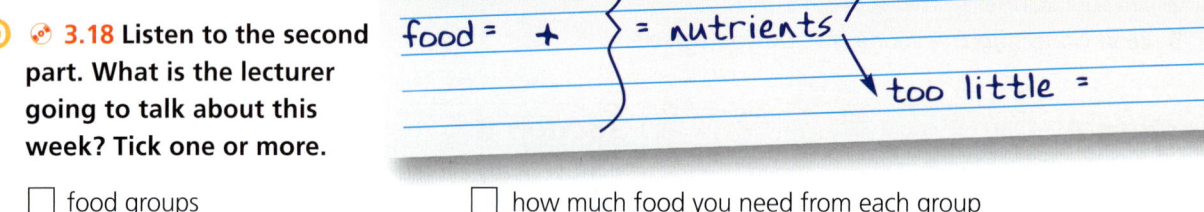

D 🔊 **3.18 Listen to the second part. What is the lecturer going to talk about this week? Tick one or more.**

☐ food groups
☐ foods that contain each nutrient
☐ how much food you need from each group
☐ different nutrients

E **Look at Table 1.**

1 Look at the name of the first nutrient. Do you know the names of the other four?
2 🔊 **3.19** Listen to the third part and complete the names of the nutrients.
3 Look at the foods. Do you know, or can you guess, which foods contain each nutrient? Many foods contain more than one. Tick any boxes that apply.
4 🔊 **3.20** Listen to the fourth part. Check and complete the table.

Table 1: *Nutrients in particular foods*

		NUTRIENTS				
		carbohydrates				
FOOD	bread	✓				
	cheese					
	eggs					
	fish					
	fruit					
	meat					
	milk					
	pasta					
	rice					
	vegetables					

F 🔊 **3.21 Listen to the fifth part. What does the lecturer want you to do before next week?**

G **How often do you eat each of the foods in Table 1? All the time? Occasionally? Never?**

Lesson 4: Listening

A **You can complete each phrase on the right from the lecture with a preposition or adverb.**
  1 Write a preposition or adverb in each space.
  2 🔊 **3.22** Listen and check your ideas.

a	talk	*about*
b	take energy	
c	the parts	
d	different types	
e	too much	
f	some examples	
g	find carbohydrates	
h	look	(on the Internet)
i	look	
j	make some notes	
k	do research	
l	note some things	

B **Can you remember any sentences from the lecture that contain the phrases in Exercise A?**
  Example: *There are several different types of nutrients.*

C **In this course, you have learnt to hear different sounds.**
  1 All these words are in the lecture. Find the odd one out from each group in standard British English. (Think about the [underlined] vowel sound.)
  2 🔊 **3.23** Listen and check your ideas.

a	t<u>a</u>lk	w<u>o</u>rk	c<u>ou</u>rse	c<u>a</u>ll
b	t<u>y</u>pe	r<u>i</u>ce	g<u>i</u>ve	f<u>i</u>nally
c	m<u>ai</u>n	cont<u>ai</u>n	h<u>a</u>ve	t<u>a</u>ke
d	s<u>o</u>	kn<u>o</u>w	d<u>oe</u>s	n<u>o</u>te
e	m<u>ea</u>t	ch<u>ee</u>se	br<u>ea</u>d	prot<u>ei</u>n
f	n<u>u</u>trient	fr<u>ui</u>t	m<u>u</u>ch	f<u>oo</u>d
g	<u>a</u>bout	am<u>ou</u>nt	h<u>ow</u>	gr<u>ou</u>p

D **In this course, you have learnt to understand spoken spellings.**
  1 🔊 **3.24** Listen to the spelling of more words from the lecture. Write the letters.
  2 Can you identify each word?

E **In this course, you have learnt to understand spoken definitions.**
  1 🔊 **3.25** Listen again to part of the lecture. Which words does the lecturer define?
  2 🔊 **3.26** Listen again. Make notes of the definition of each word.

F **In this course, you have learnt to recognize important words.**
  1 Read this part of the lecture. Underline the words you think are important.
  2 🔊 **3.27** Listen and check your ideas.

We call the energy and chemicals in food 'nutrients'. As you probably know, there are several different types of nutrient. The body needs different amounts of each nutrient. If you have too much of a particular type, you can get fat. If you have too little of a particular type, you can get ill.

Lesson 5: Speaking

A **What meals can you get in an Italian restaurant? What about an Iranian restaurant?**

B **3.28 Listen to a conversation between two friends. Choose the best answer in each case.**
   1 Gary likes *tea / coffee*.
   2 Gary went to an *Italian / Iranian* restaurant last night.
   3 He went to the *Park Mall / Garden Mall*.
   4 He had a *pizza / sandwich*.
   5 It had tomatoes and *cheese / chicken*.
   6 Gary and Yoshi are going to go there next *Tuesday / Thursday*.
   7 They are going to go in *Gary's / Yoshi's* car.
   8 They are going to meet at *7.15 / 7.30*.
   9 Yoshi has a lecture at *2.55 / 3.25*.

C **In this course, you have learnt to use the verb *like*.**
   1 Complete the sentences in Part 1.
   2 **3.29** Listen and check your answers.
   3 Practise Part 1 in pairs.
   4 Continue in pairs. Offer, accept and refuse things. Say what you like and don't like.

D **In this course, you have learnt to show that you understand or that you don't understand.**
   1 Complete the sentences in Part 2.
   2 **3.30** Listen and check your answers.
   3 Practise Part 2 in pairs.
   4 Continue in pairs. Talk about somewhere you went recently and what you did. Show that you understand/ don't understand.

E **In this course, you have learnt to say the letters of the English alphabet.**
   1 **3.31** Listen and write the name of Gary's meal.
   2 **3.32** Listen and write the names of more pizzas.
   3 Work in pairs. Choose five words from this course and spell them to your partner.

F **Gary invites Yoshi to the restaurant next week.**
   1 **3.33 Listen and complete his sentence and Yoshi's reply (Part 3).**
   2 Practise Part 3 in pairs.
   3 Continue in pairs. Invite your partner to something. Accept or refuse. Say what you like and don't like doing.

Part 1
Gary: _____ you _____ coffee, Yoshi?
Yoshi: No, thanks, Gary. But you have one.
Gary: No, thanks. I _____ coffee. I _____ tea, with three teaspoons of sugar.
Yoshi: So, you _____ tea either, then. You just _____ sugar.
Gary: Maybe.

Part 2
Yoshi: Where did you go last night?
Gary: I went to the new Italian restaurant.
Yoshi: Sorry? _____ Iranian restaurant?
Gary: No, Italian.
Yoshi: Italian? _____?
Gary: It's in the mall near the park ...
Yoshi: What did you have?
Gary: I had a pizza.
Yoshi: Pizza? _____?
Gary: It's like bread with tomatoes and cheese ... and other things.

Part 3
Gary: Would you like _____ with me next week?
Yoshi: I'd love to. I like _____ new kinds of food.

A	H	J	K			
B	C	D	E	G	P	T	V	Z*
F	L	M	N	S	X	Z**
Q	U	W				
I	Y					
O						
R						

* American English; ** British English

Lesson 6: Speaking

A In this course, you have learnt to make the main vowel sounds in English.
1 Say each group of words.
2 Which is the odd one out? Explain your answer.
3 Add one word with the same vowel sound in each group.

a live	winner	build	climb	_____
b read	dead	cheese	meeting	_____
c thank	Africa	Asia	jam	_____
d last	clerk	car	carry	_____
e behind	friend	dead	weather	_____
f work	birth	turn	where	_____
g wrong	woman	orange	watch	_____
h water	north	walk	come	_____
i name	player	captain	grey	_____
j group	move	do	look	_____
k speech	sign	guide	die	_____
l town	south	know	hour	_____
m snow	road	go	now	_____

B In this course, you have learnt to say some pairs of consonant sounds accurately.
1 Circle one of the words in each pair below.
2 Work in pairs. Say the words that you circled. Tick the words you hear.
3 Compare the circles and ticks. Try to work out why there are any differences.

a two	do		**h** shop	chop
b pray	bray		**i** wash	watch
c port	bought		**j** it's	it is
d pin	bin		**k** just	gust
e get	jet		**l** shoes	choose
f goose	juice		**m** wish	which
g angle	angel		**n** his story	history

C In this course, you have learnt to give the time in English.
Answer these questions.
1 What's the time now?
2 What time did this lesson start?
3 What time does it finish?
4 How long does it last?
5 When do you start lessons each day?
6 When do you finish?

D In this course, you have learnt to keep a conversation going.
Work in pairs.

Student A
Ask B a lot of *Yes/No* questions.
Examples:
Is this your pen?
Do you live at home?
Are you studying engineering?

Student B
Answer A's questions politely.
Examples:
Yes, I am.
No, I don't.
Then add extra information to each answer.

A Which is the odd one out? Why?

1	apples	potatoes	lemons	oranges
2	meat	juice	tea	coffee
3	chocolate	pasta	cake	sweets
4	ice cream	butter	cheese	rice
5	potatoes	eggs	crisps	chips
6	carrots	peas	cabbage	chicken

B You are going to read an article about healthy eating. Read the title. Which of these sentences do you expect to find in the text? Tick one or more. Explain your answers.

1 ☐ Don't drink anything while you are eating.
2 ☐ Eat something before you go shopping.
3 ☐ I had a good meal in a restaurant last week.
4 ☐ I love eating burger and chips.
5 ☐ I will try to eat in a more healthy way in future.
6 ☐ You must eat many different kinds of food each week.
7 ☐ You should eat fruit every day.
8 ☐ Your body slows down at night.

C Can you guess some of the advice? Cover the section headings. Make a list of *dos* (things you should do) and *don'ts* (things you should not do).

D Uncover the section headings.

1 Which section will contain each of your pieces of advice?
2 What advice will the other sections contain?
3 Do you find any of the section headings strange?

E You are going to read the text on page 147. Work in pairs.

Student A
1 Read the dos.
2 Give the advice to your partner.

Student B
1 Read the don'ts.
2 Give the advice to your partner.

F Work in the same pairs. Compare the advice in the two sections. Is any of the advice the same or similar in each section?

G Which advice do you think is …
1 good?   2 strange?   3 stupid?

The Dos and Don'ts of Healthy Eating

Eat breakfast

Eat snacks

Drink water

Think FAT!

Eat a variety of foods

Don't shop when you are hungry

Don't eat in front of the TV

Don't give up foods

Don't starve

Don't drink *and* eat

A In this course, you have learnt to deal with new words.

  1 Find and underline in the text the words in the yellow box.
  2 Is each word a noun, verb or adjective?
  3 Work out the meaning from context.

hungry	fatty	reduce
speeds up	saturated	starving
snacks	nutrients	stores
fuller	junk	chew

B In this course, you have learnt to predict content from headings. Look at each section heading below. Find the topic sentence for that section.

C In this course, you have learnt to understand the point of topic sentences. For each topic sentence in the table below, find the next sentence in the paragraph.

D In this course, you have learnt about pronoun and adverb reference. What does each of these words refer to in the text on page 147?

  1 It (line 5) _____
  2 them (line 20) _____
  3 there (line 33) _____
  4 it (line 36) _____
  5 it (line 41) _____
  6 It (line 52) _____

Section headings	Topic sentences	Next sentences
Eat breakfast	Don't drink anything while you are eating.	Eat healthy, low-fat snacks between meals.
Eat snacks	Eat something before you go shopping.	*Frequency*
Drink water	Even if you are not very hungry, eat something.	Have a piece of bread or fruit.
Think FAT!	Firstly, you will enjoy your meal better.	If you don't, you will buy a chocolate bar or some junk food while you are there.
Eat a variety of foods	If you don't eat anything for several hours, you will eat much more at the next meal.	It is strange but true – well, almost!
Don't shop when you are hungry	If you like a particular food a lot, carry on eating it.	It will make you chew for longer.
Don't eat in front of the TV	Starving makes you fat.	Reduce the portions or the number of times you eat the food each week.
Don't give up foods	When you want to eat fatty foods, think about three things:	Secondly, you will take longer to eat it, and that is good for your body.
Don't starve	Drink at least two glasses of water after your meal.	That means you must eat many different kinds of food each week.
Don't drink and eat	Your body needs more than 40 different nutrients for good health.	You will feel fuller and not go back for seconds.

Lesson 9: Writing

A **What do you normally eat for:**
  1 breakfast? **2** lunch? **3** dinner?

B **Noura Hamed is studying Food Sciences at Greenhill College. She is researching eating habits. She is writing to people in different countries. Write her research questions again, correcting the mistakes.**
  1 What your name?
  2 Where are you come from?
  3 What you do?
  4 What are you having for breakfast?
  5 Do you eats lunch?
  6 When you have dinner?

C **Noura gets replies from around the world. She makes notes in a table. Copy and complete her table, using words from the box. You can use some words more than once.**

Breakfast	Country	Dinner	Food	Job
Lunch	Name	Time		

Name	
Breakfast	Time
	Food

My name is Bani. I come from northern India. I work in a pickle factory. I get up at about 8.00 and have breakfast. I always have tea and a piece of bread. I do some cleaning and then I go to work. At the factory, I  mix the spices into the fruit or vegetable mixture – lemons, mangos or green chillis. I get lunch at work. We have a break at half past twelve. Lunch is usually bread, vegetables, rice and curry, with a glass of water. I finish work at 5.00. I do some more cleaning and other housework. We have dinner at nine p.m. It is usually the same as lunch.

D **Read these two letters to Noura. Make notes in your research table.**

E **Find these times in the two letters. What happens at each time? Write a full sentence in each case.**

4.00 a.m.	4.30 a.m.	5.30 a.m.	8.00 a.m.
12.30 p.m.	1.30 p.m.	5.00 p.m.	
7.00 p.m.	9.00 p.m.		

Example: *Lastri gets up at 4.00 a.m.*

F **Find these words in the letters. Write one sentence with each word.**

sometimes usually always

Example: *Lastri usually has rice, chilli sauce and bread for breakfast.*

My name is Lastri. I am from Indonesia. I am a tea picker. I get up at four a.m. I cook some rice. At about 4.30, I say the dawn prayer. Then I walk to the tea plantation. It's about one kilometre from my house. I have breakfast with the other tea pickers at about 5.30. We usually have rice, chilli sauce and bread. I always finish work at 1.30 and walk back home. I have lunch – a bowl of soup, rice and fried fish every day. Then I have a sleep. Between four and five p.m., I start to prepare dinner for the family. We eat at about seven p.m. We usually have rice and vegetable soup. We sometimes have salad.

Lesson 10: Writing

Ⓐ Complete these phrases from the letters in Lesson 9.

1 a piece of _____
2 a cup of _____
3 a bowl of _____
4 a glass of _____

Ⓑ In this course, you have learnt how to join sentences with *and, but, or*. Here is another letter to Noura. Complete the letter with a suitable word in each space.

Ⓒ Write full sentences to answer these questions. What does Pierre have for ...

1 breakfast?
2 lunch?
3 dinner?

Ⓓ In this course, you have learnt how to join sentences with *because* and *so*. Here is another letter to Noura. Complete the letter with *because* or *so* and a suitable sentence from the list below.

1 I have dinner very late.
2 I have pasta or rice and chilli from the restaurant kitchen.
3 I work until midnight every day except Sunday.
4 I'm not hungry at lunchtime.
5 The restaurant is closed.

My name is Sheila. I'm from Australia. I'm a waitress in a restaurant. I wake up late _____.
I don't work on Sundays _____. I have toast and coffee for breakfast. I don't have lunch _____. I just have a snack in the afternoon. I usually have a cup of coffee and a biscuit or a piece of cake. I start work at 5.30 p.m. I am too busy to eat in the evenings _____. It's too late to start cooking _____.

My name is Pierre. I'm from Belgium. I have a chocolate shop. I make chocolates _____ sell them in the shop. I get up at 7.30. I go out _____ buy my breakfast. I usually have a sandwich or a croissant. I buy a coffee from another shop _____ I make some at home. Then I go _____ open my shop. I don't have lunch _____ I eat some of the chocolates with a cup of tea. I close the shop at 5.30 _____ go home. I sometimes have a big steak for dinner with chips _____ I usually have pasta _____ a vegetable stew with potatoes.

Ⓔ Write a preposition or adverb in each space. Then check with the letters in Lessons 9 and 10.

1 I get up _____ 4 a.m.
2 I walk _____ the tea plantation.
3 It's about one kilometre _____ my house.
4 I have breakfast _____ the other tea pickers.
5 I start to prepare dinner _____ the family.
6 I work _____ a pickle factory.
7 I sell chocolates _____ my shop.
8 I go _____ and buy my breakfast.
9 I make some coffee _____ home.
10 I eat some _____ the chocolates _____ a cup of tea.
11 I sometimes have a big steak _____ dinner.
12 I don't work _____ Sundays.
13 I'm not hungry _____ lunchtime.
14 I just have a snack _____ the afternoon.
15 I am too busy to eat _____ the evenings.

Lesson 11: Grammar

Ⓐ Look at Table 1.
1 Which sentences are good advice, and which are bad?
2 How can you quickly change the bad advice into good advice? (Think about negative forms.)
3 Add the negative forms in the correct position – 1, 2 or 3.

Table 1: *Imperative (positive and negative)*

1	Verb	2	Noun/pronoun/noun phrase	3
	Eat		fatty food.	
	Drink		lots of water.	
	Choose		low-fat snacks.	
	Buy		junk food.	
	Starve		yourself	

Ⓑ Look at Table 2.
1 The doctor is talking to somebody who weighs 110 kilos. Replace the underlined words with the following modal verbs.
   • You have to ... (for something necessary)
   • You may ... (for something possible)
   • You should ... (for advising)
   • You will ... (for predicting the future)

Table 2: *Modal verbs* – have to, may, should, will

It's really very important to	lose at least 20 kilos.	You _____ ...
It's clear that you're going to	become ill if you don't.	_____ ...
'It's possible that you're going to	get heart problems.	_____ ...
I strongly suggest that you	start taking gentle exercise.	_____ ...

Ⓒ Look at Table 3.
1 Look at the underlined words. Do they mean using the present simple or continuous?
2 Complete the sentences with the words in brackets. Put the verbs in the right tenses/forms.
3 Correct these other time words and phrases.
   allways   every days   from time and time   in the moment (= now)   *sometime* (= not often)

Table 3: *Present simple and present continuous*

_____	at 6.30 every morning. (they/get up)
_____	breakfast before work each day. (she/eat)
_____	lunch right now, so he can't see you yet. (he/have)
Today, _____	a report on healthy eating. (I/write)
_____ sometimes _____	training during the week? (you ... go)

Lesson 12: Grammar

A **Look at Table 4.**

1 Complete the questions with the following.

how many   how much   how often

2 Pasta (sentence 1) and bread (sentence 2) are both uncountable. Why are the question words different?

3 Match the following.

a bowl of   Arab tea
a cup of   English tea
a glass of   cake
a piece of   cereal

Table 4: How many, How much, How often

_____	pasta do you eat in a week?
_____	pieces of bread do you have every day?
_____	do you go to the gym?

B **Look at Tables 5a and 5b.**

1 Look at the headings. Which table is about things that always happen? What is the other about?

2 Think about the verbs. What tense do you use in the *If/When* clauses in 5a and 5b? What about the other clause in 5a sentences? And how about the other clause in 5b sentences?

3 Complete the tables with the verbs in brackets.

Table 5a: *General action and general effect*

If/when clause	Other clause
If/When people _____ too much,	they usually _____ fat. (eat/get)
If/When people _____ good food,	they _____ a healthy life (not buy/not have)

Table 5b: *Particular action and particular future effect*

If clause	Other clause
If you _____ to the market,	you _____ excellent vegetables there. (go/find)
If you _____ better food,	you _____ healthier. (buy/soon feel)
If you _____ eating better	you _____ really healthy. (not start/never be)

Lesson 1: Applying listening skills

Ⓐ **Match each verb with words from the right column to make phrases about special events.**

1 give		**a** a party
2 make		**b** presents
3 wear		**c** special events
4 go to		**d** special food
5 eat		**e** speeches
6 spend		**f** time with the family
7 have		**g** traditional clothes
8 listen to		**h** special music

Ⓑ **Adriana Hernandez is in Juri's group at Greenhill. She is going to talk about a special event in Mexico. Look at the questions in the table below. Think of some sentences that you might hear in Adriana's talk.**

Example: a Where is the festival? *I'm going to talk to you today about a festival in Mexico.*

Ⓒ **Listen to Adriana's talk.**

1 🔆 **3.34** Listen to the first part. Make notes to answer the first seven questions.

2 🔆 **3.35** Listen to the second part. Complete the information about the events in order.

a Where is the festival?		*Mexico*
b What is it called?		
c What does the name mean?		
d Who is it for?		
e When is it?		
f Why is the occasion important?		
g Do the people wear special clothes?		
h What happens on the day?	First,	
	Then,	
	After that,	
	Finally,	

Ⓓ **Read the talk on page 178. Check your answers to Exercise C.**

Ⓔ **When do people come of age in your country? What happens on that day? Is there a special party?**

Lesson 2: Applying speaking skills

A Work in pairs. Say the words below. Make sure your partner can hear the difference.

1 she's	cheese
2 ship	chip
3 shoes	choose
4 shop	chop
5 shore	chore
6 wash	watch
7 wish	which
8 dish	ditch

shoes chip chop dish

B Ask the teacher about the meaning of any new words in Exercise A.
Echo any words that you don't understand (Skills Check 2 on page 75).

C Practise saying these sentences in pairs.

1 Which cheese did she choose?   **3** Is that a chip shop?

2 You wash the dishes, I'll watch TV.   **4** Was the ship near the shore?

D Work in pairs. You have both done some research into transport and found some interesting information.

1 Read your own information. Cover your partner's information.

2 Work in groups of people with the same information. Ask for help with any new words.

3 Work in pairs again. Tell your partner your information.

4 Listen to your partner's information. Ask about anything you didn't understand or didn't believe. Make notes.

Invention	The helicopter
Date	1939
Inventor	Igor Sikorsky
Nationality	Russian, but worked in America for a large part of his life
Born	1889
Facts	• began work on helicopters in 1910
	• started his own aircraft company in 1923
	• from 1925 to 1939, built flying boats = planes that could land on water
Died	1972

Invention	The motorcar
Date	1885
Name	Karl Benz
Nationality	German
Born	1844
Facts	• called his first car a 'motor carriage'
	• produced and sold the cars himself
	• continued to work in his own company until 1903, when he retired
Died	1929

Lesson 3: Applying reading skills

'Macbeth, King of Scotland'

'... when the trees come to Dunsinane'

A You are going to read about another Shakespeare play. Prepare to read the text.

B Read the text. It is on page 148.

    1 Number the illustrations in order.

    2 Find these items in the illustrations.

a castle		**d** tree	
b king		**e** witch	
c soldier		**f** wood	

C Guess the meanings of these words.

1 history		**5** guilt/guilty	
2 Lord		**6** kill	
3 Lady		**7** murder	
4 tale		**8** die	

D The writer refers to the items below in different ways. Find more ways in the text for each item.

1 Macbeth		**5** Dunsinane	
2 Lady Macbeth		**6** a wood	
3 Duncan		**7** an army	
4 three witches		**8** the murder	

E Find and underline all the pronouns. What does each pronoun refer to?

F Work in pairs. What is the story of *Macbeth*? Tell the story in your own words.

Macbeth
Tragedy or History?

Shakespeare's play *Macbeth* is a tragedy in the theatre, but it is almost a history. There was a real man called Macbeth. He lived in Scotland in around 1050. Shakespeare wrote the play in about 1605. It is a tale of murder and guilt.

[A] Lord and Lady Macbeth lived in a castle.

[B] However, one day he met three witches.

[C] Duncan came to their castle and Macbeth killed him.

[D] Macbeth met the three women again.

[E] Macbeth went home.

Lesson 4: Applying writing skills

Ⓐ Look at the illustration.

1 Do you know this game? How do you think you might play it? Discuss in pairs.

2 Read this paragraph about the game. Complete each word with the correct letter or letters. All the missing letters make the schwa sound.

The name ___f this game is *Al Ghomaid*. It comes fr___m the United Arab Emirates. It is us___lly a game f___r boys. First, the childr___n choose one boy. Then they put a cloth ___round his eyes so he cannot see. He has t___ try to catch anoth___ child. Meanwhile, the oth___ boys make noises ___nd try to c___nfuse him. When he catches ___nother child, that child has to wear the cloth.

Ⓑ Make notes about a children's game in your country.

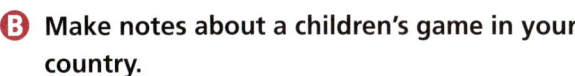

Name	
Country	
Players	
Equipment	
Rules	

Ⓒ Write a paragraph about the game. Leave a space between each line of writing. Make sure you ...

1 give the information in a logical order.

2 use pronouns/other nouns.

3 join short sentences with *and*.

4 distinguish between people and things with *one/other/another/each/all*.

Ⓓ Exchange drafts with your partner.

1 Are there any mistakes of fact?

2 Are there any spelling mistakes?

3 Do you understand what each pronoun and noun refers to?

4 Do you understand who does what?

5 Correct any mistakes. Write on the line above the mistake.

Ⓔ Look at the corrections on your first draft. Are they correct? Write the second draft, correcting the mistakes if necessary. Leave a space between each line of writing.

Ⓕ Show your second draft to your teacher/instructor.

Reading Resources

Crosswords

Tapescript

Word Lists

Advice for New Students

Introduction

First, consider these questions:

1 Are you living away from home for the first time?

If *yes*, read paragraph 1 opposite. ✓

2 Are you sharing a bedroom for the first time?

If *yes*, read paragraph 2 opposite. ✓

3 Is your college work harder than your school work?

If *yes*, read paragraph 3 opposite. ✓

4 Have you made a lot of new friends at college?

If *no*, read paragraph 4 opposite. ✗

5 Do you go to bed early?

If *no*, read paragraph 5 opposite. ✗

6 Do you eat sensibly?

If *no*, read paragraph 5 opposite. ✗

7 Do you understand everything in the classes?

If *no*, read paragraph 6 opposite. ✗

Advice

1 **College life means … living away from home**
   You are responsible for managing your time now. Buy a calendar and mark all the important dates and times on it – the start of the semester, the times of classes, the dates for assignments, the dates of tests.

2 **College life means … sharing a room**
   Perhaps you have your own bedroom at home, but at college you must share a room. You do not have to make friends with your roommate, but you must respect him or her. Always be polite. Always ask before you borrow things from your roommate.

3 **College life means … working harder**
   Don't worry if you find college work hard at first. It is not a problem with you or your intelligence. All first-year students feel the same.

4 **College life means … making new friends**
   You will make new friends at college, but it takes time. Don't worry if you don't have any friends at first. It is not a problem with you or your personality. All first-year students feel the same.

5 **College life means … taking care of yourself**
   You must take care of your health. Get enough sleep. Eat sensibly. Work hard, but relax, too, with sports and leisure activities.

6 **College life means … having a second chance**
   If you don't understand something the first time, you can:
   - check it out in the library.
   - look it up on the Internet.
   - ask the people in your group.
   - ask your instructor.
   - ask a student advisor.

College Life Is Not Just College Work

You are an adult now. You make your own weekly schedule. But in that schedule, you must make time for four areas of your life.

The four areas are:

- **personal care** – looking after yourself
- **college work** – doing assignments, studying, revising
- **family responsibilities** – keeping in touch, helping family members
- **social life** – enjoying yourself!

Each area of your life is important. Are you neglecting any of the parts? Answer the questions in our check list to find out.

Check list of activities in your weekly schedule

Important area	Do you ...	
personal care	have regular meals?	
	take exercise regularly?	
	get enough sleep?	
college work	do assignments on time?	
	attend all classes?	
	revise for tests?	
social life	meet friends regularly?	
	play sports?	
	relax at the weekend?	
family responsibilities	keep in touch regularly?	
	spend time with the family?	
	deal with family problems?	

personal care

college work

Your weekly schedule

family responsibilities

social life

Get Set

WORK EXPERIENCE COMPANY

We are looking for students for work experience jobs this summer.

The Jobs

There are two types of work experience jobs at Get Set.

5 Firstly, there are holiday jobs in the tourist industry. For example, you can work in a hotel or a restaurant. The jobs are hard but very interesting.

10 Secondly, there are career-entry jobs in many different fields. For example, you can work in teaching, the law or engineering. You get experience in these jobs before you choose a career.

15

Length of Employment

Most holiday jobs last through the summer. They usually start in late June and end in early August. They are full-time.

20 Career-entry jobs are shorter. They usually last for three or four weeks. They are part-time. You work for two or three hours a day.

Requirements

You must have a secondary certificate. You must be in full-time education. You must be 18 for a holiday job. You must be 19 for a career-entry job.

25

Benefits

You earn between $10 and $15 per hour. You also get free accommodation.

30

Work Schedule

You work a five-day week in both holiday jobs and career-entry jobs. You usually work from 9 a.m. to 5 p.m. You can do overtime at the weekends and in the evenings in a holiday job. You receive extra money for this work. You cannot do overtime in a career-entry job.

35

40

Get Set
WORK EXPERIENCE COMPANY

Why Is It So Hot?

Table 2:
Average temperature in selected capital cities

Capital cities	Average temperature (in °C)	Line of latitude °N	Distance from the Equator (in km)
Muscat	28.6	23	2,530
Abu Dhabi	27.1	24	2,640
Doha	26.6	25	2,750
Manama	26.1	26	2,860
Kuwait	25.6	29	3,190
Baghdad	22.7	33	3,630
Damascus	17.0	33	3,630

Source: Average temperature information from worldweather.com

WHY ARE SOME PLACES HOTTER than other places? Is there one single factor that affects the average temperature at a location? The simple answer is no.

There are many factors that affect the average temperature. These factors include:
- Is the city surrounded by mountains?
- Is the city on the coast?
- How high is the city above sea-level?

However, there is one main factor that strongly influences the average temperature. That factor is the distance of the city from the Equator. Take Kampala, the capital of Uganda, for instance. It is almost on the Equator, and the average temperature is extremely high, at 29 degrees centigrade.

As you travel north or south from the Equator, the average temperature falls. In Muscat, for example, which is 2,500 kilometres north of the Equator, the average temperature is 28.6. In Damascus, the capital of Syria, which is another 1,100 kilometres north, the average is down to 17.0. So places close to the Equator are generally hotter than places close to the poles. But that still leaves one question.

Why is it so hot at the Equator? It is because the sun is much higher in the sky during the day at the Equator. At the poles, the sun is close to the horizon, so less heat reaches the ground.

5

10

15

20

25

Saudi Arabia – A Brief Introduction

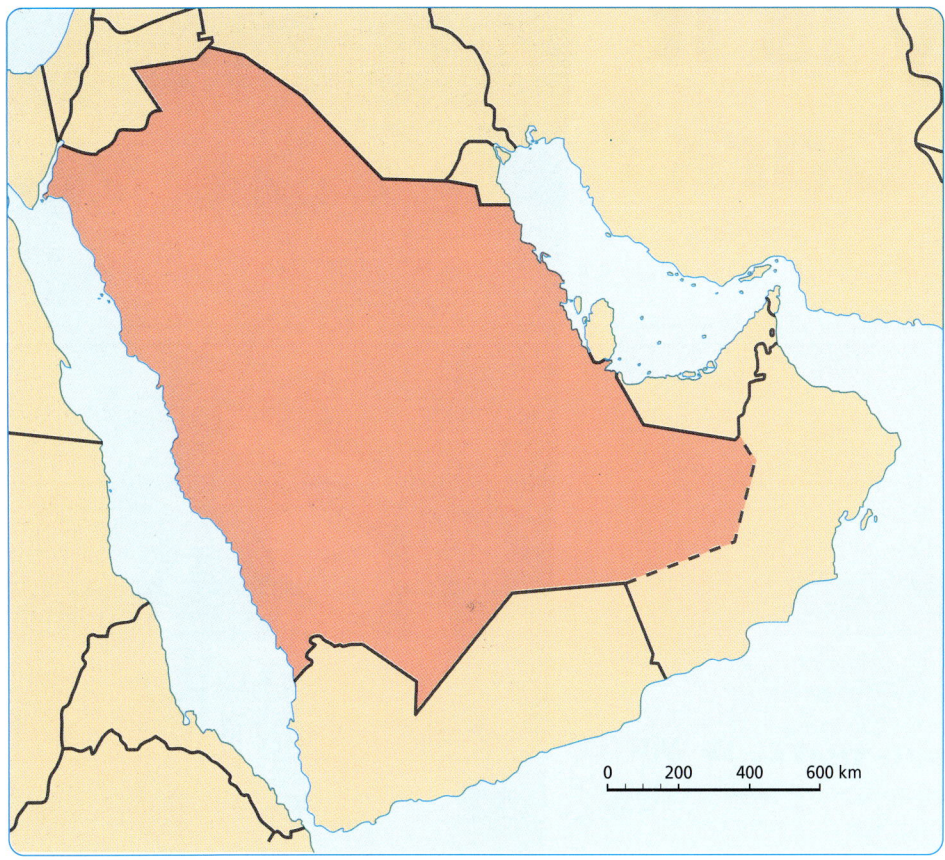

Location	Saudi Arabia is a large country situated in the region called the Middle East. It occupies the majority of the Arabian peninsula. It is located between latitudes 16° and 32° North and longitudes 35° and 55° East.
Capital and other main cities	The capital is Riyadh. The city is located in the centre of the country. There is another large city, Jeddah, on the Red Sea. It is southwest of Riyadh. 5 Just over 70 kilometres inland from Jeddah is the holy city of Makkah.
Area and borders	The country covers an area of nearly 2 million square kilometres. In the west, the country has a long coastline on the Red Sea. To the south, it is bordered by Yemen and Oman. The countries of the United Arab Emirates and Qatar are to the east. There is also a long coastline on the Gulf. To the north, the 10 country is bordered by Jordan, Iraq and Kuwait.
Landscape	There are mountains along the coast in the west of the country. The highest point of these mountains is Jebel Sawda, in the southwest corner of the country. It reaches a height of 3,133 metres. There are two large sand deserts. In the north there is the An Nafud and in the south the enormous Rub al 15 Khali desert. The land slopes down to the Gulf in the east. On the eastern coast, there are swamps and salt marshes. There are no permanent rivers in the country. Fresh water comes from oases, wells and wadis.

Why Is It Still Dark?

Table 3:
Sunrise on July 1ˢᵗ in selected capital cities

Capital cities	Sunrise on July 1ˢᵗ	Line of longitude °E	Distance from Greenwich longitude (in km)
Muscat	5.22	59	6,490
Abu Dhabi	5.40	54	5,940
Doha	5.46	52	5,610
Manama	5.48	51	5,720
Kuwait City	5.53	48	5,280
Baghdad	5.55	45	4,950
Damascus	6.31	36	3,960

Source: Sunrise times from worldtime.com

PEOPLE WHO TRAVEL IN WINTER from the Gulf to London are often surprised that the sun does not rise in London until 7.30 or 8.00. Why does the sun rise at different times in different places?

There are two factors that affect the time of sunrise. The first factor is related to the distance of the place from the Greenwich meridian. A meridian is a line of longitude. The Greenwich meridian, which runs through London, is the 0° line of longitude. The second factor is related to the distance of the place from the Equator.

Let's consider the first factor. The sun rises in the east. This means that, as we travel to the west, we leave the sun behind, so sunrise is later. For example, in Muscat on July 1ˢᵗ, sunrise is at 5.22, whereas in Damascus, sunrise on the same day of the year is at 6.31. This is because Damascus is around 2,500 kilometres closer to Greenwich than Muscat.

What about the second factor? The Earth is tilted slightly towards the sun. So if you travel north from the Equator, you are actually moving closer to the sun. Take Tehran, for example. The capital of Iran is on almost the same line of longitude as Abu Dhabi, but it is 1,400 kilometres north. Sunrise on July 1ˢᵗ is 5.25 – a quarter of an hour earlier than in Abu Dhabi.

GREAT TRADITIONAL EVENTS
≈ AROUND THE WORLD ≈

1: The Palio in Siena

Siena is a city of around 56,000 people. It is situated in central Italy, 65 kilometres south of Florence and 271 kilometres northwest of Rome. It is built on a high hilltop.

Siena was once an important centre for banking and for art. The Black Death of 1348, however, killed thousands of people. In some ways, the city never recovered.

Siena is famous today for a horse race. It is as old as Siena: in other words, nearly 3,000 years old. It takes place in July and August each year. The race is called the Palio. It is famous throughout the world. Thousands of visitors come to the city every year just to see it.

For three days before the event, flags fly from houses and shops. The flags belong to the 17 areas of the city. Young men from ten of the areas take part in each race.

On the day of the event, the young men and women of the city dress up in colourful clothes from the Middle Ages. First, in the morning they walk around the streets, looking like actors from a Shakespeare play. Then, in the late afternoon, there is a parade in the Piazza del Campo. This is the main square in the centre of the city. After that, there is an exhibition of flag throwing, with lots of drumming.

Finally, at exactly 6.30 p.m., the race begins. It only lasts 90 seconds. In that time, the horses and jockeys race three times around the piazza. After the race, the men and women from the winning area carry their flags through the city. Then there are special dinners in each area. The most special, of course, is in the restaurants of the winning area.

A Brief History of Space Travel

PART 1

Fireworks, Cannons and Rockets

Cannon of the Middle Ages

Fireworks

In about 800 BCE, a Chinese person mixed sulphur (S) and potassium nitrate (KNO_3), and carbon (C). He set fire to the mixture. It exploded. The mixture was gunpowder.

The Chinese mainly used the new invention in fireworks, but they also made rockets. They sometimes fired the rockets at their enemies. They didn't know it, but their invention led, over 1,000 years later, to space travel.

Between the 10th and 13th centuries, Arab traders in China learnt about gunpowder. They took it to Europe. People there used it for fireworks.

The Europeans also put gunpowder in new guns called cannons. Cannons could blow huge holes in castle walls. The arrival of gunpowder, therefore, led to the end of castles because there was no safety inside a castle anymore. But what has all this got to do with space travel?

Werner von Braun, a German scientist, studied the rockets of the ancient Chinese and the cannons of medieval Europe. In December 1934, von Braun invented a rocket that travelled a long way. Its fuel was not gunpowder but liquid oxygen. The Germans attacked London with the rocket at the end of the Second World War. But what about space travel?

On September 8th, 1944, the first rocket hit London. Von Braun turned to one of his colleagues and said, 'The rocket worked perfectly but it landed on the wrong planet.'

Castle

Love Story Lasts 400 Years

R omeo *and Juliet* is one of the most famous tragedies in the world. William Shakespeare wrote it between 1590 and 1595. There
5 have been thousands of performances in the 400 years since then. The story is simple and very sad.

Romeo Montague fell in love with Juliet Capulet. This was a big problem because the
10 Montagues and Capulets hated each other. The two young people got married in secret.

Then something terrible happened. Romeo tried to stop a sword fight and killed a young Capulet by accident. He left the city.

Juliet's father wanted her to marry a man 15
called Paris. He didn't know about her
marriage to Romeo. Of course, Juliet couldn't
marry him.

Juliet's friend had an idea. 'I will give you
something to drink,' he told her. 'You will 20
sleep, but people will think you're dead. Then
I will wake you and take you to your husband.'

However, the plan went wrong. Romeo heard
that his wife was dead. He came back to the
city and found her 'body'. He took poison and 25
died. Juliet woke up and found Romeo dead.
She killed herself, too.

Something good came out of the tragedy. The
two families agreed to stop fighting.

Can You Play Four Army Groups?

HISTORY

People first played this game in India over 2,000 years ago. They used real soldiers then, and horses
5   pulling chariots. It was called Chaturanga in the ancient Indian language of Sanskrit. It means 'four army groups'. This Sanskrit word is the origin of the modern name in Arabic.

From India, it moved to Persia in the 6th
10   century. There, Arab traders learnt the pastime. They took it back to their own countries in the 7th century. Then it spread to China and from there to Korea and Japan. Arabs carried it to Spain. People played it there by the 12th century. From Spain, it
15   spread to the rest of Europe. There are now more than 40 million players in Russia alone.

THE PLAYING PIECES

The names of the pieces show the history of the game. The name of the main piece in many
20   languages, including Arabic, comes from the Persian word shah. The name of another piece comes from the word roka, which is 'ship' in Sanskrit. Eight of the men are called pawns. This word comes from a Spanish word for 'farm worker'.

HOW TO PLAY
25

The game is for two players. Play starts with all the pieces in two lines on opposite sides of the board. One player moves, then the other player. A player takes an opponent's piece when he lands on the
30   same square. A player gets a piece back when one of his pawns reaches the opposite side of the board. The most important piece is the king.

HOW TO WIN

The objective of the game is simple. One player
35   must trap the opponent's king so he cannot move. When a player gets close to that position, he says 'Check'. The word is a form of the Persian word shah, which means 'king'. If the opponent's king cannot move, then the player says 'Checkmate'.
40   This word comes from a sentence in Persian, shah mat. This means 'The king is dead.'

The Dos and Don'ts of Healthy Eating

Eat breakfast

Even if you are not very hungry, eat something. Have a piece of bread or fruit. Your body slows down at night. It speeds up again when you eat something. If you wait until lunchtime to eat, that is four or five more hours of slow body rate.

Eat snacks

If you don't eat anything for several hours, you will eat much more at the next meal. Eat healthy, low-fat snacks between meals.

Drink water

Drink at least two glasses of water after your meal. You will feel fuller and not go back for seconds.

Think FAT!

When you want to eat fatty foods, think about three things:

Frequency	Don't eat them so often.
Amount	Don't eat so much.
Type	Don't eat saturated fats – check food labels.

Eat a variety of foods

Your body needs more than 40 different nutrients for good health. That means you must eat many different kinds of food each week. Every day you should eat bread and fruits, vegetables, dairy products, meat or fish.

Don't shop when you are hungry

Eat something before you go shopping. If you don't, you will buy a chocolate bar or some junk food while you are there.

Don't eat in front of the TV

Firstly, you will enjoy your meal better. Secondly, you will take longer to eat it, and that is good for your body. Thirdly, you will not eat as much.

Don't give up foods

If you like a particular food a lot, carry on eating it. Reduce the portions or the number of times you eat the food each week.

Don't starve

Starving makes you fat. It is strange but true – well, almost! If you don't eat for long periods of time, you may put on weight. On the one hand, while you are starving, your body slows down and stores fat. On the other hand, when you eat again, you will eat more than normal.

Don't drink *and* eat

Don't drink anything while you are eating. It will make you chew for longer. You will enjoy the food more then.

Macbeth Tragedy or History?

Shakespeare's play *Macbeth* is a tragedy in the theatre, but it is almost a history. There was a real man called Macbeth. He lived in Scotland in around 1050. Shakespeare wrote the play in about 1605. It is a tale of murder and guilt.

Lord and Lady Macbeth lived in a castle called Dunsinane, near a wood. At that time, Duncan was King of Scotland. Macbeth was an important man, but he could never become king.

However, one day he met three witches. They said to him, 'You will be king one day.' He told his wife about the old women. She told her husband to kill the king.

Duncan came to their castle and Macbeth killed him, but he felt guilty after the murder. Duncan's sons heard about the murder and they sent an army to kill Macbeth.

Macbeth met the three women again. 'You will only die when the wood comes to Dunsinane,' they told him. He was happy. 'I cannot die,' he thought, 'because trees cannot move.'

Macbeth went home. He looked at the wood. He saw the trees move but they weren't trees! They were soldiers. The 'trees' came to Dunsinane and the soldiers killed him.

Student A

Example:

One across and thirteen across – a person who teaches languages.

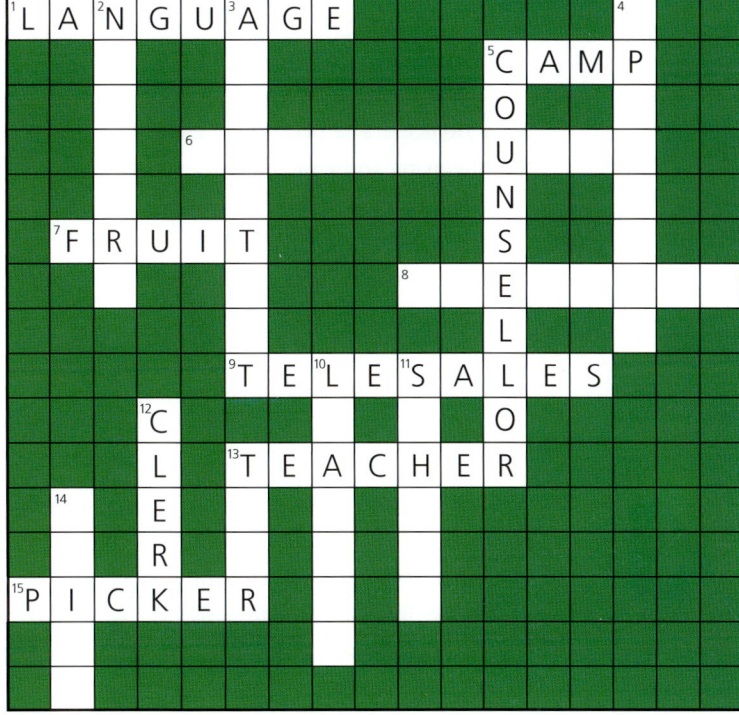

Student B

Example:

Two down, eleven down and three down – a person who helps in a school for young children.

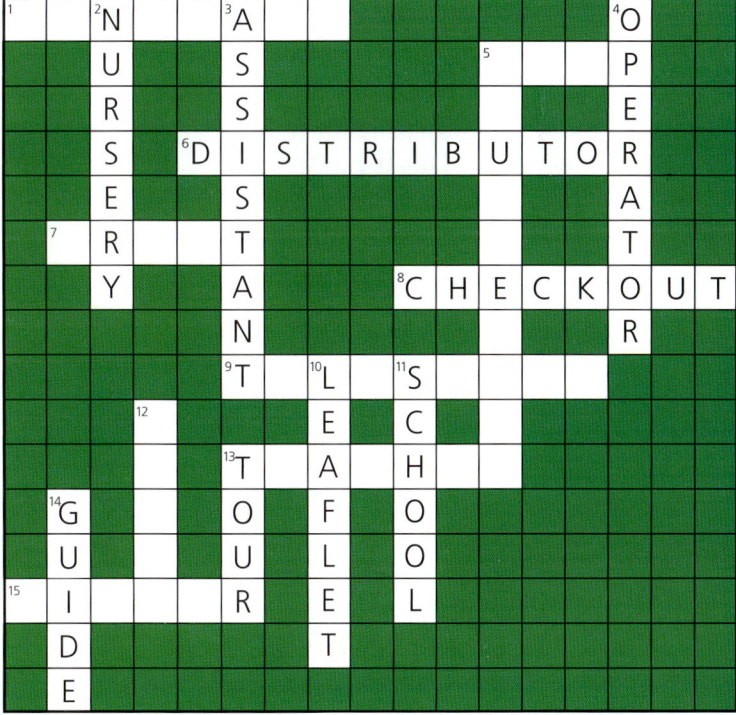

Presenter: Unit 1: Education

Lesson 1

B Listen to the following sentences. Then complete each one using some of the Key Vocabulary.

Voice: 1 The academic year in my country starts in October. All the students go back to high school then.

2 When does the second semester start? Is it in February?

3 Which room is the lecture in? The one about learning English?

4 Mr Jones is in charge of the library. He is responsible for all the books and CD-ROMs.

5 Who is the head of Year 1? Is it Mrs Wright? Or is she in charge of Year 2?

Presenter: Lesson 3

C It is the start of the college year at Greenhill College. The principal is welcoming the new students. Listen and add the missing information.

Peter Bean: OK. Let's begin. Welcome to Greenhill College. I am very pleased to see you all here. My name is Peter Bean. I'm the principal – that means I am in charge of the whole place. You come and see me if you have any problems with the fees – that means the money you must pay. My office is on the first floor, Room 15, by the stairs. The people behind me are some of my staff. This is Mrs Polly Penn. She's the head of Year 1. She is responsible for the schedule. After this meeting, Mrs Penn will give you the schedule for the first term. The schedule tells you the times of all your lectures. Mrs Penn will also give you the name of your instructor. We call the teachers at Greenhill instructors. She will also tell you the name of your personal advisor – that's a person who helps you if you have problems. Finally, this is the registrar, Mr Bill Beale. He's in charge of attendance. If you can't come to college one day, tell Mr Beale. OK, that's it from me. Now I'll hand over to Mrs Penn … Oh, I nearly forgot. Mr Beale's room is on the first floor, next to my room – Room 16.

Presenter: E The principal explains the meaning of the words in Exercise D. Listen to his speech again and check your answers. [REPEAT OF EXERCISE C]

Presenter: Lesson 4

A Listen and tick the words you hear. If you get three ticks in a line, say Bingo! [REPEAT OF LESSON 3 EXERCISE C]

Presenter: B 2 Listen and check your answers.

Voice:	
pay	– letter p
Bill	– letter b
Penn	– letter p
personal	– letter p
Bean	– letter b
Peter	– letter p
people	– letter p
place	– letter p
pleased	– letter p
Beale	– letter b
Polly	– letter p
principal	– letter p
problems	– letter p
behind	– letter b

Presenter: B 3 Listen to these words connected with education. Is the missing letter p or b?

Voice:
a book
b paper
c begin
d spell
e pass
f period
g subject
h explain

Presenter: C 2 Look at these pairs of words. Listen. Which do you hear in each case? Don't worry about the meanings.

Voice:
a hill
b steal
c will
d meal
e pill
f kill
g feel
h feet
i Bill
j beat

Presenter: D Listen to the first part of the principal's speech again. It's much slower this time. Put your left hand up every time you hear /p/. Put your right hand up every time you hear /b/.

Peter Bean: OK. Let's begin. Welcome to Greenhill College. I am very pleased to see you all here. My name is Peter Bean. I'm the principal. You come and see me if you have any problems with the fees – that means the money you must pay. My office is on the first floor, Room 15, by the stairs. The people behind me are some of my staff. This is Mrs Polly Penn. She's the head of Year 1. She is responsible for the schedule. After this meeting, Mrs Penn will give you the schedule for the first term. The schedule tells you the times of all your lectures.

Presenter: E Listen to the second part of the speech again. Say /ɪ/ every time you hear the short sound. Say /iː/ every time you hear the long sound.

Peter Bean: Mrs Penn will also give you the name of your instructor. We call the teachers at Greenhill instructors. She will also tell you the name of your personal advisor – that's a person who helps you if you have problems. Finally, this is the registrar, Mr Bill Beale. He's in charge of attendance. If you can't come to the college one day, tell Mr Beale. OK, that's it from me. Now I'll hand over to Mrs Penn … Oh, I nearly forgot. Mr Beale's room is on the first floor, next to my room – Room 16.

Presenter: Lesson 5

B Paula and Barbara are both starting at Greenhill College today. Listen to their conversation. Tick any of your underlined words from the leaflet.

Paula: Hello.
Barbara: Hello, I'm Barbara.
Paula: Hi, I'm Paula.
Barbara: Is this your first day?
Paula: Yes, it is. What about you?
Barbara: Yes, me too.
Paula: What happens today?
Barbara: Well, first there's a speech from the principal.
Paula: What's a principal?
Barbara: The head of a college. He's going to welcome us and introduce the staff.
Paula: What does staff mean?

Barbara:	The staff are the people who work at a college.
Paula:	Right. Then what?
Barbara:	Then there's a meeting with the head of Year 1.
Paula:	The head?
Barbara:	Yes, the person in charge. She's going to give us the schedule.
Paula:	Does schedule mean the subjects and times?
Barbara:	That's right. She's also going to tell us the name of our instructor and our personal advisor.
Paula:	Is an instructor a teacher?
Barbara:	Yes. It's the word for teacher at a college or university.
Paula:	What about a personal advisor?
Barbara:	It's the person you go to if you have any problems with your studies.
Paula:	Ah, I see. How do you know all this?
Barbara:	I read the leaflet. Look!

Presenter:	**C Listen again. Match each word from the leaflet with its meaning.** [REPEAT OF EXERCISE B]

Presenter:	Lesson 6 **D 2 Listen to Barbara's speech to the tutor group. Make full sentences from Barbara's notes.**
Barbara:	My name is Barbara Peters. I'm British. I'm from Birmingham. My favourite subject is P.E. I don't like Biology.

Presenter:	Unit 2: Daily Life Lesson 1 **B Listen to eight sentences using words from *Key vocabulary*. Number the words in the order you hear them.**

Voice:	1 There is a very good restaurant in North Road. The food is excellent.
	2 I don't like chess. In fact, I don't like any games like that.
	3 Do you play any sports? Football, basketball, handball?
	4 My sister is excellent at music. She plays the piano, the flute and the guitar.
	5 Have you joined the college computer club yet?
	6 This university has a very big campus – there are about twenty college buildings and several houses for students to live in.
	7 It is very important to plan your day. Make sure there is time for college work and family life.
	8 I watched the new Indian film at the cinema yesterday.

Presenter:	Lesson 3 **C 2 Listen to Mrs Penn's definitions and check your answers.**
Mrs Penn:	a I'm going to give you your schedule – that's the days and times of your classes – for this semester, OK?
	b First I want you to write the start time and the end time of each period – in other words, each part of the day.
	c Lunch is served in the cafeteria – that's the restaurant on the campus.
	d You have a short recess – I mean, a short break between classes.

Presenter:	**D Mrs Penn is going to give you your schedule. Listen and answer these questions.**	
Mrs Penn:	OK. Is everybody ready? Have you all got a pencil? Good. I'm going to give you your schedule – that's the days and times of your classes – for this semester, OK? Can you fill it in as I read it out? If you're not sure about anything, ask your friends after this talk. OK. First I want you to write the start time and the end time of each period – in other words, each part of the day. As you can see, there are six periods, three in the morning and three in the afternoon. There's also a lunch period which lasts an hour. Lunch is served in the cafeteria – that's the restaurant on the campus. OK. Each period is one hour, so that's three hours in the morning and … how many hours in the afternoon?	
Student 1:	Three.	
Mrs Penn:	Good. The first period begins at 9 o'clock. So can you write 9 o'clock in the first morning space? When does the first period end?	
Student 2:	Half past nine.	
Mrs Penn:	No, not half past nine.	
Student 3:	9.45?	
Mrs Penn:	No! Come on, think!	
Student 1:	10 o'clock.	
Mrs Penn:	Why?	
Student 1:	Because each period is one hour.	
Mrs Penn:	Right. Good. So the next period begins at 10 o'clock, right?	
Student 1:	Yes.	
Mrs Penn:	Wrong. You have a short recess – I mean, a short break between classes. The recess is 10 minutes long. So the next period begins at …?	
Student 2:	Five past ten.	

Student 3:	Ten past ten.	
Mrs Penn:	That's right. OK. So now you can fill in the other times …	

Presenter:	**E Listen again.**	
	[REPEAT OF EXERCISE D]	

Presenter:	**F 2 Listen and check your ideas.**	
Voice:	a each	column 2
	b give	column 1
	c mean	column 2
	d read	column 2
	e see	column 2
	f six	column 1
	g this	column 1
	h three	column 2
	i begins	column 1
	j between	column 2

Presenter:	**G 2 Listen and check your ideas.**	
Voice:	a about	letter b
	b because	letter b
	c begins	letter b
	d pencil	letter p
	e between	letter b
	f break	letter b
	g space	letter p
	h campus	letter p
	i part	letter p
	j period	letter p

Presenter:	**Lesson 4**	
	B 1 Listen to eight times. Letter the clocks A to H.	
Voice:	a twenty to ten	
	b quarter past seven	
	c six o'clock	
	d twenty past four	
	e It's ten to four.	
	f ten past eight	
	g half past eleven	
	h quarter to three	

Presenter: **B 3 Listen to the times again and check.**
[REPEAT OF EXERCISE B1]

Presenter: **C 3 Listen and check your ideas.**
Mrs Penn: a Have you all got a pencil?
b ask your friends
c after this talk
d the start time
e each part of the day
f in the afternoon
g it lasts an hour
h in the cafeteria
i on the campus
j half past nine

Presenter: **Lesson 5**
B 2 Listen to Martino talking about his day. Fill in the missing times.
Martino: It's Monday tomorrow. I've got a really busy day. From nine o'clock to eleven ten, I've got General Studies. Then I've got a free period – that's a period with no class – from eleven twenty to twelve twenty. I have to revise for a test in the afternoon. Lunch starts at twenty past twelve. It lasts an hour. Then I've got P.E. from twenty past one to twenty past two, followed by English from half past two to half past three. I've got another free period from twenty to four to twenty to five, then I'm playing handball with Peter from quarter to five to quarter past.

Presenter: **D Listen again and check your answers.**
[REPEAT OF EXERCISE B2]

Presenter: **Lesson 6**
A 2 Listen and check your order.
Voice: 1 nine o'clock

2 ten ten
3 eleven fifteen
4 quarter to twelve
5 five past one
6 half past two
7 twenty to three
8 four forty-five

Presenter: **Unit 3: Work and Business**
Lesson 3
B Gerald Gardiner is a management consultant. He is at Greenhill College today. He is talking to the first-year students about work. Listen to the first part of his talk.
1 How many points does he make?
2 Can you remember any of the points?
Gerald How do you get a good job when you leave college?
Gardiner: You start thinking about it NOW! Change the way that you think about college. Think of college as a job – your job. You will find it much easier then to live in the world of work in two or three years' time. So college should be a job. But what is a job? What must you do in a job? I'm going to tell you nine things.

Number 1: You must go to work every day.
Number 2: You must be punctual – that means, you must always be on time.
Number 3: You must respect your manager – the person who gives you orders – and your colleagues – that is, the people you work with.
Number 4: You must also respect the customers, in other words, the people who buy things from the company.

Number 5: You must do all the tasks or pieces of work that your manager gives you.
Number 6: You must complete all your tasks on time.
Number 7: You are responsible for the quality of your work – whether it is good or bad.
Number 8: You must keep your workplace tidy – your desk, and any shelves or cupboards that you use.
Number 9: You must organize your work files sensibly – in alphabetical order or chronologically – in other words, by date.

Presenter: C Listen again. How does he define these words? Match each word to a definition.
[REPEAT OF EXERCISE B]

Presenter: E Listen again and check your answers.
[REPEAT OF EXERCISE B]

Presenter: F 2 Listen and check your ideas.
Voice:

are	column D
bad	column C
colleagues	column B
gives	column A
keep	column B
leave	column B
manager	column C
people	column B
pieces	column B
start	column D
that	column C
think	column A

Presenter: G 2 Listen and check your ideas.
Voice:

a	punctual	letter p
b	respect	letter p
c	buy	letter b
d	pieces	letter p
e	sensibly	letter b
f	people	letter p
g	job	letter b
h	company	letter p
i	responsible	letter p
j	workplace	letter p
k	complete	letter p
l	person	letter p

Presenter: **Lesson 4**
B 2 Listen and check your ideas.
Voice: a You must go to work every day.
b You must be punctual.
c You must respect your manager and your colleagues.
d You must also respect the customers.
e You must do all the tasks or pieces of work that your manager gives you.
f You must complete all your tasks on time.
g You are responsible for the quality of your work.
h You must keep your workplace tidy.
i You must organize your work files sensibly.

Presenter: C 2 Listen and check your answers.
Voice:

go	row A
give	row A
college	row B
get	row A
change	row B
colleague	row A
organize	row A

Presenter: C 4 Listen and check your answers.
Voice:

age	row B
page	row B
begin	row A
charge	row B
ago	row A
again	row A

large	row B	
big	row A	

Presenter: C 6 Listen and check your answers.

Voice:	danger	row B
	angry	row A
	wage	row B
	magazine	row A
	rig	row A

Presenter: Lesson 5

C Julia's friend, Carla Fernandez, is talking to her. Listen.

Carla: Hi, Julia. What are you doing?

Julia: I'm using this web page to help me find a summer job. It says a good summer job for me is … nursery school assistant or shop assistant. I think that's a stupid suggestion! I don't like working with children and I don't like selling things.

Carla: Are you going to get a job in the college holidays?

Julia: I'd like to. What about you?

Carla: Yes, I think so.

Julia: What would you like to do?

Carla: I'm not sure.

Julia: OK. I'll ask you the questions and let's see what the computer suggests.

Carla: OK.

Julia: Question 1. Would you like to work in your own country or abroad?

Carla: What does it mean, abroad?

Julia: It means in another country – Greece or France, for example.

Carla: Oh, I'd like to work abroad.

Julia: Question 2. Do you like working alone or with other people?

Carla: With other people, definitely. I don't like working alone.

Julia: Question 3. Do you like working inside or outside?

Carla: Um, let me think. Inside. No, I'll change that. Outside.

Julia: OK. So I just click 'Find' and …

Carla: Why are you laughing?

Julia: It says … a good job for you is … a camp counsellor.

Carla: Well … I agree. I think that is a good suggestion.

Presenter: E Listen to this part of the conversation again and check your answers.

Carla: Are you going to get a job in the college holidays?

Julia: I'd like to. What about you?

Carla: Yes, I think so.

Julia: What would you like to do?

Carla: I'm not sure.

Julia: Would you like to work in your own country or abroad?

Carla: Oh, I'd like to work abroad.

Julia: Do you like working alone or with other people?

Carla: With other people, definitely. I don't like working alone.

Julia: Do you like working inside or outside?

Carla: Um, let me think. Inside. No, I'll change that. Outside.

Presenter: Unit 4: Science and Nature
Lesson 1

D Listen to a paragraph. Then write one of the *Key vocabulary* words in each space.

Voice: Science is the study of how things work in the world. A scientist usually works in a laboratory. He or she tests things to find out the facts. He or she often puts the facts in a table, with columns of information, or in a graph, with blocks or lines that represent the information.

Presenter: Lesson 3

C 1 Listen to the introduction to the programme. Tick each

	point in the programme information on the left when Arthur mentions it.
Arthur Burns:	This week on *So you want to be…* we are looking at the job of the scientist. What is science? What do scientists do? What is scientific method? And the most important question of all: Is science the right career for you?
Presenter:	**C 2 Listen to the first part of the programme. Put your hand up when Arthur starts to talk about a new point.**
Arthur Burns:	First, what is science? Science is the study of how things work in the world. The word science comes from Greek and Latin words meaning 'to know'.

What do scientists do? Well, scientists are not satisfied just to think something is true. They must prove it. Proving means showing that something is always true. In this way, scientists are different from other people. Let me show you the difference.

I know that plants need sunlight and water to live. At least, I think that's true. But thinking is not enough for a scientist. If a scientist thinks something is true, he or she wants to prove it.

How can scientists prove that something is true? They must follow the scientific method. A method is a way of doing something. But what is the scientific method? It works like this: Firstly, a scientist makes a hypothesis, which means an idea of the truth. Then he or she tests the hypothesis. Scientists can test hypotheses in two main ways. They can do an experiment, which means a test in a laboratory. Scientists study what happens during the experiment. Or they can do research, which means looking up information. They usually do research in a library or, nowadays, on the Internet. With research, scientists look at what happened in the past.

In both cases – experiments and research – they collect data. Data is information before it is organized. Then they display the results in a table or a graph. Then they draw conclusions. Conclusions are what you learn from an experiment. The hypothesis is proved – or disproved.

Does this sound interesting to you? Is science the right career for you?

Presenter:	**D Listen again. How does Arthur Burns define these words?** [REPEAT OF EXERCISE C 2]
Presenter:	**E Look at the student notes on the right. Listen to the first part of the programme again. Complete the notes by writing one word in each space.** [REPEAT OF EXERCISE C2]
Presenter:	**F 2 Listen and check your ideas.**
Voice:	display column A
	even column B
	enough column A
	graph column D
	Greek column B
	happen column C

if	column A
lab	column C
past	column D
plant	column D

Presenter: **G 2 Listen and check your ideas.**

Voice:

a	prove	letter p
b	display	letter p
c	both	letter b
d	table	letter b
e	past	letter p
f	disprove	letter p
g	hypothesis	letter p
h	experiment	letter p
i	lab	letter b
j	happen	letter p

Presenter: **Lesson 4**

C 2 Listen to some of Arthur's sentences. Choose the next word from the yellow box each time Arthur pauses. Write the number beside the word.

Arthur Burns:
1 Science is the study of how things work in the [PAUSE] world.
2 The word 'science' comes from Greek and Latin words meaning to [PAUSE] know.
3 Scientists must prove that something is [PAUSE] true.
4 They must follow the scientific [PAUSE] method.
5 Scientists must collect [PAUSE] data.
6 They display the results in a table or [PAUSE] graph.

Presenter: **D 2 Listen and check your answers.**

Voice:

that	column B
the	column B
they	column B
both	column A
then	column B

there	column B
hypothesis	column A
with	column B
thing	column A
truth	column A

Presenter: **E 2 Listen and check your answers.**

Voice:
test
when
then
pen
she
bed
many
any
head
again

Presenter: **Lesson 5**

B Martha's friend, Ruth, comes into the cafe. Listen to the conversation. Which question can Ruth answer?

Ruth: Hi, Martha. How are you?

Martha: I'm fine, thanks. Have a seat.

Ruth: Thanks. What are you doing?

Martha: I'm thinking about this competition.

Ruth: Oh, a competition. I like competitions.

Martha: Could you help me, then?

Ruth: Yes, of course. I'll give you a hand.

Martha: Thanks. Do you know anything about science and nature?

Ruth: You mean birds and weather and things?

Martha: Yes, things like that.

Ruth: Oh, no. Sorry. I'm afraid I don't.

Martha: That's a pity. Neither do I.

Ruth: Well, let's try, anyway. What are they asking?

Martha: OK. This is the first one. Question A. Why is the sky blue?

Ruth: Well, it's because … it's the colour

	of … it's … I have no idea.
Martha:	Oh. Question B. Why is the sky red at sunrise and sunset?
Ruth:	Ah, that's easier. It's red because … the red colour comes from … No, I don't know that one either. Do you know?
Martha:	No, I don't. OK. Question C. Why are the clouds white or grey?
Ruth:	I really don't know.
Martha:	Well, here's the last one. Why does it rain?
Ruth:	Oh, I know that one.
Martha:	You know this one?
Ruth:	Yes, I do.
Martha:	So what's the answer?

Presenter:	**C 2 Listen again to the first part of the conversation and check your ideas.**
Ruth:	Hi, Martha. How are you?
Martha:	I'm fine, thanks. Have a seat.
Ruth:	Thanks. What are you doing?
Martha:	I'm thinking about this competition.
Ruth:	Oh, a competition. I like competitions.
Martha:	Could you help me, then?
Ruth:	Yes, of course. I'll give you a hand.
Martha:	Thanks. Do you know anything about science and nature?
Ruth:	You mean birds and weather and things?
Martha:	Yes, things like that.
Ruth:	Oh, no. Sorry. I'm afraid I don't.
Martha:	That's a pity. Neither do I.
Ruth:	Well, let's try, anyway. What are they asking?

Presenter:	**Unit 5: The Physical World** **Lesson 1**
	D Listen to descriptions of six countries. Look at the map above. Find each country.
Voice:	1 It is in North America. It is

north of the USA.

2 It is in Asia. It is southeast of Pakistan.

3 It is in Africa. It is west of Egypt.

4 It is in Europe. It is west of Spain.

5 It is in Australasia. It is a large island. It is on the Tropic of Capricorn. It is near New Zealand.

6 It is in South America. It is between the Equator and the Tropic of Capricorn. It is north of Argentina.

Presenter:	**Lesson 3**
	B 1 Listen. Donna pauses a few times in her questions. Guess the word she is going to say next on each occasion. Listen and check your ideas.
Donna:	Where are you [PAUSE] from, Anita?
Anita:	I'm from Venezuela.
Donna:	Where's [PAUSE] that?
Anita:	It's in the north of South America. It's north of Brazil, east of Colombia and west of Guyana.
Donna:	And where do you come [PAUSE] from in Venezuela?
Anita:	I come from San Fernando.
Donna:	How do you spell [PAUSE] that?
Anita:	S-A-N F-E-R-N-A-N-D-O.
Donna:	Which part of the [PAUSE] country is that in?
Anita:	It's in the centre of the country.
Donna:	Is San Fernando the capital?
Anita:	No. The capital is Caracas.
Donna:	What about you, Maria?
Maria:	I'm from Peru.
Donna:	Is that in South America, [PAUSE] too?
Maria:	Yes. North of Colombia and Ecuador.
Donna:	Does it have a long coastline?

Maria:	Yes, that's right. It has a coastline on the Pacific Ocean.
Donna:	And what's your home [PAUSE] town?
Maria:	I'm from Tacna.
Donna:	Sorry. What did you [PAUSE] say?
Maria:	I said, Tacna.
Donna:	How do you spell [PAUSE] that?
Maria:	T-A-C-N-A.
Donna:	Is that the [PAUSE] capital?
Maria:	No, the capital is Lima.
Donna:	Which part of the country is Tacna [PAUSE] in?
Maria:	It's in the south.

Presenter:	**B 3 Listen again. Complete the information about Venezuela and Peru.**
	[REPEAT OF EXERCISE B1 WITHOUT PAUSES]

Presenter:	**C 2 Listen and check your ideas.**	
Voice:	city	columns A and B
	did	column A
	east	column B
	exactly	columns A, C and B
	said	column E
	spell	column E
	west	column E

Presenter:	**D 2 Listen and check your ideas.**	
Voice:	a about	letter b
	b capital	letter p
	c north	letters t and h
	d part	letter p
	e south	letters t and h
	f spell	letter p

Presenter:	**E Listen and complete these words from earlier units.**
Voice:	1 college
	2 display
	3 experiment
	4 job
	5 manager
	6 method

	7 past
	8 prove
	9 think
	10 punctual

Presenter:	**Lesson 4**
	B 3 Listen and put the other letters of the alphabet into the correct column, according to the vowel sound.
Voice:	A B C D E F G H I J K L M N O P Q R S T U V W X Y Z

Presenter:	**C 1 Listen to the spellings.**
Voice:	1 U-K
	2 V-E-N-E-Z-U-E-L-A
	3 U-S-A
	4 K-O-R-E-A
	5 Q-A-T-A-R
	6 P-O-R-T-U-G-A-L
	7 C-H-I-L-E
	8 U-G-A-N-D-A
	9 J-A-P-A-N
	10 C-H-I-N-A
	11 S-R-I L-A-N-K-A
	12 M-A-L-A-Y-S-I-A

Presenter:	**D 3 Listen and check your ideas.**
Voice:	it's
	is
	small
	south
	has
	east
	coast
	what's
	sorry
	does
	spell
	say
	towns

Presenter:	**E 4 Listen to the words in Questions 1 and 2.**
Voice:	Question 1:

on
not
from
what
come
of
sorry
want
was
wash
Question 2:
for
before
more
small
talk
war
August
taught
north

Presenter: Lesson 5

C 1 Listen to the conversation. Does Simon ask any of your questions from Exercises A or B?

Simon: Hi. My name's Simon. Simon Shepherd.

Zeki: Hello. I'm Zeki.

Simon: Can I help you?

Zeki: No, it's OK I can manage.

Simon: Are you going to the Geography lecture?

Zeki: Yes, I am. What about you?

Simon: Yes, me too. When does it start?

Zeki: Ten past ten, I think.

Simon: Where are you from, Zeki?

Zeki: I'm from Turkey.

Simon: Where's that?

Zeki: It's in Europe. It's north of Syria and Iraq.

Simon: And where do you come from in Turkey?

Zeki: I come from Mersin.

Simon: Sorry. What did you say?

Zeki: I said Mersin.

Simon: How do you spell that?

Zeki: M-E-R-S-I-N.

Simon: And how do you say it?

Zeki: Mersin.

Simon: Mersin. Which part of the country is that in?

Zeki: It's in the south.

Presenter: C 2 Listen again. Complete the information about Zeki in the table.
[REPEAT OF EXERCISE C1]

Presenter: D 2 Listen again and check your order.
[REPEAT OF EXERCISE C1]

Presenter: E 2 Listen and check your answers.

Voice:
a think in hi it's
The odd one out is *hi*.
b part what Iraq past
The odd one out is *what*.
c me help said spell
The odd one out is *me*.
d am about that manage
The odd one out is *about*.
e think north south that
The odd one out is *that*.

Presenter: Revision 1
Lesson 1

C Mrs Penn runs the extracurricular activities at Greenhill College. Listen and find out:
1 the meaning of *extracurricular*
2 the extracurricular activities at the college – tick the activities on the notice board.

Mrs Penn: OK, so that's the schedule. Now, some other information for you. We have extracurricular activities – that means extra things you can do after college work – every evening, so can you make a note of these? If you want to do any of the activities, just come along to the first meeting this week. Right. First, we have Sports Club on Saturday at 8 o'clock in the evening – you can do basketball, handball, table tennis and lots of other sports.

Then there's Film Night on Sunday, starting at 8.30. We have a different film every week and after the film, there's a discussion.

It's Quiz Time on Monday. Come with a friend and take part in a General Knowledge quiz. That starts at quarter to eight.

Computer Club is on Tuesday. It doesn't matter whether you are a beginner or an expert. Come and learn or just have fun. Computer Club starts at quarter past eight.

Finally, we have Music Makers on Wednesday night. If you play an instrument or want to learn, join the music makers at half past seven. I'll run through those again in case you missed anything.

Presenter: **D Listen again and write in the days and times for each activity that you ticked.**
[REPEAT OF EXERCISE C]

Presenter: **Unit 6: Culture and Civilization**
B Listen to a paragraph. Then complete each space using words from *Key vocabulary 1*.

Voice: In some parts of Pakistan there are traditional events for children. The first event is called Bismillah Khawni. It takes place when the child is four years and four months. The boy or girl wears special clothes with flowers on, and family and friends watch him or her say the first chapter of the Holy Qur'an. The celebration ends with a special dinner. The second event is called Khtme Qur'an. This event celebrates the child's ability to say the complete Holy Qur'an. The child receives gifts and, once again, there is a special dinner.

Presenter: **D Read and listen to the text below. Then complete the text using words from *Key vocabulary 2*. Make any changes necessary.**

Male lecturer: In some cultures, birthdays are very important. In Western cultures, for example, people give presents to relatives and friends on their birthday. They often have special parties for the lucky person. People say Congratulations or Happy Birthday even to people they don't know well. Are birthdays important in your culture?

Some people even believe that date of birth is connected in some way to luck. These people know how birthdays relate to star signs and they read 'the stars' every day in the newspaper. Do you know your star sign? Do you read 'the stars' every day?

Presenter: **Lesson 3**
B Listen to the talk once.
1 Juri pauses a few times during her talk. Guess the word that she is going to say next. Listen and check your ideas.

Juri: I'm going to talk to you today

about a festival in Japan. The festival is called Seijin-no-hi, which is spelt S-E-I-J-I-N N-O H-I. The name means the Coming of Age festival. This festival is for all girls and [PAUSE] boys who become 20 years old in that year. It takes place on the second Monday of January each year. The festival celebrates the change from being a child to being an [PAUSE] adult. At the age of 20, a person in Japan can vote and smoke! There is a ceremony in a town hall. Town halls – H-A-L-L-S – are the local government offices. First, government officials make speeches. Then they give small presents to the new [PAUSE] adults. Young women wear traditional dresses called kimonos. The word is spelt [PAUSE] K-I-M-O-N-O. They usually rent the kimonos, because they can cost as much as a [PAUSE] car. Young men wear business suits or, occasionally, dark kimonos. Later, after the ceremony, the new adults go to special [PAUSE] parties. Finally, the young people go [PAUSE] home. They go out in the morning as children. They come back in the evening as [PAUSE] adults.

Presenter: C 2 **Listen to the talk again, without the pauses. Make notes in the table below.**
[REPEAT OF EXERCISE B1 WITHOUT PAUSES]

Presenter: E 2 **Listen and check your answers.**

Voice:		
after	column A	
all	column B	
although	column B	
called	column B	
dark	column A	
first	column C	
girl	column C	
hall	column B	
or	column B	
parties	column A	
person	column C	
small	column B	

Presenter: F **What are the missing letters in each of these sentences? Listen and write the letters.**

Juri: 1 I'm going to talk to you about the Coming of Age festival.
2 It takes place on the second Monday of January.
3 It celebrates the change from being a child to being an adult.
4 Town halls are local government offices.
5 First, officials make speeches.
6 Then they give small presents.
7 Young women wear traditional dresses.
8 They usually rent the kimonos.
9 They can cost as much as a car.

Presenter: **Lesson 4**
B 3 **Listen and check.**

Juri: I'm going to talk to you today about a festival in Japan. First, government officials make speeches. Then they give small presents to the new adults. Later, after the ceremony, the new adults go to special parties. Finally, the young people go home.

Presenter: C 1 **Listen to the words in the blue box. Which consonant is missing in each case?**

Voice: talk
take
twenty
vote
festival

party

after

later

Presenter: C 2 Listen to the words in the yellow box. Which consonant is missing in each case?

Voice: dark

adult

traditional

dinner

day

idea

die

understand

Presenter: Lesson 5

B 1 Listen to the conversation. Does Dario use any of the expressions from Exercise A?

Dario: Hi, Tony. What's the matter?

Tony: I can't open this.

Dario: I'll give you a hand.

Tony: Thanks.

Dario: What is it?

Tony: It's a present.

Dario: A present. That's nice. Who's it from?

Tony: My father.

Dario: Your father? Lovely. Is it your birthday, then?

Tony: Yes, it is. Well, actually, my birthday's next Thursday.

Dario: Next Thursday? The fourth of August?

Tony: Yes.

Dario: Great. Happy birthday!

Tony: Thank you. Oh, it's a shirt.

Dario: A shirt? That's smart. I'll give you a card tomorrow.

Tony: You don't have to do that.

Dario: I want to. Would you like to have a party?

Tony: No, thanks. Just a card.

Dario: Are you sure?

Tony: Yes, I'm sure.

Dario: OK. By the way …

Tony: Yes?

Dario: My birthday's on the third of March.

Tony: I'll remember that!

Presenter: B 2 Listen again. Answer the questions.
[REPEAT OF EXERCISE B1]

Presenter: Unit 7: Technology
Lesson 1

B Listen to the paragraph. Then complete the text using the *Key vocabulary*. Make any necessary changes.

Voice: Nowadays, we can travel in many different ways. On land, we can ride on a bicycle or drive in a car. In many countries, we can also go along special tracks in a train. On the sea, we can sail in a small boat or cruise in a large ship. In the air, we can fly in a small plane or in a huge one. How did we get all these forms of transport? Who invented them? When did each invention happen?

Presenter: Lesson 3

B 1 What is the lecturer going to talk about? Look at the notebook. Listen and number the points in order.

Lecturer: I'm going to talk to you today about inventions; that is, new ways of doing something. All the inventions are in the field, or area, of transport. First, I'm going to talk about different methods or types of transport. After that, I'll tell you when each method was invented. Finally, I'm going to say which invention was the most important, as far as I am concerned – I mean, in my opinion.

Presenter: **B 2 Listen again and check your answers.**
[REPEAT OF EXERCISE B1]

Presenter: **B 3 Listen to the second part. When the lecturer stops, guess the next word. Then check your guesses.**

Lecturer: OK. So, first, what are the main methods of transport that we use today? We can travel on land, on the sea and in the [PAUSE] air. We use cars and bicycles, trains, boats and, of course, [PAUSE] planes. OK. So, there are several methods of [PAUSE] transport. But when was each method [PAUSE] invented?

Presenter: **B 4 Copy Table 1. Then listen to the third part and complete the table.**

Lecturer: The first method of transport was of course, walking. But about 40,000 years ago – yes, that's right, 40,000 – some Indonesian natives made a boat and sailed from one island to another. For centuries, man sailed the seas using only the power of the wind. Then, in 1775, J.C. Perier – that's P-E-R-I-E-R – invented the steamship. Steam also powered the first train. In 1830, George Stephenson, which is spelt S-T-E-P-H-E-N-S-O-N, drove his engine, called the Rocket, along a track, and the Railway Age began. Just nine years later, in 1839, a man called Macmillan, spelt M-A-C-M-I-L-L-A-N, invented the bicycle. Fifty years after that, in 1888, Karl Benz – that's B-E-N-Z – invented the motor car. So now man could move quickly on land and on the sea. Finally, at the beginning of the 20th century, in 1903, the Wright

brothers conquered the air. That's Wright with a silent W – W-R-I-G-H-T. Their plane, called Flyer, flew a distance of 35 metres and went down in history.

Presenter: **B 5 Listen to the final part.**

Lecturer: So we have heard about the main inventions in the field of transport. But which invention was the most important? In my opinion, it was the last invention, the plane. This invention has made the world into a much smaller place. People can travel right to the other side of the world in a day. Why is that important? Because the more we travel, the more we understand other people and other cultures.

Presenter: **C 2 Listen and check your answers.**

Voice: Column A
      ship which wind history
      engine
  Column B
      land track transport that
  Column C
      tell when went engine
  Column D
      on was what because

Presenter: **D 2 Listen and check your answers.**

Voice: Column A
      sea steam each people
  Column B
      car after last far
  Column C
      first world concerned
  Column D
      talk course transport called
  more walk
  Column E
      new flew move use

Presenter: **Lesson 4**

B 2 Listen to the introduction again and check your answer.
[REPEAT OF LESSON 3 EXERCISE B1]

Presenter: **D 2 Listen and check your ideas.**
Voice: a check
b each
c English
d match
e much
f ship
g short
h which

Presenter: **Lesson 5**

C Richard Shaw, Charles' friend, has just come into the library. Listen to the conversation between Charles and Richard. Complete the missing information on the website.

Richard: Hi, Charles.
Charles: Oh, hi, Richard. This is amazing.
Richard: What is?
Charles: This website. It has information about famous inventions.
Richard: Oh. You're doing research for the next lecture.
Charles: That's right. Did you know that there are over a billion bicycles in the world?
Richard: Sorry? How many bicycles are there?
Charles: One billion. It says here that Kirkpatrick Macmillan invented it in 1839.
Richard: Pardon? When did he invent it?
Charles: In 1839. But it seems that Leonardo da Vinci drew a picture of a bicycle more than 300 years earlier.
Richard: Who drew a picture of a bicycle?
Charles: Da Vinci. D-A V-I-N-C-I. He was a painter and inventor from Italy. Good heavens!
Richard: What?

Charles: Apparently, the speed record for a bicycle is 268 kilometres an hour.
Richard: Sorry? How many kilometres an hour?
Charles: Two hundred and sixty-eight kilometres an hour.
Richard: Are you sure?
Charles: Absolutely. According to this, he was riding behind a car.
Richard: Maybe. But you shouldn't believe everything you read on the Web.

Presenter: **D 2 Listen and check your ideas.**
Charles: Did you know that there are over a billion bicycles in the world?
Richard: Sorry? How many bicycles are there?
Charles: One billion. It says here that Kirkpatrick Macmillan invented it in 1839.
Richard: Pardon? When did he invent it?
Charles: In 1839. But it seems that Leonardo da Vinci drew a picture of a bicycle more than 300 years earlier.
Richard: Who drew a picture of a bicycle?
Charles: Da Vinci. D-A V-I-N-C-I. He was a painter and inventor from Italy. Good heavens!
Richard: What?
Charles: Apparently, the speed record for a bicycle is 268 kilometres an hour.
Richard: Sorry? How many kilometres an hour?
Charles: Two hundred and sixty-eight kilometres an hour.
Richard: Are you sure?
Charles: Absolutely. According to this, he was riding behind a car.
Richard: Maybe. But you shouldn't believe everything you read on the Web.

Presenter: **E 2 Listen and check your answers.**
Voice: believe   B
car   C

drew	A
earlier	D
more	E
example	C
forty	E
pardon	C
read	B
sure	E
speed	B
thirty	D
two	A
who	A
world	D

Presenter: Unit 8: Art and Literature
Lesson 1

Presenter: B **Listen to the paragraph. Then complete it using** *Key vocabulary 1.*

Voice: Everybody likes a good story. There are stories in the literature of every culture. Children learn them at home or at school. Many of these stories have a moral – in other words, a lesson for life. For example, help people and they will help you. There is usually one main character – one person who does most of the actions. We often don't know the name of the writer of these traditional stories. People often translate the best stories into many languages so, in the end, the same story appears all around the world.

Presenter: Lesson 3

C 2 **Listen to the first part of the programme and check your answers.**

Jenny Ingram: In this programme, we're going to hear about *The Arabian Nights.* First, I'm going to talk about the history of the stories. After that, we're going to listen to one of the stories.

So first, the history. *The Arabian Nights*, or *The Thousand and One Nights*, is a collection of stories from Persia, Arabia, India and Egypt. The stories are anonymous – in other words, nobody knows who made up the stories, who wrote them. For centuries, they have been part of the folklore – that means, the traditional stories passed, by word of mouth, from generation to generation, from father to son and mother to daughter. A few of the stories appeared around 800 AD. Then, in around 1500, an unknown Egyptian wrote down the stories that we know today. This collection included stories of Aladdin – the boy who found a wonderful lamp, Sindbad the sailor, who met a fabulous bird, the Roc, and Ali Baba and his problems with the Forty Thieves. The stories were translated from Arabic into French in 1717. The person who translated them was a Frenchman and his name was Galland – that's G-A-L-L-A-N-D. Later, in 1885, they were translated from Arabic into English. This translation was by the English explorer Sir Richard Burton. His surname is spelt B-U-R-T-O-N.

The Arabian Nights is the most widely known piece of Arabic literature in the Western World.

Presenter: D **Listen again. Complete the table.**
[REPEAT OF EXERCISE C2]

Presenter: F Listen to the story. Which sentence about the story is true?

Jenny Ingram: Here is one of the stories from *The Arabian Nights*. It is called *The Thieves and the Donkey*. There were once two thieves, a young man and an old man. They were at a market. They saw a poor man buy a donkey. The poor man put a rope around the donkey's neck and led the donkey away from the market.

'We can steal that donkey easily,' the young thief said to the old thief.

The young thief went up behind the poor man and untied the rope from the donkey. He put the rope around his own neck. The old thief took the donkey away.

The young thief walked behind the poor man for some time. Suddenly, the young thief stopped and the poor man looked round. He was very surprised to see a man at the end of the rope, not the donkey.

'Who are you?' he asked. 'And where's my donkey?' 'I am your donkey,' the young thief said. 'I was rude to my mother and, suddenly, I became a donkey. I was a donkey for several years and then you bought me. Just now, I became a man again.'

The man untied the rope from the young thief's neck. 'Go back to your home. And do not be rude to your mother again.'
The poor man still wanted a donkey, so he went back to the market the next day. He was surprised to see his donkey for sale again. He went up to the donkey and said: 'I told you not to be rude to your mother again.'

Presenter: G 1 Listen to the words in Column A.

Voice: lived, means, led, words, man, passed, not, called, young, rude, took

Presenter: G 2 Listen to the words in the orange box. Write each word in a space in Column B.

Voice: back, bought, his, looked, market, mother, problem, thief, went, who, world

Presenter: G 3 Write each word from the yellow box in a space in Column C. Listen and check.

Voice: English, steal, said, bird, lamp, father, stopped, story, son, few, put

Presenter: Lesson 4

C Who did what? Listen to the story in Lesson 3 again. Answer each question with 1, 2 or 3. [REPEAT OF LESSON 3 EXERCISE F]

Presenter: D Look at these words from the talk. Listen. Tick the correct column, according to the stressed vowel sound.

Voice: away, became, behind, buy, eighty, famous, generation, made, tie, time, translate

Presenter: Lesson 5

B Leila, an Iranian, is talking to her friend, Meliai. Listen to the start of the conversation. Answer the questions.

Leila: What's your favourite Joha story?

Meliai: I don't know. I like lots of them.

Leila:	Do you know the one about Joha and the tiger? It's my favourite.
Meliai:	What are tigers?
Leila:	They're big cats with black stripes.
Melia:	Oh, yes. Joha and the tiger. I haven't heard that one.
Leila:	Really, it's so funny. Would you like to hear it?
Meliai:	I'd love to.
Leila:	OK.

Presenter:	**C Listen to the next part of the conversation. Define these words: *hunting, shooting, guns.***
Leila:	Joha was old and his eyes were poor. But he still liked to go hunting.
Meliai:	I'm sorry. Did you say hunting?
Leila:	Yes, you know – shooting animals or birds.
Meliai:	No, I don't understand. What does shooting mean?
Leila:	You know. Shooting. Bang bang!
Meliai:	How do you say it?
Leila:	Shooting. Shooting.
Meliai:	Shooting. OK. Go on.
Leila:	So … one day he saw some men. They had guns.
Meliai:	Sorry? What did they have?
Leila:	Guns. You know, things for shooting.
Meliai:	I see.

Presenter:	**D Listen to the final part of the conversation. Number the events from the story in order.**
Leila:	Now, where was I?
Meliai:	You said the men had guns.
Leila:	Oh, yes. Joha saw some men with guns. Joha said to the men, 'Are you going hunting?' 'Yes, we are,' they replied. 'What are you hunting?' he asked. 'Tigers,' they replied. 'Can I come with you?' asked Joha. 'You can,' said the leader. 'But you must be careful with your gun.'

Meliai:	Sorry. Who said that?
Leila:	The leader.
Meliai:	What's a leader?
Leila:	The person in charge.
Meliai:	I see.
Leila:	So Joha said, 'I'll be careful,' and he went and got his gun. One of the villagers decided to make fun of Joha. He got a big piece of paper. He tied it to a rope. He put the rope around his neck.
Meliai:	Sorry. Where did he put it?
Leila:	Around his neck – here.
Meliai:	Right.
Leila:	Oh, I forgot to say. He wrote on the paper in big letters: I AM NOT A TIGER. Then he put the rope around his neck. A few minutes later, Joha shot him and hurt his arm. 'What is the matter with you?' said the man. 'Didn't you see the sign?' Joha looked at the man, then came closer and looked at the sign. 'Oh, sorry,' he said. 'I didn't see the word NOT.'
Meliai:	That's really funny. So Joha read 'I AM a tiger!'

Presenter:	**Unit 9: Sport and Leisure Lesson 1**
	C Listen to a paragraph. Then complete with words from the *Key vocabulary* or others you know. Change the form of the word if necessary.
Voice:	There are many different kinds of sport. We play some sports with a ball – for example, football, tennis, rugby and golf. We play some sports with other players in a team. For example, football is a team sport. Sometimes we need a piece of equipment to take part in a sport. We need a bicycle, of course, for cycling, and we need a stick for ice hockey.

Presenter: Lesson 3

B 1 Listen to the introduction. Write the missing words in *Categories* and *Definitions*. Part 1

Lecturer: Today I'm going to talk about sport. As you know, there are many different sports, but it is possible to classify them into three groups – classify is spelt C-L-A-S-S-I-F-Y. It comes from the word 'class'. Classifying means putting into groups. The first group contains racing sports – R-A-C-I-N-G – which means trying to go faster than another person. The second group of sports is opponent sports. An opponent – that's O-P-P-O-N-E-N-T – is someone you play against. Finally, there are achievement sports. Achievement, of course, means reaching a certain level, a good level. Oh, sorry. Achievement is A-C-H-I-E-V-E-M-E-N-T. So, I'm going to classify sports into three groups and give examples of sports in each category or group.

Presenter: **B 2 Listen to Part 2. When the lecturer stops, guess the next word. Then listen and check. Part 2**

Lecturer: OK. So let's look at the first [PAUSE] group – racing. Trying to go faster than another [PAUSE] person. There are two sub-categories here. Sub means 'under'. So a sub-category is under a category. Some racing sports just use the power of the human [PAUSE] body. For example, running and [PAUSE] swimming. Other sports in this category use the power of [PAUSE] machines. Cycling uses [PAUSE] bicycles,

motor racing uses [PAUSE] cars.

What about the second group – opponent sports? Once again, with opponent sports, there are two sub-[PAUSE] categories. The opponent might be a person or a [PAUSE] team. For example, we play tennis against one [PAUSE] person, but we play football against a [PAUSE] team. Finally, there are achievement [PAUSE] sports. In achievement sports, there are also two [PAUSE] sub-categories. Sometimes we try to reach a target – T-A-R-G-E-T. For example, in golf, we try to get a white ball into a [PAUSE] hole. So that's a target [PAUSE] sport. Sometimes we try to achieve a particular quantity – distance, for example or [PAUSE] height. Quantity is Q-U-A-N-T-I-T-Y. In the long jump, we try to jump farther than all the other [PAUSE] people.

Presenter: **B 3 Listen to Part 2 again. Complete the *sub-categories* section with headings under each arrow.**
[REPEAT OF EXERCISE B2 WITHOUT PAUSES]

Presenter: **B 4 Listen to Part 2 again and write one example for each sub-category.**
[REPEAT OF EXERCISE B3]

Presenter: **B 5 Listen to the summary of the lecture and check your answers. Part 3**

Lecturer: OK. So we have heard about three categories of sports – racing, opponent and achievement. We have seen that each category has two sub-categories. In racing it's human body and machine, in opponent sports it's person or team, and in achievement sports it's target or quantity.

Before next time, can you think of ten sports and classify each one into one of the sub-categories from today's lecture?

Presenter: **D 2 Listen and check your answers.**

Voice:		
against	column 6
ball	column 5
class	column 3
heard	column 7
quantity	column 4
racing	column 8
reach	column 1
target	column 3
team	column 1
that	column 2

Presenter: Lesson 4

B Listen to Part 1 of the lecture from Lesson 3 again. Put your hand up when you hear an important word.
[REPEAT OF LESSON 3 EXERCISE B1]

Presenter: **C Listen to Part 2 of the lecture again. How does the lecturer show that these words are important? Tick one or more ways.**
[REPEAT OF LESSON 3 EXERCISE B3]

Presenter: **D 2 Listen and check your ideas.**

Voice:		
so	column A
power	column B
opponent	column A
how	column B
know	column A
go	column A
also	column A
OK	column A

Presenter: Lesson 5

A Listen to the first part of Mino and Munira's conversation. Answer the questions.

Munira: Hi Mino. How are you?
Mino: Hello, Munira. I'm fine.
Munira: What are you watching?
Mino: It's Brazil versus Germany.
Munira: Who's winning?
Mino: Brazil. Two goals to one. Germany scored just now, but the referee said it wasn't a goal.
Munira: Is it a good game?
Mino: Yes, it's quite exciting. But the pitch is terrible.
Munira: Sorry. What's a pitch?
Mino: The place where they play.
Munira: How do you spell it?
Mino: P-I-T-C-H.
Munira: How do you say it? Pitich?
Mino: No, pitch.
Munira: Pitch. I love football. It's my favourite game.
Mino: Really? I like football, but my favourite sport is baseball.
Munira: Baseball? What's that?

Presenter: **B 3 Listen to the second part of the conversation. Complete the information about baseball.**

Mino: Don't you know the game?
Munira: No, I don't. I've never heard of it.
Mino: It's very popular in my country.
Munira: Is it a team game?
Mino: Yes, it is. There are nine players on each team.
Munira: Is it a ball game?
Mino: Yes, it is. You play it with a small, hard ball.
Munira: Do you play it indoors?
Mino: No, you don't. You play it outside because you hit the ball a long

way.

Munira: Do you play it in a special place?

Mino: Yes, you do. You play on a big pitch with a diamond shape on one side.

Munira: A diamond shape?

Mino: Yes, that's like a square on its side.

Munira: How do you spell it?

Mino: D-I-A-M-O-N-D.

Munira: And how do you say it? Dee-a-mond.

Mino: No, diamond.

Munira: So what's the … diamond … for?

Mino: There are special places called bases at each corner.

Munira: Ah, that's why it's called baseball.

Mino: Yes. You need bases and a ball.

Munira: Do you need any other equipment?

Mino: Yes, you do. You need a baseball bat.

Munira: Is it a long bat?

Mino: Yes, it is. It's long and thin. Well, it's a bit thicker at one end. You hold the thin end. It's made of wood.

Munira: So, do you hit the ball with the bat?

Mino: Yes, you do. You hit the ball and you run round the bases.

Munira: Do you score goals?

Mino: No, you don't. You get one run each time you go round all the bases. The team with the most runs wins.

Munira: I'd like to play it.

Mino: OK. Let's ask about it at the college sports club.

Presenter: C 2 Listen to the first part of the conversation again and check your answers.

Munira: Hi Mino. How are you?

Mino: Hello, Munira. I'm fine.

Munira: What are you watching?

Mino: It's Brazil versus Germany.

Munira: Who's winning?

Mino: Brazil. Two goals to one. Germany scored just now, but the referee said it wasn't a goal.

Munira: Is it a good game?

Mino: Yes, it's quite exciting. But the pitch is terrible.

Munira: Sorry. What's a pitch?

Mino: The place where they play.

Munira: How do you spell it?

Mino: P-I-T-C-H.

Munir: How do you say it? Pitich?

Mino: No, pitch.

Presenter: D 2 Listen and check your ideas.

Voice: all, any, ask, ball, base, bat, called, each, favourite, game, hand, hard, heard, place, play, really, say, shape, team, that, watch, what

Presenter: Unit 10: Nutrition and Health Lesson 1

B Listen to a paragraph. Then complete the text using the *Key vocabulary* and other appropriate words.

Voice: Why do we eat? What a silly question! We eat because we are hungry. Well, that answer is true, in a way. But why do we feel hungry? We feel hungry because the body needs more energy. The whole body needs energy to move. Every part of the body needs energy to work correctly. We get energy from food. However, we have to be careful. If we don't use all the energy from food, the body keeps it. How does it keep it? It keeps it as fat. It is easy to use new energy from food. It is much harder to use the energy in fat. So, what's the answer? We must eat the right amount of food, and we must take exercise to use the extra energy. The food we normally eat is called our diet. Of course, we must eat the right kind of food as well. If we eat the right amount of the right kind of food, we will have a healthy diet. But what's the right kind of food? That's another question.

Presenter: Lesson 3

B Noura Hamed is studying Food Sciences at Greenhill College. She has a lecture today about food. Listen to the first part. When the lecturer stops, guess the next word. Did you guess correctly?

Lecturer: Today I'm going to talk about food. Why does the human body need [PAUSE] food? Of course, the body needs food to [PAUSE] live. The body takes energy from [PAUSE] food. Energy is the ability to do [PAUSE] work. It also takes important [PAUSE] chemicals. Chemicals are things like calcium and magnesium. These chemicals help the parts of the body to work [PAUSE] correctly. We call the energy and chemicals in food [PAUSE] nutrients. As you probably know, there are several different types of [PAUSE] nutrient. The body needs different amounts of each [PAUSE] nutrient. If you have too much of a particular type, you can get [PAUSE] fat. If you have too little of a particular type, you can get [PAUSE] ill.

Presenter: C 2 Listen to the first part again and check.
[REPEAT OF EXERCISE B WITHOUT PAUSES]

Presenter: D Listen to the second part. What is the lecturer going to talk about this week? Tick one or more.

Lecturer: So, this week, I'm going to name the different nutrients. Then I'm going to give you some examples of foods that contain each type of nutrient. Next week, I'm going to talk about food groups and how much food you need from each group.

Presenter: E 2 Listen to the third part and complete the names of the nutrients.

Lecturer: OK. First, what are the different nutrients? There are five main types. Firstly, there are carbohydrates. Secondly, there is protein. We spell that P-R-O-T-E-I-N. That's E-I-N, not I-E-N. Thirdly, we have vitamins – V-I-T-A-M-I-N-S. Fourthly, there are fats. Meat and fish contain fats. Finally, there are minerals – M-I-N-E-R-A-L-S.

Presenter: E 4 Listen to the fourth part. Check and complete the table.

Lecturer: Where do we find the main nutrients? We find carbohydrates in food like bread, pasta and rice. There is protein in meat and fish. There is also protein in cheese. What about vitamins? Fruit, like apples and oranges, contains vitamins. So do vegetables like carrots and peas. Next, fats. Meat and fish contain fats. There are also fats in products like milk and cheese. Finally, there are minerals. We find minerals in many foods, but particularly in milk, meat and eggs.

Presenter: F Listen to the fifth part. What does the lecturer want you to do before next week?

Lecturer: OK. So, we have looked at nutrients and foods that contain them. Next week, food groups and how much food you need from each group. Before next week, could you look up food groups on the Internet and make some notes of different ideas about them? OK. So I want you to do some research on food groups on the Internet and note some things down.

Presenter: Lesson 4

A 2 Listen and check your ideas.

Lecturer: Today I'm going to talk about food. Why does the human body need food? Of course, the body needs food to live. The body takes energy from food. Energy is the ability to do work. It also takes important chemicals. Chemicals are things like calcium and magnesium. These chemicals help the parts of the body to work correctly. We call the energy and chemicals in food nutrients. As you probably know, there are several different types of nutrient. The body needs different amounts of each nutrient. If you have too much of a particular type, you can get fat. If you have too little of a particular type, you can get ill.

So, this week, I'm going to name the different nutrients. Then I'm going to give you some examples of food that contain each type of nutrient. Next week, I'm going to talk about food groups and how much food you need from each group.

Where do we find the main nutrients? We find carbohydrates in food like bread, pasta and rice.

There is protein in meat and fish. There is also protein in cheese. What about vitamins? Fruit, like apples and oranges, contains vitamins. So do vegetables like carrots and peas. Next, fats. Meat and fish contain fats. There are also fats in products like milk and cheese. Finally, there are minerals. We find minerals in many foods, but particularly in milk, meat and eggs.

OK. So, we have looked at nutrients and foods that contain them. Next week, food groups and how much food you need from each group. Before next week, could you look up food groups on the Internet and make some notes of different ideas about them? OK? So I want you to do some research on food groups on the Internet and note some things down.

Presenter: C 2 Listen and check your ideas.
Voice: a talk work course call
b type rice give finally
c main contain have take
d so know does note
e meat cheese bread protein
f nutrient fruit much food
g about amount how group

Presenter: D 1 Listen to the spelling of more words from the lecture. Write the letters.
Voice: H-U-M-A-N
N-U-T-R-I-E-N-T
C-H-E-M-I-C-A-L-S
O-R-A-N-G-E
C-A-R-R-O-T
P-A-S-T-A
B-O-D-Y
F-I-N-A-L-L-Y
E-N-E-R-G-Y

Presenter: **E 1 Listen again to part of the lecture. Which words does the lecturer define?**

Lecturer: Today I'm going to talk about food. Why does the human body need food? Of course, the body needs food to live. The body takes energy from food. Energy is the ability to do work. It also takes important chemicals. Chemicals are things like calcium and magnesium. These chemicals help the parts of the body to work correctly. We call the energy and chemicals in food nutrients. As you probably know, there are several different types of nutrient. The body needs different amounts of each nutrient. If you have too much of a particular type, you can get fat. If you have too little of a particular type, you can get ill.

Presenter: **E 2 Listen again. Make notes of the definition of each word.**
[REPEAT OF EXERCISE E1]

Presenter: **F 2 Listen and check your ideas.**

Lecturer: We call the energy and chemicals in food, nutrients. As you probably know, there are several different types of nutrient. The body needs different amounts of each nutrient. If you have too much of a particular type, you can get fat. If you have too little of a particular type, you can get ill.

Presenter: Lesson 5

B Listen to a conversation between two friends. Choose the best answer in each case.

Gary: Would you like coffee, Yoshi?

Yoshi: No, thanks, Gary. But you have one.

Gary: No, thanks. I don't like coffee. I like tea, with three teaspoons of sugar.

Yoshi: So, you don't like tea either, then. You just like sugar.

Gary: Maybe.

Yoshi: Where did you go last night?

Gary: I went to the new Italian restaurant.

Yoshi: Sorry? Did you say Iranian restaurant?

Gary: No, Italian.

Yoshi: Italian? Where's that?

Gary: It's in the mall near the park. The Park Mall?

Yoshi: No, it's called the Garden Mall!

Gary: Yes, that's right. The Garden Mall. I love that place.

Yoshi: So do I. What did you have?

Gary: I had a pizza.

Yoshi: Pizza? What's that?

Gary: It's like bread with tomatoes and cheese… and other things.

Yoshi: Bread with tomatoes and cheese. Like a sandwich?

Gary: No, you cook it in an oven. It's hot.

Yoshi: Hot? Oh, is it round?

Gary: That's right.

Yoshi: Oh, yes. I know. They have it in the canteen sometimes. What kind did you have?

Gary: They called it a Pizza Margharita.

Yoshi: Sorry? What do they call it?

Gary: Pizza Margharita.

Yoshi: How do you spell it?

Gary: P-I-Z-Z-A M-A-R-G-H…

Yoshi: H?

Gary: Yes, M-A-R-G-H-A-R-I-T-A.

Yoshi: How do you say the word?

Gary: Mar-gha-RI-ta.

Yoshi: Mar-GHA-ri-ta

Gary: No, Mar-gha-RI-ta.

Yoshi: Right. Mar-gha-RI-ta. How do you make it?

Gary: I don't know but it's delicious.

Yoshi: I must go there and try it.

Gary: Would you like to come with me

next week?

Yoshi: I'd love to. I like trying new kinds of food. Which day?

Gary: Thursday?

Yoshi: Yes, great. What time?

Gary: Half past seven?

Yoshi: Oh. I forgot. My car's in the garage on Thursday. Could you give me a lift?

Gary: Yes, of course.

Yoshi: Could you pick me up at seven fifteen from my house?

Gary: Sure.

Yoshi: That reminds me. What's the time, now?

Gary: It's quarter to three.

Yoshi: Oh, no! I must go. My lecture starts in 10 minutes.

Presenter: **C 2 Listen and check your answers.**

Gary: Would you like coffee, Yoshi?

Yoshi: No, thanks, Gary. But you have one.

Gary: No, thanks. I don't like coffee. I like tea, with three teaspoons of sugar.

Yoshi: So, you don't like tea either, then. You just like sugar.

Gary: Maybe.

Presenter: **D 2 Listen and check your answers.**

Yoshi: Where did you go last night?

Gary: I went to the new Italian restaurant.

Yoshi: Sorry? Did you say Iranian restaurant?

Gary: No, Italian.

Yoshi: Italian? Where's that?

Gary: It's in the mall near the park. The Park Mall?

Yoshi: No, it's called the Garden Mall!

Gary: Yes, that's right. The Garden Mall. I love that place.

Yoshi: So do I. What did you have?

Gary: I had a pizza.

Yoshi: Pizza? What's that?

Gary: It's like bread with tomatoes and cheese… and other things.

Presenter: **E 1 Listen and write the name of Gary's meal.**

Voice: Pizza Margharita: P-I-Z-Z-A M-A-R-G-H-A-R-I-T-A

Presenter: **E 2 Listen and write the names of more pizzas.**

Voice: 1 Marinara: M-A-R-I-N-A-R-A

2 Napolitana: N-A-P-O-L-I-T-A-N-A

3 Quattro Stagione: Q-U-A-T-T-R-O S-T-A-G-I-O-N-E

4 Prosciutto: P-R-O-S-C-I-U-T-T-O

Presenter: **F 1 Gary invites Yoshi to the restaurant next week. Listen and complete his sentence and Yoshi's reply (Part 3).**

Gary: Would you like to come with me next week?

Yoshi: I'd love to. I like trying new kinds of food.

Presenter: **Revision 2**

C 1 Listen to the first part. Make notes to answer the first seven questions.

Adriana: I'm going to talk to you this morning about a festival in Mexico. It is called Quinceañera, spelt Q-U-I-N-C-E-A-N-E-R-A. The name means fifteen years. The festival is for girls. It happens when a girl becomes 15 years old. It is a coming of age celebration. In the past in Mexico, parents expected a daughter to get married after she was 15, but today it just means the child has become an adult. The girl usually wears a long pink or white dress.

Published by
Garnet Publishing Ltd.
8 Southern Court
South Street
Reading RG1 4QS, UK

First published 2010.
Reprinted 2012.

ISBN 978 1 85964 631 1

British Library Cataloguing-in-Publication Data
A catalogue record for this book is available from
the British Library.

Production

Project managers:	Rod Webb, Richard Peacock
Editorial team:	Emily Clarke, Natalie Griffith, Sarah Margetts, Katherine Mendelsohn, Nicky Platt, Lucy Thompson
Design:	Mike Hinks, Nick Asher
Illustration:	Beehive Illustration (Dave Bowyer/Janos Jantner/Mark Ruffle/Simon Rumble/Roger Wade Walker), Janette Hill, Doug Nash, Karen Rose, Ian West
Photography:	Banana Stock, Corbis (Chris Lisle/Stapleton Collection/Dennis Marsico/Wolfgang Kaehler/Hulton-Deutsch Collection/ Bettman), Digital Vision, Flat Earth, Getty Images, Image Source, Ingram Publishing, Photodisc, Stockbyte, Istockphoto

Every effort has been made to trace the copyright
holders and we apologize in advance for any
unintentional omissions. We will be happy to
insert the appropriate acknowledgements in
any subsequent editions.

Audio production: John Green TEFL Tapes
                 Matinée Sound & Vision Ltd

Printed and bound
in Lebanon by International Press: interpress@int-press.com

UNIT 1
Education

academic (adj)
/ækə'demɪk/

advice (n)
/əd'vaɪs/

advisor (n)
/əd'vaɪzə/

assignment (n)
/ə'saɪnmənt/

college (n)
/'kɒlɪdʒ/

consider (v)
/kən'sɪdə/

head (n)
/hed/

in charge (of) (adj)
/ɪn 'tʃɑːdʒ (əv)/

instructor (n)
/ɪn'strʌktə/

intelligence (n)
/ɪn'telɪdʒəns/

lecture (n)
/'lektʃə(r)/

literature (n)
/'lɪtrətʃə(r)/

meeting (n)
/'miːtɪŋ/

polite (adj)
/pə'laɪt/

principal (n)
/'prɪnsəpl/

relax (v)
/rɪ'læks/

respect (n and v)
/rɪ'spekt/

responsible (for)
(adj)
/rɪ'spɒnsəbl (fɔː, fə)/

semester (n)
/sɪ'mestə/

speech (n)
/spiːtʃ/

studies (n)
/'stʌdiz/

subject (n)
/'sʌbdʒɪkt/

term (n)
/tɜːm/

year (n)
/jɪə/

UNIT 2
Daily Life

always (adv)
/'ɔːlweɪz/

break (n)
/breɪk/

breakfast (n)
/'brekfəst/

diary (n)
/'daɪəri/

dinner (n)
/'dɪnə/

film (n and v)
/fɪlm/

last (adj and v)
/lɑːst/

never (adv)
/'nevə/

often (adv)
/'ɒfn, 'ɒftən/

once (adv)
/wʌns/

on time (prep)
/ɒn 'taɪm/

period (n)
/'pɪəriəd/

regular (adj)
/'regjələ/

regularly (adv)
/'regjələli/

restaurant (n)
/'restrɒnt/

schedule (n)
/'ʃedjuːl/

second (n)
/'sekənd/

social (adv)
/'səʊʃl/

social life (n)
/'səʊʃl laɪf/

sometimes (adv)
/'sʌmtaɪmz/

spend (v)
/spend/

sport (n)
/spɔːt/

sports (n)
/spɔːts/

twice (adv)
/twaɪs/

usually (adv)
/'juːʒuəli/

weekend (n)
/wiːk'end/

weekly (adv)
/'wiːkli/

UNIT 3
Work and Business

applicant (n)
/'æplɪkənt/

assist (v)
/ə'sɪst/

benefit (n)
/'benəfɪt/

career (n)
/kə'rɪə/

colleague (n)
/'kɒliːg/

employ (v)
/ɪm'plɔɪ/

employable (adj)
/ɪm'plɔɪəbl/

employee (n)
/ɪm'plɔiiː/

employer (n)
/ɪm'plɔɪə/

employment (n)
/ɪm'plɔɪmənt/

experience (n)
/ɪk'spɪəriəns/

overtime (n)
/'əʊvətaɪm/

papers (n)
/'peɪpəz/

product (n)
/'prɒdʌkt/

qualification (n)
/kwɒlɪfɪ'keɪʃn/

rely on (v)
/rɪ'laɪ ɒn/

requirement (n)
/rɪ'kwaɪəmənt/

salary (n)
/'sæləri/

service (n)
/'sɜːvɪs/

urgent (adj)
/'ɜːdʒənt/

UNIT 4
Science and Nature

average (adj)
/'ævərɪdʒ/

decrease (n)
/'diːkriːs/

diagram (n)
/'daɪəgræm/

experiment (n)
/ɪk'sperɪmənt/

explain (v)
/ɪk'spleɪn/

explanation (n)
/eksplə'neɪʃn/

graph (n)
/grɑːf/

increase (n)
/'ɪŋkriːs/

laboratory (n)
/lə'bɒrətri/

large (adj)
/lɑːdʒ/

latitude (n)
/'lætɪtjuːd/

longitude (n)
/'lɒŋgɪtjuːd/

natural (adj)
/'nætʃrəl/

science (n)
/ˈsaɪəns/

scientific (adj)
/saɪənˈtɪfɪk/

scientist (n)
/ˈsaɪəntɪst/

small (adj)
/smɔːl/

steady (adj)
/ˈstedi/

sunrise (n)
/ˈsʌnraɪz/

sunset (n)
/ˈsʌnset/

table (n)
/ˈteɪbl/

test (n and v)
/test/

the Earth (n)
/ðiː ˈɜːθ/

the Equator (n)
/ðiː ɪˈkweɪtə/

unit of measurement (n)
/juːnɪt əv ˈmeʒəmənt/

UNIT 5
The Physical World

Africa (n)
/ˈæfrɪkə/

America (n)
/əˈmerɪkə/

Asia (n)
/ˈeɪʒə/

celebrate (v)
/ˈselɪbreɪt/

celebration (n)
/selɪˈbreɪʃn/

ceremony (n)
/ˈserəməni/

compass (n)
/ˈkʌmpəs/

continent (n)
/ˈkɒntɪnənt/

Europe (n)

/ˈjʊərəp/

event (n)
/ɪˈvent/

festival (n)
/ˈfestɪvl/

landscape (n)
/ˈlændskeɪp/

latitude (n)
/ˈlætɪtjuːd/

location (n)
/ləʊˈkeɪʃn/

longitude (n)
/ˈlɒŋɡɪtjuːd/

Oceania (n)
/əʊʃiˈɑːniə/

region (n)
/ˈriːdʒən/

special (adj)
/ˈspeʃl/

take place (v)
/teɪk ˈpleɪs/

the Equator (n)
/ðiː ɪˈkweɪtə/

the Middle East (n)
/ðə mɪdl ˈiːst/

traditional (adj)
/trəˈdɪʃnəl/

UNIT 6
Culture and Civilization

birth (n)
/bɜːθ/

celebrate (v)
/ˈselɪbreɪt/

culture (n)
/ˈkʌltʃə/

event (n)
/ɪˈvent/

festival (n)
/ˈfestɪvl/

happen (v)
/ˈhæpən/

invent (v)
/ɪnˈvent/

invention (n)
/ɪnˈvenʃn/

luck (n)
/lʌk/

lucky (adj)
/ˈlʌki/

prepare (v)
/prɪˈpeə/

relative (n)
/ˈrelətɪv/

ride (v)
/raɪd/

special (adj)
/ˈspeʃl/

star sign (n)
/ˈstɑː saɪn/

take place (v)
/teɪk ˈpleɪs/

traditional (adj)
/trəˈdɪʃnəl/

UNIT 7
Technology

appear (v)
/əˈpɪə/

captain (n)
/ˈkæptɪn/

character (n)
/ˈkærəktə/

control (n)
/kənˈtrəʊl/

cyclist (n)
/ˈsaɪklɪst/

drove (v – past)
/drəʊv/

flew (v – past)
/fluː/

helicopter (n)
/ˈhelɪkɒptə/

invent (v)
/ɪnˈvent/

invention (n)
/ɪnˈvenʃn/

inventor (n)
/ɪnˈventə/

jet (n)
/dʒet/

literature (n)
/ˈlɪtrətʃə(r)/

moral (n)
/ˈmɒrəl/

navy (n)
/ˈneɪvi/

planet (n)
/ˈplænɪt/

ride (v)
/raɪd/

rider (n)
/ˈraɪdə/

rode (v – past)
/rəʊd/

row (a boat) (v)
/rəʊ/

sailed (v – past)
/seɪld/

satellite (n)
/ˈsætəlaɪt/

Solar System (n)
/ˈsəʊlə sɪstəm/

space (n)
/speɪs/

star (n)
/stɑː/

story / stories (n)
/ˈstɔːri, ˈstɔːriz/

submarine (n)
/sʌbməˈriːn/

the Earth (n)
/ðiː ˈɜːθ/

the moon (n)
/ðə ˈmuːn/

the sun (n)
/ðə ˈsʌn/

translate (v)
/trænsˈleɪt/

UNIT 8
Art and Literature

character (n)
/ˈkærəktə/

comedy (n)
/ˈkɒmədi/

golf (n)
/gɒlf/

history (n)
/ˈhɪstri/

ice hockey (n)
/ˈaɪs hɒki/

kill (v)
/kɪl/

literature (n)
/ˈlɪtrətʃə(r)/

play (n and v)
/pleɪ/

player (n)
/ˈpleɪə/

playwright (n)
/ˈpleɪraɪt/

plot (n)
/plɒt/

riding (n)
/ˈraɪdɪŋ/

rugby (n)
/ˈrʌgbi/

running (n)
/ˈrʌnɪŋ/

team (n)
/tiːm/

tragedy (n)
/ˈtrædʒədi/

writer (n)
/ˈraɪtə/

UNIT 9
Sports and Leisure

body (n)
/ˈbɒdi/

choose (v)
/tʃuːz/

court (n)
/kɔːt/

cycling (n)
/ˈsaɪklɪŋ/

diet (n)
/ˈdaɪət/

energy (n)
/ˈenədʒi/

equipment (n)
/ɪˈkwɪpmənt/

exercise (n)
/ˈeksəsaɪz/

fat (n)
/fæt/

game (n)
/geɪm/

hit (n)
/hɪt/

hungry (adj)
/ˈhʌŋgri/

indoors (adv)
/ɪnˈdɔːz/

land (v)
/lænd/

net (n)
/net/

outdoors (adv)
/aʊtˈdɔːz/

out of court (prep)
/aʊt əv ˈkɔːt/

piece (n)
/piːs/

player (n)
/ˈpleɪə/

point (v and n)
/pɔɪnt/

rule (n)
/ruːl/

score (n and v)
/skɔː(r)/

serve (v)
/sɜːv/

team (n)
/tiːm/

try (v)
/traɪ/

winner (n)
/ˈwɪnə/

UNIT 10
Nutrition and Health

add (v)
/æd/

biscuit (n)
/ˈbɪskɪt/

bowl (n)
/bəʊl/

burger (n)
/ˈbɜːgə/

cake (n)
/keɪk/

cereal (n)
/ˈsɪəriəl/

chip (n)
/tʃɪp/

chocolate (n)
/ˈtʃɒklət/

cook (v)
/kʊk/

crisp (n)
/krɪsp/

cut (v)
/kʌt/

dinner (n)
/ˈdɪnə/

fried (adj)
/fraɪd/

gram (n)
/græm/

lunch (n)
/lʌntʃ/

pasta (n)
/ˈpæstə/

pepper (n)
/ˈpepə/

piece (n)
/piːs/

potato(es) (n)
/pəˈteɪtəʊ(z)/

put on (v)
/pʊt ˈɒn/

salad (n)
/ˈsæləd/

soup (n)
/suːp/

steak (n)
/steɪk/

sweet (n)
/swiːt/

tomato (n)
/təˈmɑːtəʊ/

academic (adj)
/æˈkəˈdemɪk/

add (v)
/æd/

advice (n)
/ədˈvaɪs/

advisor (n)
/ədˈvaɪzə/

Africa (n)
/ˈæfrɪkə/

always (adv)
/ˈɔːlweɪz/

America (n)
/əˈmerɪkə/

appear (v)
/əˈpɪə/

applicant (n)
/ˈæplɪkənt/

Asia (n)
/ˈeɪʒə/

assignment (n)
/əˈsaɪnmənt/

assist (v)
/əˈsɪst/

average (adj)
/ˈævərɪdʒ/

benefit (n)
/ˈbenəfɪt/

birth (n)
/bɜːθ/

biscuit (n)
/ˈbɪskɪt/

body (n)
/ˈbɒdi/

bowl (n)
/bəʊl/

break (n)
/breɪk/

breakfast (n)
/ˈbrekfəst/

burger (n)
/ˈbɜːgə/

cake (n)
/keɪk/

captain (n)
/ˈkæptɪn/

career (n)
/kəˈrɪə/

celebrate (v)
/ˈselɪbreɪt/

celebration (n)
/selɪˈbreɪʃn/

cereal (n)
/ˈsɪəriəl/

ceremony (n)
/ˈserəməni/

character (n)
/ˈkærəktə/

chip (n)
/tʃɪp/

chocolate (n)
/ˈtʃɒklət/

choose (v)
/tʃuːz/

colleague (n)
/ˈkɒliːg/

college (n)
/ˈkɒlɪdʒ/

comedy (n)
/ˈkɒmədi/

compass (n)
/ˈkʌmpəs/

consider (v)
/kənˈsɪdə/

continent (n)
/ˈkɒntɪnənt/

control (n)
/kənˈtrəʊl/

cook (v)
/kʊk/

court (n)
/kɔːt/

crisp (n)
/krɪsp/

culture (n)
/ˈkʌltʃə/

cut (v)
/kʌt/

cycling (n)
/ˈsaɪklɪŋ/

cyclist (n)
/ˈsaɪklɪst/

decrease (n)
/ˈdiːkriːs/

diagram (n)
/ˈdaɪəgræm/

diary (n)
/ˈdaɪəri/

diet (n)
/ˈdaɪət/

dinner (n)
/ˈdɪnə/

drove (v – past)
/drəʊv/

employ (v)
/ɪmˈplɔɪ/

employable (adj)
/ɪmˈplɔɪəbl/

employee (n)
/ɪmˈplɔɪiː/

employer (n)
/ɪmˈplɔɪə/

employment (n)
/ɪmˈplɔɪmənt/

energy (n)
/ˈenədʒi/

equipment (n)
/ɪˈkwɪpmənt/

Europe (n)
/ˈjʊərəp/

event (n)
/ɪˈvent/

exercise (n)
/ˈeksəsaɪz/

experience (n)
/ɪkˈspɪəriəns/

experiment (n)
/ɪkˈsperɪmənt/

explain (v)
/ɪkˈspleɪn/

explanation (n)
/ekspləˈneɪʃn/

fat (n)
/fæt/

festival (n)
/ˈfestɪvl/

film (n and v)
/fɪlm/

flew (v – past)
/fluː/

fried (adj)
/fraɪd/

game (n)
/geɪm/

golf (n)
/gɒlf/

gram (n)
/græm/

graph (n)
/grɑːf/

happen (v)
/ˈhæpən/

head (n)
/hed/

helicopter (n)
/ˈhelɪkɒptə/

history (n)
/ˈhɪstri/

hit (n)
/hɪt/

hungry (adj)
/ˈhʌŋgri/

ice hockey (n)
/ˈaɪs hɒki/

in charge (of) (adj)
/ɪn ˈtʃɑːdʒ (əv)/

indoors (adv)
/ɪnˈdɔːz/

increase (n)
/ˈɪŋkriːs/

instructor (n)
/ɪnˈstrʌktə/

intelligence (n)
/ɪnˈtelɪdʒəns/

invent (v)
/ɪnˈvent/

invention (n)
/ɪnˈvenʃn/

inventor (n)
/ɪnˈventə/

jet (n)
/dʒet/

kill (v)
/kɪl/

laboratory (n)
/ləˈbɒrətri/

land (v)
/lænd/

landscape (n)
/ˈlændskeɪp/

large (adj)
/lɑːdʒ/

last (adj and v)
/lɑːst/

latitude (n)
/ˈlætɪtjuːd/

lecture (n)
/ˈlektʃə(r)/

literature (n)
/ˈlɪtrətʃə(r)/

location (n)
/ləʊˈkeɪʃn/

longitude (n)
/ˈlɒŋgɪtjuːd/

luck (n)
/lʌk/

lucky (adj)
/ˈlʌki/

lunch (n)
/lʌntʃ/

meeting (n)
/ˈmiːtɪŋ/

moral (n)
/ˈmɒrəl/

natural (adj)
/ˈnætʃrəl/

navy (n)
/ˈneɪvi/

net (n)
/net/

never (adv)
/ˈnevə/

Oceania (n)
/əʊʃiˈɑːniə/

often (adv)
/ˈɒfn, ˈɒftən/

once (adv)
/wʌns/

on time (prep)
/ɒn ˈtaɪm/

outdoors (adv)
/aʊtˈdɔːz/

out of court (prep)
/aʊt əv ˈkɔːt/

overtime (n)
/ˈəʊvətaɪm/

papers (n)
/ˈpeɪpəz/

pasta (n)
/ˈpæstə/

pepper (n)
/ˈpepə/

period (n)
/ˈpɪəriəd/

piece (n)
/piːs/

planet (n)
/ˈplænɪt/

play (n and v)
/pleɪ/

player (n)
/ˈpleɪə/

playwright (n)
/ˈpleɪraɪt/

plot (n)
/plɒt/

point (v and n)
/pɔɪnt/

polite (adj)
/pəˈlaɪt/

potato(es) (n)
/pəˈteɪtəʊ(z)/

prepare (v)
/prɪˈpeə/

principal (n)
/ˈprɪnsəpl/

product (n)
/ˈprɒdʌkt/

put on (v)
/pʊt ˈɒn/

qualification (n)
/kwɒlɪfɪˈkeɪʃn/

region (n)
/ˈriːdʒən/

regular (adj)
/ˈregjələ/

regularly (adv)
/ˈregjələli/

relative (n)
/ˈrelətɪv/

relax (v)
/rɪˈlæks/

rely on (v)
/rɪˈlaɪ ɒn/

requirement (n)
/rɪˈkwaɪəmənt/

respect (n and v)
/rɪˈspekt/

responsible (for)
(adj)
/rɪˈspɒnsəbl (fɔː, fə)/

restaurant (n)
/ˈrestrɒnt/

ride (v)
/raɪd/

rider (n)
/ˈraɪdə/

riding (n)
/ˈraɪdɪŋ/

rode (v – past)
/rəʊd/

row (a boat) (v)
/rəʊ/

rugby (n)
/ˈrʌgbi/

rule (n)
/ruːl/

running (n)
/ˈrʌnɪŋ/

sailed (v – past)
/seɪld/

salad (n)
/ˈsæləd/

salary (n)
/ˈsæləri/

satellite (n)
/ˈsætəlaɪt/

schedule (n)
/ˈʃedjuːl/

science (n)
/ˈsaɪəns/

scientific (adj)
/saɪənˈtɪfɪk/

scientist (n)
/ˈsaɪəntɪst/

score (n and v)
/skɔː(r)/

second (n)
/ˈsekənd/

semester (n)
/sɪˈmestə/

serve (v)
/sɜːv/

service (n)
/ˈsɜːvɪs/

small (adj)
/smɔːl/

social (adv)
/ˈsəʊʃl/

social life (n)
/ˈsəʊʃl laɪf/

Solar System (n)
/ˈsəʊlə sɪstəm/

sometimes (adv)
/ˈsʌmtaɪmz/

soup (n)
/suːp/

space (n)
/speɪs/

special (adj)
/ˈspeʃl/

speech (n)
/spiːtʃ/

spend (v)
/spend/

sport (n)
/spɔːt/

sports (n)
/spɔːts/

star (n)
/stɑː/

star sign (n)
/ˈstɑː saɪn/

steady (adj)
/ˈstedi/

steak (n)
/steɪk/

story / stories (n)
/ˈstɔːri, ˈstɔːriz/

studies (n)
/ˈstʌdiz/

subject (n)
/ˈsʌbdʒɪkt/

submarine (n)
/sʌbməˈriːn/

sunrise (n)
/ˈsʌnraɪz/

sunset (n)
/ˈsʌnset/

sweet (n)
/swiːt/

table (n)
/ˈteɪbl/

take place (v)
/teɪk ˈpleɪs/

team (n)
/tiːm/

term (n)
/tɜːm/

test (n and v)
/test/

the Earth (n)
/ðiː ˈɜːθ/

the Equator (n)
/ðiː ɪˈkweɪtə/

the Middle East (n)
/ðə mɪdl ˈiːst/

the moon (n)
/ðə ˈmuːn/

the sun (n)
/ðə ˈsʌn/

tomato (n)
/təˈmɑːtəʊ/

traditional (adj)
/trəˈdɪʃnəl/

tragedy (n)
/ˈtrædʒədi/

translate (v)
/trænsˈleɪt/

try (v)
/traɪ/

twice (adv)
/twaɪs/

unit of measurement (n)
/juːnɪt əv ˈmeʒəmənt/

urgent (adj)
/ˈɜːdʒənt/

usually (adv)
/ˈjuːʒuəli/

weekend (n)
/wiːkˈend/

weekly (adv)
/ˈwiːkli/

winner (n)
/ˈwɪnə/

writer (n)
/ˈraɪtə/

year (n)
/jɪə/

Presenter: C 2 Listen to the second part.
Complete the information
about the events in order.

Adriana: On the girl's 15ᵗʰ birthday, there
are several special events. First,
the girl's family and friends go to a
ceremony in a church. There are
speeches in the church. Then,
fourteen couples walk with the
birthday girl – one couple for each
year of her life. After that, the girl
gives a small doll to her younger
sister. Finally, after the ceremony,
there is a party in a local hall, or
at the home of the girl's parents.